The Bread of the Strong

CATHOLIC PRACTICE IN NORTH AMERICA

This series aims to contribute to the growing field of Catholic studies through the publication of books devoted to the historical and cultural study of Catholic practice in North America, from the colonial period to the present. As the term "practice" suggests, the series springs from a pressing need in the study of American Catholicism for empirical investigations and creative explorations and analyses of the contours of Catholic experience. In seeking to provide more comprehensive maps of Catholic practice, this series is committed to publishing works from diverse American locales, including urban, suburban, and rural settings; ethnic, post-ethnic, and transnational contexts; private and public sites; and seats of power as well as the margins.

The Bread of the Strong

LACOUTURISME AND THE FOLLY OF THE CROSS, 1910–1985

Jack Lee Downey

FORDHAM UNIVERSITY PRESS
New York 2015

Fordham University Press also publishes its books in a variety of electronic formats. Some content that appears in print may not be available in electronic books.

Visit us online at www.fordhampress.com.

Library of Congress Cataloging-in-Publication Data

Downey, Jack Lee.
The bread of the strong : Lacouturisme and the folly of the Cross, 1910–1985 / Jack Lee Downey. — First edition.
pages cm — (Catholic practice in North America)
Includes bibliographical references and index.
ISBN 978-0-8232-6543-5 (hardback)
1. Pacifism—Religious aspects—Catholic Church—History—20th century. 2. Catholic Worker Movement. 3. Day, Dorothy, 1897–1980. 4. Catholic Church—United States—History—20th century. 5. United States—Church history—20th century. 6. Lacouture, Onésime, 1881–1951—Influence. 7. Hugo, John, 1911–1985—Influence. 8. Catholic Church—Québec (Province)—History—20th century. I. Title.
BX1407.P24D69 2015
267'.182—dc23

2015002944

Printed in the United States of America

17 16 15 5 4 3 2 1

First edition

for Mom & Dad

Contents

Acknowledgments

Whenever I think about questions of method and scholarship—which, honestly, is not incredibly often—I am reminded of a paraphrase of the great American Catholic historian John Tracy Ellis that Tom Shelley, another great American Catholic historian, recounted during a graduate seminar some years back: "You can't be a good historian unless you like reading dead people's mail." I have been very lucky to have a constellation of resources and support align to allow me the space to do the archival research and analysis that formed the backbone of this project, and which has brought me great joy, along with no small amount of anxiety, during the past few years. And I am happy to have the opportunity to (briefly) express my gratitude.

Pride of place easily goes to my parents, whom I love very dearly. Of all the undeserved privileges I have experienced by virtue of having been born their child, I think the greatest has been a kind of presumption of genetic moral integrity by those who know them—that I would be good because they are good. And although I have done my best to obliterate this preconception over the years, I have received the benefit of the doubt many more times than I have earned.

I have been very lucky to have basked in the glow of some brilliant and kind souls. To all my teachers, thank you. I am most profoundly grateful to Jetsunma Tenzin Palmo for caring for me and personifying compassionate wisdom. My mentor James T. Fisher has been a wonderful guide and friend—along with the rest of his clan, Kristina Chew and Charlie. I am very grateful to Robert Orsi for having played matchmaker between me and Jim and for being another great teacher. Along with Jim, Mark Massa, SJ, and the incomparable Maria Terzulli gave me a welcoming home at Fordham University's Curran Center for American Catholic Studies. There is a litany of people who made my experience at Fordham remarkable, but in a particular way Reg Kim, Mara Brecht, Catherine

Osborne, Jim Keane, Catherine Petrany, and Kyle Haden, OFM, have been precious conversation partners and friends who kept me more or less afloat.

Tom Banchoff and Georgetown University's Berkley Center for Religion, Peace, and World Affairs were very hospitable in supporting my research on the tail end and allowing me to tag along with some of their tremendous work. My current colleagues at La Salle University have been outrageously generous, fun, and inspiring. Margaret McGuinness, Anthony Paul Smith, Jordan Copeland, Julie Regan, and Maureen O'Connell—and the entire rest of our department . . . I couldn't ask for better friends to work with. And considering that the acknowledgments section is an exercise in sentimentality, I should say that I am deeply appreciative of all of the students I have gotten to learn with, who have made my life better, even when they are making fun of me directly to my face.

Much thanks to Angela Alaimo O'Donnell and John Seitz, co-editors of the Catholic Practice in North America series at Fordham University Press, under the auspices of which the present work is being published, as well as to Fred Nachbaur, Will Cerbone, and everyone at Fordham University Press. I owe a special debt of gratitude that may be impossible to pay to the two anonymous reviewers of my original manuscript, whose comments and suggestions have been invaluable in the process of forming this book.

I have been blessed with a life-giving activist community, especially my Ruckus Society family (but also plenty of others) who challenge, comfort, provoke, and inspire. Jack Hill has helped me try to keep it together for almost my entire life, and he has gotten help from many other dear ones, like Stuart DeVan, Sarah Dunagan, Adam Blasavage, Rose Hodwitz, Robby Diesu, Hayfa Abichahine, and John Watterberg. There are scores of others who deserve better than to be glossed over like this but, you know, sorry: I appreciate you more than my word count allows me to express. Finally, my everlasting thanks to Omi Hodwitz for keeping me from wasting away throughout this project and introducing me to the zany animal kingdom of cat, python, and fish cohabitation, interspersed with visits from bunnies, possums, raccoons, all manner of birds, and the occasional fox.

The Bread of the Strong

Introduction

Conversion and Catholic Pacifism

In 1976, while researching for the second installment in a historical trilogy on Dorothy Day (1897–1980) and the Catholic Worker movement, William Miller interviewed a diocesan priest from Pittsburgh named John Hugo, who had served for a time as her confessor and spiritual director. Hugo had gained some notoriety as the arch-apologist for a controversial contemplative retreat that Day once described as "like hearing the Gospel for the first time."[1] During their conversation, Hugo reminisced about his first encounters with Day in 1940: "I don't know how many times Dorothy made the retreats. I would say perhaps a dozen times, or two dozen. . . . That [their introduction] was before we got involved in the war [World War II] too much, I think. . . . I guess she converted me completely to pacifism; I had been on the fence about it."[2] Hugo credited Day for introducing him to the antiwar movement, and himself for inspiring her to give up smoking. And then a rather bold claim: "I think I was the first priest to defend conscientious objectors. I don't want to boast unduly, but I think I was."[3] Now, although pacifism would not even be formally recognized as a legitimate conscientious option for Roman Catholics until 1965, this was—strictly speaking—not quite true.[4] Hugo might be forgiven for his ignorance on the matter, given the scant and poorly-networked clerical support for COs throughout the war, but his depiction of the reciprocal, symbiotic relationship with Day was telling. While Hugo would develop a strong portfolio as an agitator, his singular passion and talent lay in his capacity as a conduit for and translator of the maximalist Christian doctrine known at first pejoratively as *Lacouturisme*—which created a kind of feedback loop by forging a spiritual generator for Day's radical praxis, which in turn pushed Hugo further toward a pacifist application of Christian principles.

John Hugo was born and raised in the suburbs, a dozen miles southeast of Pittsburgh, in the long shadow of St. Vincent's Archabbey in nearby

Latrobe—the Bavarian Benedictine St. Michael's (Metten) Abbey's original US satellite, and original brewers of Rolling Rock beer.[5] He enrolled at St. Vincent's prep school in 1924 and spent over a decade there—eventually at the college and seminary. Although he never entered into vowed Benedictine life, the contemplative charism impressed deeply on his future ministry as diocesan priest.[6] And when John Hugo first encountered the iconoclastic Québécois Jesuit evangelist Onésime Lacouture in September 1938—under coincidental or auspicious circumstances, depending on perspective—his receptivity to Lacouture's maximalist spirituality and moral perfectionism was piqued.

Lacouture's impact on Hugo, from the very beginning, was practically sacramental, and radicalized Hugo, transfiguring him from a conventional, if socially-minded, cleric into a barnstorming revivalist. Lacouture introduced Hugo to a new way of reading Scripture, as well as to the litany of Catholic mystics, such as John of the Cross.[7] The austere dichotomies of Lacouturite theology—between nature and grace, between true Christianity and so-called paganism, between the two eternal destinies of the soul—would deeply shape Hugo's vision of the interior transformation that was the heart of the retreat, but also—and consequently—of practical ethics.

One of the principle framing concepts of Lacouturite theology was its notion of the Gospel—and the Christian vocation—as a countercultural sign of contradiction to domesticating mediocrity. In some more recent meditations, Judith Butler has considered nonviolence as an existential refusal to reproduce the mechanisms by which we are molded as subjects. We are socialized into group norms through cycles of perceived, experienced, and imagined punishments, wherein we learn behavioral standards and taboos. In doing so, we become ourselves symbols of that violence: as objects, expressions of that process of conditioning, but also—as subjects—its perpetuators and purveyors. Butler writes:

> We are at least partially formed through violence. . . . But even if this is true, and I think it is, it should still be possible to claim that a certain crucial breakage can take place between the violence by which we are formed and the violence with which, once formed, we conduct ourselves. Indeed, it may be that precisely because one is formed through

> violence, the responsibility not to repeat the violence of one's formation is all the more pressing and important.[8]

Although a Christian framework—particularly one as fervently Augustinian as Lacouturite theology—would likely demand some doctrine of grace to be inserted into such a formulation, Hugo provided Dorothy Day with a practical means of effecting something analogous to this form of radical nonparticipation in her own interior life and for persevering in her taxing apostolate. While the United States as we know it may have been forged through waves of structural injustice, Catholic Worker pacifist social ethics aspired to intervene in the cycles of violence conventionally considered by realists to be inevitable, necessary, even noble, in our imperfect, fallen world—recalling Walter Benjamin's laconic assertion that "there is no document of culture which is not at the same time a document of barbarism."[9] And Lacouturite asceticism, particularly the "*nada, nada, nada*" of Sanjuanist detachment—a formulation whose emphasis may obscure underlying *pro*activity (withdrawing from one form of life in favor of another that is valued higher)—dovetails with Butler's description of the paradigmatic nonviolent act as, in fact, a non-act (a cessation of the reproduction of violence in relationships with self and others), or, conceived slightly differently, an intervention in an act. This is mirrored in nonviolent direct action's frequent manifestation as transgressive intransigence (not relocating to designated parts of buses or lunch counters, not dispersing when instructed to by police, noncompliance with air raid drills, not abiding one's conscription into military service). The Catholic Worker's conscientious precarity plunged the community into a liminal position, estranged from normative American and American Catholic tides, and appearing to outsiders as alternatingly quixotic, heroic, treasonous, and narcissistic.

The Evolution of the Retreat

The irony behind the history of the Lacouture retreat movement was that through its southward migration from Québec, an insular, ascetic, almost *a*social theology morphed into spiritual fodder for what is arguably US Catholicism's most profound expression of liberationist praxis. It was a delicate sequence of events that furnished the causes and conditions whereby Lacouturisme was born, and matured into the provocative phenomenon that it was.[10] The story comes in several acts, each the product of radically contingent circumstances that were crucial to the movement's development and circulation. Born in 1881 just outside of Montréal, Onésime Lacouture immigrated to the United States during his early childhood—as part of New England's Canadien diaspora—where he gained his first exposure to the secular social environment that would later serve as a foil for his doctrines of self-abnegation and spiritual revivalism. This first border crossing also set the stage for his movement's transnational fluidity. As a young adult, Lacouture would return to Québec as a Jesuit scholastic and, later, a priest. A forced relocation to a remote village in western Alaska during clerical formation appeared to derail his scholarly aspirations, but it was in this desolate environment, which Lacouture dubbed the White Desert, that he had a formative series of mystical revelations, which fundamentally recalibrated his sense of vocation.

Lacouture returned to the mainland as a countercultural, anti-intellectual militant, bent on resuscitating lapsed Catholic masses and restoring the Church to its primitive spiritual rigor. In time, his reputation as a Gospel preacher drew enthusiastic seminarians and clergy from around the provinces and United States, but also led to his censure and eventual exile south of the border. Among his young, bright-eyed disciples was John Hugo—newly minted as a priest—who came to Lacouture in 1938, and cited the experience as *the* pivotal event of his life:

> Perhaps I may best explain my indebtedness to Father Lacouture by saying that he *fertilized* my mind, until then rendered barren by a spirit of rationalism and inhibiting minimalism such as has in fact long dominated practically all Catholic spirituality.[11]

His discipleship under Lacouture effectively torpedoed Hugo's future in academia, and this loss, coupled with Lacouture's vigorous affective spirituality seems to have played a foundational role in cultivating Hugo's anti-intellectual pedigree, which deepened exponentially through his confrontations with a laundry list of future theological adversaries. Hugo's mentality shifted from socially-conscious but respectably safe to wildly prophetic—some would say fundamentalist. The rest of his life would be consumed with propagating his maximalist Christian doctrine and Lacouturite apologetics. But in terms of posterity, much of Hugo's legacy is refracted through his relationship with Dorothy Day, his most renowned student.

"Read the *Catholic Worker* Daily!"

Debuting in Lower Manhattan on May Day 1933, the *Catholic Worker* monthly newspaper hit the streets with a peculiar amalgamation of radical politics and ultra-supernaturalist Christian spirituality. Cofounded by a loquacious autodidact and precocious journalist, the *Catholic Worker* soon expanded its apostolate from the printing press to the street, organically morphing into a clearing house for communitarian activism and DIY social services—inspired by a maximalist interpretation of the Sermon on the Mount, Catholic social teaching, and the lives of the saints. Dorothy Day was the Catholic Worker movement's public face, largely resulting from her practical responsibilities and enthusiasm for social protest, which her mentor, French émigré Peter Maurin (1877–1949), did not particularly share. As indoctrinated by Maurin, Day inherited a rigorous philosophy of labor, voluntary poverty, and personalist ethics, which she extended to include absolute pacifism and a mandate for active participation in structural change. Her exposure to the French personalists Emmanuel Mounier and Nicholas Berdyaev (albeit of Russian extraction), as well as Catholic Worker patrons Jacques and Raïssa Maritain, inspired an emphasis on human dignity and visceral aversion to the bourgeois obsession with leisure.[12] Day rejected modern consumerism as fundamentally oppressive—economically, socially, and spiritually—echoing Berdyaev: "The will to power, to well-being, to wealth, triumphs over the will to holiness, to genius."[13] In Day's view, society's misplaced notion of self fostered a disordered pathology of insatiable greed that feeds into a round of perpetual acquisition. This is doubly tragic because it leads us to objectify and manipulate others for our needs—stripping their inherent subjectivity, agency, and dignity.

Against this, Dorothy Day developed a model of rehabilitated psychology that accepted the accountability conditional with human freedom and struggled against the bondage of psychological necessity. In opposition to cultural materialism, wherein we unwittingly give up our capacity to choose the good and bind ourselves to psychological compulsion, personalism courageously asserted the right and responsibility to act with purpose.[14] The Catholic Worker movement's personalist ethos expanded upon the notion of individual accountability for oneself to include, at least theoretically, all the needy (which is to say, all)—akin to Levinas's "anarchic responsibility":

> Responsibility for the Other, for the naked face of the first individual to come along. A responsibility that goes beyond what I may or may not have done to the Other or whatever acts I may or may not have committed, as if I were devoted to the other man before being devoted to myself. . . . A responsibility for my neighbor, for the other man, for the stranger or sojourner, to which nothing in the rigorously ontological order binds me—nothing in the order of the thing, of the something, of number or causality.[15]

Dorothy Day conceived of work in the public sphere as an extension of the sacramental life, and as a communitarian anarchist was—unlike her New Dealing counterparts—wary of relying on the institutional benevolence of "Holy Mother the State."[16]

Rejecting the predatory impulse of capitalist upward mobility, the bourgeois spirit of leisure, and crippling hardship of *in*voluntary poverty, Day sought out a liminal *via media* that reinforced mutual interdependence but also liberated individuals from abject destitution. The protocols of Catholic Worker houses intentionally blurred the division between worker and guest so that often the two were indistinguishable, which embodied their antagonism to both the hierarchical model of philanthropic charity and the consolidation of state power:[17]

> In our fight against such a concept as Christian charity, we have been accused of lining up with Wall Street and private enterprise, and the rich opponents of state control and taxation. But, anarchists that we are, we want to decentralize everything and delegate to smaller bodies and groups what can be done far more humanely and responsibly through mutual aid, as well as charity, though Blue Cross, Red Cross, union cooperation, parish cooperation.[18]

Catholic Worker thought was dedicated to an intense rendition of subsidiarity, which demanded the practitioner willingly locate herself in a position of existential precarity, refusing both stability and security. This was expressed collectively in the early movement's hallowed tradition of abstaining from nonprofit tax exemption, federal tax payment, and voting.[19] These practices, along with the embrace of a life of evangelical poverty, were remixes of the traditional Christian "Works of Mercy," but also spiritual exercises and ascetic techniques that that both expressed and facilitated an ongoing conversion toward holiness and a different way of being community.

Porous Borders

The narrative of the Lacouture retreat involves multiple border crossings between Québec and New England, along with forays into other parts of the contiguous United States and Alaska. Onésime Lacouture grew up largely within the Canadien diaspora in Rhode Island and Massachusetts, but migrated back and forth between Canada and the United States. His points of residency largely clustered within the Laurentia bioregion, Lacouture was a product of alternating hybridities, a semi-itinerant insider-outsider in communities experiencing moments of cultural flux. The network that he built was both geographically and chronologically fluid—his primary interlocutors being just as much the pantheon of the Catholic communion of saints as any of his contemporaries. Within the contemporary field of lived or popular American religious history, Robert Orsi's work has received singular recognition for its capacity to articulate the real presence of the communion of saints in the Catholic lifeworld. And while some assimilationist respectability narratives might shudder at the rugged persistence of such antiquated phenomena, the incorporation of predeceasing archetypes into supernatural worldviews was not the sole purview of devotional Catholics, but is a practice shared much more widely. It is not even particular to Catholicism or, even more broadly, Christianity. However, in some recent work, Orsi contends that the orientation toward a collapse of time and space through processes of memory and prayer differentiated American Catholics from their Protestant contemporaries:

> The fact that Catholics in the United States possessed their own traditions of national myth and memory has been consequential for how they have acted in the U.S. public sphere. Philip Berrigan had more in common with Saint Isaac Jogues . . . than he did with his fellow antiwar

activists Benjamin Spock and William Sloane Coffin. Coming to national participation, memory, and identity by different routes, Catholics became other kinds of citizens.[20]

That many of the primary referents for Catholics in the realms of spiritual counsel and intervention in material concerns were not only transnational (as famously illustrated by the sensationalist rumormongering during 1926 that a Vatican army lay primed to invade the United States in anticipation of a win by Catholic presidential candidate Al Smith, which went some way into galvanizing the anti-papist vote and torpedoing Smith's campaign) but also transtemporal—belying the presumption that Christian notions of time are simply one-directional and linear. And while these were not unique characteristics, they did render Catholics culturally peculiar, relative to US norms, which at least affected a cultivated historical amnesia and forward-looking supercessionism—the forgetting-as-purification that Bruno Latour identifies as a characteristic of Modernism, which erects an impermeable barricade between natural and supernatural realms.[21] While Lacouture, Hugo, and Day articulated overlapping but diverse countercultural positions, one point of commonality was their shared affectionate and studied engagement with spiritual ancestors as exemplars and consultants in the construction of their visions of the heroic Christian vocation.

Ultra-supernaturalism and Christian Enthusiasm

> There is, I would say a recurrent situation in Church history—using the word "church" in the widest sense—where an excess of charity threatens unity. You have a clique, an *élite*, of Christian men and (more importantly) women who are trying to live a less worldly life than their neighbours; to be more attentive to the guidance (directly felt, they would tell you) of the Holy Spirit. More and more, by a kind of fatality, you see them draw apart from their co-religionists, a hive ready to swarm.
>
> —Ronald A. Knox, *Enthusiasm: A Chapter in the History of Religion with Special Reference to the XVII and XVIII Centuries*

In 1950, after more than thirty years of self-admittedly obsessive labor, British cleric Ronald A. Knox (1888–1957) published his maximum opus, *Enthusiasm: A Chapter in the History of Religion with Special Refer-*

ence to the XVII and XVIII Centuries.[22] In this text, Knox identifies a particular *genus* of Christianity, marked by what he calls ultra-supernaturalism. This chronic strain of reactionary, charismatic Christianity dissents from the mainstream, and inevitably challenges Church unity. Knox's project, which originated as an apologetic assault on various forms of illuminism and their threat to Christian orthodoxy, mutated—over the course of several decades—into a profound sympathetic investigation into a dozen or so enigmatic spiritual prodigies.[23] Characteristic of Knox's vision of enthusiasm is the expectation of intense religious experience—more tangible evidence of the divine—compared to what is typical, even among the devout. This is grounded on a vigorously supersessionist vision of the relationship between grace and nature, in which the former obliterates, rather than perfects, the latter: "It is the attempt to root up nature and plant the seed of grace in fallow soil, instead of grafting the supernatural on to the natural, after the timorous fashion of orthodoxy."[24] Extraordinary revelations, visions, and so forth are not prerequisites per se, but are popular hallmarks of the enthusiast. Ecclesiastically, as charismatic individuals evolve into spiritual leaders and garner local support, an "invisible church within the church" arises, and—in Knox's model—a new faction of Christianity emerges. Herein lies the threat to Church harmony that Knox originally set out to combat, whether the community that forms be overtly schismatic or not. As the sect becomes increasingly confident in its spiritual authority, it minimizes, or rejects outright, the more conventional sensibilities of the mainline faithful. In the most extreme cases, the new communities turn on their host churches, ascribing diabolic motives or sinister allegiances to them. Disciplinary measures and attempts to rein in perceived excesses are interpreted as malevolent assaults on the "true" Body of Christ. Eventually, what may have originated as a peculiar but unthreatening revivalist movement within the larger Church becomes viciously sectarian and divisive. As the sect, which associates lack of enthusiasm with tepidity, expands its influence and power—builds muscle—it migrates from the margins to the center and evolves into a hegemonic threat that may persecute the "ungodly" at will, under the rationale that error has no rights.[25] Given Christendom's history of dispensing with heterodoxy, Knox's anxieties about enthusiastic sects' hypothetical propensity for persecution was just a bit incongruous. But while Knox seems to have found the ultra-supernaturalists alternately abhorrent and appealing, repulsive and attractive, his (and his readers') fascination with them was symptomatic of more pervasive trends toward esotericism during the industrial era.[26]

Although there is no indication that he was at all conscious of the contemporaneous revivalist phenomenon that was Lacouturisme/Lacouturism, Knox's enthusiast model finds a hospitable analogue in the narrative history of the movement—whose rise signaled the heated re-emergence of perennial Christian debates, rooted in North American soil. Among the theological hazards was authoritative teaching on the relationship between nature and grace, ordered affections, self-mortification, and both the universality and gravity of the call to Christian perfection. Fused onto these subjects was Lacouturism's extreme critique of free-market capitalism, which ran against the grain of mainline Catholicisms in both Québec and the United States, which had been working overtime to demonstrate their respectable secular values.[27] Additionally, the movement's protagonists, particularly in its US iteration, confounded critics by simultaneously presenting as both excessively liberal and conservative. The controversies surrounding Lacouturism elicited a peculiar role reversal for some conventional sentries of the faith, who found themselves in the unaccustomed position of defending progressivism and cultural assimilation.[28]

Hyphenated Modernisms

As with Knox's decades-long research into ultra-supernaturalism, the Lacouturite movement belongs to the resurgence of interest in maximalist spirituality in the opaque taxonomy of Christian engagements with the Modern.[29] More focused, the subject of Modernism has been a seemingly perennial preoccupation of American Catholic historians (although certainly not our sole domain), which has inspired a proliferation of theoretical and source-based scholarship that has helped illuminate the mediation between past and present, the forces that have constructed the social, political, and interior realities that form Catholic culture. Even the term and the phenomenon it signifies are, as R. Scott Appleby has noted, "slippery": it may be employed as a signifier for any number of objects of collective anxiety or, conversely, a euphemism for progress and social improvement—leviathan and messiah.[30] As Latour notes, "the adjective 'modern' designates a new regime, an acceleration, a rupture, a revolution in time," which stands in contrast to the ancient, remote past.[31] Nevertheless, as Orsi notes, it is a formidable obsession in contemporary scholarship, it exerts a powerful imaginative force as an axis of intellectual conversation:

> Contemporary religious are modern, anti-modern, alternately modern, one of a multiple of moderns, or (less often) pre-modern; but they are always defined in relationship to the modern (which includes the fundamentalist modern, in [Robert W.] Hefner's words, the party of "conquest"). Discourse about modernity and secularization theory (and its inadequacies and limitations) has become like a woven finger-trap toy, impossible to extricate oneself from, especially the harder one tries.[32]

To add to Orsi's list of hyphenated -modernisms, Paula Kane has recently added "off-modern"—a term borrowed from Stephen Schloesser's study of interwar Paris (and coined by Svetlana Boym)—to describe the manner in which Catholics incorporated supernatural markers of difference, contra Protestant and secular hegemony.[33] Catholic debates were distinct but not isolated from Protestant and non-Christian analogues, coupled historiographical and philosophical interrogations of the roles of memory, forgetting, progress, and the relationship between faith and science with the Church's history of formal antagonism to various permutations of Modernism. These were codified in a veritable anthology of opposition papers: Pope Pius IX's *Syllabus of Errors* (1864), Leo XIII's condemnation of Americanism in *Testem Benevolentiae Nostrae* (1899), and Pius X's *Lamentabili sane exitu* (1907) and *Pascendi Dominici Gregis* (1910)—which was enforced by the institution of an anti-Modernist oath, mandatory for clergy and religion teachers, and later undergirded by an index of forbidden books that persisted until the 1960s.

That any two-thousand-year-old superstructure would react inhospitably to what Theodor Adorno pithily described as the "authority of the new" is not particularly mind-bending, although this should be tempered by some sympathy for the lived experience of anti-Catholicism in shaping Catholic antagonism to the modern. Some scholarship has argued that the rise of "evangelical Catholicism" embodied in the *Catholic Worker*, the Berrigan brothers, the Camden 28—and possibly by contemporary extension DignityUSA, the Plowshares movement, Catholics for Choice, and School of the Americas Watch—represents an evolutionary stage in the progression of Catholics in the United States, with the rise of the counterculture being inadvertently confirmative of the shifting ground that bolstered Catholics' sense of place, their comfort level within Will Herberg's "triple melting pot" of American civil religion.[34] No longer consumed by their outsider status, a minority of Catholics felt secure enough to renounce normative cultural aspirations and critique the American project from within—as illustrated in Dorothy Day's not-so-subtly titled 1948 essay "We Are Un-American: We Are Catholics," which seemed tailored to court antagonism, corroborating James T. Fisher's description of her as "radically separatist."[35] However, that she felt empowered to scribe it in the first place can be read as indicative of identity confidence, although as a Waspy convert Day was not exactly a representative demographic sample.

Ways of Proceeding

This study originated as an attempt to contribute to the ongoing excavation of the spiritual lifeworld of Dorothy Day, whom renowned American Catholic historian David O'Brien famously—perhaps too famously—once dubbed "the most significant, interesting, and influential person in the history of American Catholicism."[36] Some years ago, like thousands of people before me, I thumbed through Day's memoir *The Long Loneliness* for the first time, including a trim twenty-page chapter in part 3 called, simply, "Retreat." The present study is a history of that retreat—"*the* retreat," as Day often referred to it. Although it might be more magisterial to claim that this work emerged from an epic metacritical impulse to revise dominant historical narratives or argue an alternate grand unified theory, the goals of this project are much more meager: to better understand the mind of someone who I find endlessly fascinating by investigating the retreat movement that she loved dearly, and which she claimed was so integral to her spiritual formation. However, in doing so, this work also attempts to gather together several broader questions about the relationship between contemplative theology, asceticism, and radical activism. Although I do offer some thoughts which I hope may be helpful for a larger field of inquiry, it seems worth noting that this work is rooted in a desire to bolster the increasingly thick descriptions we have of Dorothy Day and her environs. In doing so, I hope I am somewhat successful in navigating the historiographic tension between treating my primary subjects as purely isolated phenomena—incapable of telling us anything about the deeply complex workings of North American Catholicism—and overexaggerating their capacity to be illustrative of any major trends in the tectonic social phenomena that is modern Catholicism. This text is not meant to be a normative anything, but a minor contribution to a conversation already well in progress, which I hope will be built upon and debunked as appropriate, as scholarship in the field advances further.

In both the US and Canadien contexts, although with considerable narrative difference to be explored in subsequent chapters, Modernism was in many ways an imagined threat that reinforced Catholic self-identity as underdog outsiders—sojourners—but also reified notions of Modernism as a concrete, real entity—with its own subjectivity and agency that was hostile to core Catholic principles, and therefore an adversarial object of Catholic hostility—even if sometimes also an object of envy and desire. The conventional trajectory of American Catholicism depicts a linear progression of impoverished immigrant communities living in tension with their Anglo-Protestant host, eventually assimilating into American civil religion, punctuated most notably by John F. Kennedy's presidential election in 1960—a triumphant point of arrival in Catholics' respectability narrative. Subsequently, the narrative plods on with the increased suburbanization of white Catholics, the short-lived triumph of liberal Catholicism in the Vatican II era, subsequent culture wars set off by *Humanae vitae* (1967), flight from the Church, revelations of clerical abuse and cover-ups, and the concentration of non-white Catholic demographics within the American Church. This normative but almost comically limited narrative has been the subject of deep revision, to complicate and nuance it in the interest of a more representative treatment of the diversity of sub-identities, experiences, and alternate trajectories within Catholic life. In addition to being overly simplistic, the endurance of this linear assimilation trajectory is irksome because it appears to embrace a neocolonial framework of success through domination—that the only way to thrive in the United States is to become powerful, and the only way to become powerful is to mimic and appropriate the practices of those who already hold power. Although an extreme example because he champions a concept of race as pure social construction, Noel Ignatiev's *How the Irish Became White* illustrates this, by arguing essentially that mid-nineteenth century Philadelphia Irish accessed upward mobility into

Anglo-Protestant-dominated society by allying themselves against black Americans. The presumption in the linear model is that the logical goal for all communities is to aspire to become wealthy, patrician WASPs. Thus, returning to transassimilationist proof text thesis (the counterculture as indicative of ciscultural vitality), in this general framework, even the emergence of radical communities that opt out from or against the norms of systematic domination are themselves evidence of the vitality of those trends—antibodies that confirm the presence of normative cultural shifts. This differs from its "ethnic ghetto Catholic" predecessors and contemporaries (populated often by the most recent waves of migration), because the counterculture's core identity as American is never really in question, even if they might renounce it—not least because it is already presumed as theirs to disavow. It may often be the metahistorian's job to lump and draw wide-ranging connections—but the tendency toward universalism benefits by being tempered by a diasporic recognition of the particularity of enculturation, and the often thin bonds that undergird pan-identity group narratives—but it may be worth interrogating whether the depiction of the margins as reifying the center unnecessarily itself further solidifies anti-liberationist cultural presumptions.[37]

For the purposes of the present work, and suspending the digression of whether one can ever actually be anti-Modern—because even that position is mediated by the context that gives it rise—it is important to note that the Lacouturite movement often imagined itself in just those terms and framed its mission in terms of a retrieval of a more vital, authentic spirituality than it saw ascendant in mainstream, so-called pagan Catholicism.[38] It was evangelical in its prophetic call—although at times insular, more interested in in revitalizing Roman Catholicism than proselytizing. In their more extreme moments, some Lacouturites betrayed the sentiment that any tepidity was fundamentally incompatible with the heroic mandates of Christianity—the not-too-subtle implication being that antagonists were imperfectly, or incompletely, Christian. Although William Halsey contends that the disorientation of liberal Protestantism in the wake of World War I opened a space for Catholic ascendency in the form of Thomism, ascetical mysticism such as Lacouture's "Sermon on the Mount" theology was an alternate way.[39] In a toxic postwar environment that seemed to some as suddenly hypermodern, theological primitivists, such as Lacouture, Hugo, and—arguably less so—Day, found themselves drawn to antique, artisanal mysticism, which they perceived as a purer way, saturated within the framework of a nostalgic declension narrative. Like Eastern religions and esotericism, the appeal of alternate worldviews like Knox's ultra-supernaturalists came at least partially from their radical disconnect with the perceived prevailing winds of modernism: hyper-rationalism, technology, individualism, acceleration—the urbanization of the mind and spirit. Although there are profound drawbacks to the gravitational pull of Modernism as the normative historiographic axis, under both Lacouture's and Hugo's stewardship, the retreat's "Sermon on the Mount" ethic was self-consciously hostile to Modernism as they defined it, and cultivated an identity based on contrast. In Dorothy Day, we witness less of the hypersensitivity around the theme of the Modern: although many of her primary points of critique—free-market capitalism, militarism, racism—were products of modernity, her capacity to lead as a Catholic lay*woman* was itself prefigurative of a progressive vision for intersectional equality.

With a couple of wonderful exceptions, the very small amount that has been written about the Lacouturite retreat has relied almost exclusively on Day's published reflections, and therefore has viewed the movement refracted through her lens—and the lens of her public persona. Additionally, as Dan McKanan has argued, much of the bibliography on Day is explicitly biased, and whether or not this is accurate and to what extent that matters is up for debate.[40] However, Lacouture and Hugo are very much more susceptible to such historiographic bias because of their trickle-down historical relevance in the imaginations of those who care: that they are solely important because they were important to Dorothy Day, and therefore little is required except to tease out what she got from them. Leon Hooper, SJ, has penned one of the rare treatments of the movement, but primarily, it seems, in the interest of drawing a contrast between Day and her allegedly Jansenist influences. While he sees apologetics and revelry in Lacouturite Jansenism in the seminal works of William Miller and James T. Fisher, respectively, Hooper distances Day from the influence of Lacouture and Hugo by rooting her in the more bona fide orthodoxy of Saint Thérèse of Lisieux.[41] However, Hooper restricts his primary sources to Day's published essays on Lacouture and Hugo, giving him scant basis for any real assessment of its orthodoxy, which would not necessarily be all that problematic if it was not so instrumental to his larger argument:

that Day's association with Lacouture's "Sermon on the Mount" theology ought not tarnish her reputation, because its influence was marginal. Leaving Day unsullied by her affiliation with Jansenists is instrumental for Hooper to mount his case against the "romanticism of suffering" depiction of Day that he finds in Fisher. Although he does not cite her directly, he would presumably object even more vigorously to Paula Kane's insertion of Day into her study of spiritual victimhood—although the presupposition that Saint Thérèse's spirituality of self-annihilation is somehow immune from "suffering romanticism" seems puzzling.[42]

If Hooper seems preoccupied with trying to distance Day from the imputations of heresy that her Lacouturite affiliation brought, this study will emphasize continuity, even while recognizing some points of distinction and rupture. Furthermore, normative questions of orthodoxy are not primary concerns, except as theological phenomena: what heresy does, how it is socially situated, how it functions as a form of boundary maintenance, and the like. The primary allegation of Jansenism that was leveled against Lacouturisme interests me historically, but my purpose here is not to mount an argument that either condemns or exonerates Lacouturism from this charge. This is not the least because I harbor some skepticism that Jansenism was actually something real or simply *un fantôme*—and even if it was, that it was something inherently malevolent. And while the term was created, and continues to be employed, as a pejorative bludgeon that is now associated with a dour, rigorist, possibly gnostic, resentment of embodiedness as a locus of estrangement—being theologically glum—its common contemporary employ is now so vague that it seems to have passed its use as a meaningful category, if there ever was such a time. Considering virtually nobody has ever accepted the term as a personal descriptor, vindicating a movement or any individual from the taint of Jansenist heresy seems more of an ecclesiological project than a scholarly one, beyond the scope of this investigation. That does not mean, however, that I do not find these to be compelling questions.

The subject of Day's orthodoxy is now often integrally linked to her cause for canonization, and one suspects that Hooper's attempt to distance her from Lacouturism at least subconsciously relates to debates about her suitability for advancement. In this case, the attempt to frame our memory of Day also inevitably bleeds over into the formation of other memories, and in the case of Lacouture and Hugo it may be instrumental in dispelling imputations of her as dangerous to insulate her from them. It is true that there is a tug-of-war in process over Day's legacy, rife with potential pitfalls for those who want to protect her dangerous memory from the sanitization that is Church institutional incorporation, such as perpetually threatens the birdbath saint, Francis of Assisi.[43] Now, it would be deeply hypocritical to denounce the utility of Day as a point of entrance into the subject of Lacouturite theology—it is virtually the only entrance point, and was certainly my own. However, I hope that this work and that of Benjamin Peters and Charles Strauss will help bolster the historical record of Onésime Lacouture and John Hugo beyond simply their impact on Day, and retrieve a bit more of their agency.[44] What kind of a saint (even if a non-officially-recognized one) we want her to be may inevitably retroactively color how we view her supporting characters, but we bear some responsibility to push back against those impulses.

Much like Leon Hooper, my point of curiosity into the Lacouture retreat movement was piqued by what I initially perceived to be incongruities and peculiarities in Dorothy Day, particularly that an anarchist liberation theologian, whose radical activism was infused by an incarnational spirituality—the conviction that we literally encounter Christ in the suffering subject—could also be accused of harboring Jansenist sympathies. Additionally, anarchism's stereotypically positive anthropology—that humanity is naturally ethical and cooperative in the absence of external coercion—seems to contrast markedly from the suspicion of natural (read: pagan) motives and deep sense of the human predisposition toward sin, which was characteristic of allegations made against the Lacouturites. But although Day does play a major role in the narrative of this study (which should be perhaps irritatingly clear by now), this project is structured as more a biography of the Lacouture retreat itself: its origins, development, controversies, and influence.

The current work was conceived as essentially tripartite, following the interwoven lifestreams of Lacouture, Hugo, and Day. In each case, I have attempted to reconstruct some of the backstory—both biographical and social-historical—in order to contextualize the episodes, but also to connect trends and influences that often seem disciplinarily segregated. Although Roman Catholicism is a paradigmatically transnational religious tradition, and all American history is a history of colonization and migration, there seems to be a profound absence of consciousness of the migratory tides between our contiguous borders—particularly, for the purposes of this study, as related to les Canadiens in the Laurentia bioregion. There may be linguistic reasons for this, coupled with broader cultural blinders regarding our northward neighbors and the historic dominance of other ethnic populations in US Catholicism in terms of the acquisition of ecclesiastical power and popular influence—criteria which still set the standard for who and what gets foregrounded in the historical record. The goal here is not to replace, say, the history of Irish Catholics with the Canadien narrative, in a kind of dueling Catholic diaspora competition for historiography preeminence, but rather to shed some light on the broad—sometimes fragmented—spectrum that composes the experience of Catholics in North America.

The format of the text oscillates between focused examination of the life and work of my three primary characters and some grounding social history, in order to help situate them more clearly. In conceptualizing the progression of the retreat, this wavering back and forth has been helpful to me as a means of acknowledging the continuity throughout its stages of development, without flattening the distinct shifts that arose as it fertilized different soils. Hopefully readers will also find this telescoping between macro- and micro-history helpful, and not just irritating and stilted. Throughout the different sections, I have also attempted to turn step back from the narrative and turn a critical eye toward the retreat and its actors, as I describe them. I hope that some of this analytical gaze will be taken in the spirit in which it is offered and not be interpreted as snide, opportunistic, or slanderous—although this caveat may be more a reflection of my own neuroses than a sound-minded foreshadowing of things to come in the book. While it has certainly not been my objective to compose a hagiography of the movement, these are characters to whom I feel profoundly close, after years of spending time with some of their most intimate thoughts, which is the voyeuristic treasure of archival work. If primary historical research is largely about building relationships with subjects and coming to understand their minds, this process often follows an arc of ignorance-based idealization, followed by inevitable disillusionment (even if slight) that is resuscitated into a more informed, appreciative solidarity.

As a type of Catholic revivalism, the Lacouture retreat's practical theology was interested foremost in the formation of a particular type of subjectivity that its stewards viewed as a cosmically-significant rebuttal to the spirit of Christian minimalism pervading contemporary life. It was frankly ascetic in that it promoted a withdrawal from habitual patterns of behavior as part of a deeper intervention into existentially disordered ways of being. Much as the Judith Butler quote earlier in this introduction frames nonviolence as an offensive against the self-perpetuating cycles of behavior policing through which we are socialized into cultural norms, Lacouturism saw itself as fundamentally contra prevailing cultural tides. The climate of supernaturalism that forged Onésime Lacouture as a supple receptacle for mystical transformation was augmented by trends in Canadien Catholic life that provided a foil for his revivalist iconoclasm and social critique. Both the receptivity and hostility that greeted his maximalist spirituality teachings and doctrine confirmed his sense of divine mission and inspired a small but militant retinue of devotees—led by John Hugo—to import Lacouture's radical theology and translate it into American idioms somewhat more suited to their liberationist analysis. This lays the groundwork for Lacouturisme's encounter with Dorothy Day, who further radicalized the retreat's stewards and provided a social-political platform for this praxis of confrontational public theology. The narrative is not simply linear, but the job of the rest of this book is to shed some light on the Lacouturite movement in the hope that it will give some clarity to what has been largely opaque, and consider what it might have to say about modern Catholic history and the radical praxis of liberation.

1 *Canadien* Identity, Nationalism, and Muscular Catholicism

> At the sight of those men and women who had ostentatiously taken on a mentality that wasn't their own, I felt that an iron hand had descended on the soul of my people. My young pride revolted. I was reading our history at the time. In it I discovered, every day, the old soil in which my spirit had its natural roots. . . . The sight of that little group of Frenchmen, surrounded by a hundred or so millions of Anglo-Saxons, but magnificently persistent in not giving in, . . . the sight of a people that places above all material ambitions the pride of its cultures and the worth of its soul, that is a sight which I assure you I found to be of stirring beauty, superior to anything that the other civilization had shown me until then.
>
> —Lionel Groulx, *The Iron Wedge*

Although self-styled as a reactionary movement pitted against then-ascendant mainline social Catholicism, Lacouturisme emerged from the very same muscular, supernatural *mentalité* that undergirded the collective lifeworld of post-Confederation Québec. The narrative of Canadian—and particularly Québécois—Catholic history dovetails occasionally with its counterpart in the United States but simultaneously also mirrors those of colonized native Catholic environs such as Ireland. Its origins are bound up with French migration and displacement of indigenous peoples but by the late nineteenth and early twentieth centuries Québécois Catholicism under British rule adopted many conventional stereotypes of American "ghetto Catholicism": racially insular, sectarian, largely uneducated, proletarian, politically conservative, and clannish. In the decades bookending World War I, French Canadians—les Canadiens—displayed a somewhat confounding self-identity that was simultaneously immigrant and xenophobic, colonizer and colonized, nationalist (relative to Québec) and assimilationist (relative to Canada), socially and politically conservative while revolutionary and messianic. Many Canadiens conveniently glossed over their own invasive identity and appropriated indigenous status in the face of Protestant British occupation. As such, even without raising the specter of Québécois nationalism—an issue that precipitated a broad spectrum of responses within the province since Canadian Confederation in 1867—French Canada largely maintained a partisan sensibility and siege mentality defensiveness regarding its adoptive sibling. While constituting a sizable minority in Canada as a whole, Catholics were so dominant within Québec that the Church hierarchy controlled virtually the entire public sector, and religious and social identities were essentially united. Perhaps most important, Canadiens saw themselves as a vestige of authentic Catholic Christianity from a modernized Europe that had been overrun by secular humanism and materialist individualism.[1] Somewhat ironically, this remnant identity all but collapsed during the rapid cultural and political overhaul of Québec society in the 1960s that has been dubbed the "Quiet Revolution"—in many respects spearheaded by the very individuals who had trumpeted Catholic exceptionalism decades earlier.

Unlike its American coreligionists—save perhaps those of early colonial Maryland—Canadiens inhabited a socio-political climate that was comprehensively Roman Catholic. What initially began as a botched expedition to China in the 1520s rapidly developed into a trade settlement for French entrepreneurs and missionaries, precipitating the establishment of the colony of Nouvelle-France. Its development along the Saint Lawrence River instigated an almost perpetual conflict with indigenous communities, later compounded by the flagrant hostility of British colonials. Roman Catholicism was virtually ubiquitous within the urban areas of Montréal and Québec City, with the Church playing a dominant role in public works, education, and governance. A liturgical round of feast days and almost compulsory mass attendance reinforced Church authority and power of both the hard and soft varieties.[2] The clerical Catholic establishment sustained a thoroughly religious tone of life in New France, which included what now seems a somewhat peculiar debate over the amphibious nature of the beaver and its function as a potential Friday meat substitute. By all significant measures, the New French inhabited a holistically Catholic social environment. This is not, of course, to say that all Canadien colonials were particularly doctrinaire in terms of their adherence to clerical standards (and there is substantial evidence that they, in fact, were not)—an admittedly reductive criteria of what constitutes vigorous religiosity.

The Seven Years' War and eventual British capture of New France brought about the progressive dismantling of Church-State integration, although this was obscured by a cloak of religious tolerance, presented in the Treaty of Paris in 1763.[3] The reality on the ground simulated a diluted, North American version of the English Penal Laws implemented most famously—though not exclusively—in Ireland during the eighteenth century. Acadian French were relocated to Louisiana, the Oath of Allegiance to the Crown was implemented (essentially barring professing Catholics from taking public office), male religious orders were disbanded, and ordinations were forbidden, assuring that the Catholic priesthood would eventually self-extinguish. Furthermore, English citizens were encouraged to settle in the region, diluting French ethnic normativity in a textbook Machiavellian population transfer tactic.[4] However, French Canadians benefited from the political turmoil to the south and Britain's subsequent attempt to placate the province in the face of the looming American Revolution. In 1774, the British project of Canadien assimilation was prematurely aborted by the Quebec Act. This substantially expanded the province's territory, crafted a more inclusive oath, restored the use of French civil law, and guaranteed free practice of the Catholic faith—albeit "under the supremacy of the King."[5] This established (a qualified) freedom of religion in French Canada and laid the foundation for the restoration of the Catholic machine to its previously enjoyed position of authority.

The nineteenth century was largely an era of political consolidation in Lower Canada, as the Québec region of New France was then called. The Act of Union in 1840 merged Upper (what is essentially now Ontario) and Lower Canadas into a single United Province. This coincided with, and potentially facilitated, an upshift of French nationalism (and the widespread use of the newly coined term "French Canadian") along with a revival of religious fervor among Roman Catholics that proved hospitable to a myriad of Catholic religious communities:

> The revolutionary movements in Europe in 1848 were also an incentive for members of religious orders to take refuge in Quebec, where they were welcomed by both Church authorities and the British colo-

> nial officials. This consolidated the revival of religious practice that had ebbed in the first half of the 19th century. Soon thereafter, the Jesuits returned, followed by the Clerics of Saint Viator, the Oblates, and the Congregation of the Sacred Cross. Religious orders for women were also established in Lower Canada, including the sisters of the Sacred Heart and the Sisters of the Good Shepherd of Angers. New indigenous orders were also founded such as the Sisters of Providence, the Congregation of the Sisters of the Holy Names of Jesus and Mary, the Institut des sœurs de la Miséricorde, and the Sisters of Sainte-Anne. Religious organization became the backbone of education and social services.[6]

In the political sector, the clergy vilified the newly formed Liberal Party and attempted to rally an increasingly uniform ultramontane community against modernization and liberalism, invoking the collective nightmare of the French Revolution. The Confederation of Canada in 1867—which established Canada's relative independence—was followed soon by the First Vatican Council and a period of enhanced clerical dominance in Canadien culture. Québécois superiority was fostered by a collective sense of ideological and political encroachment—by English cultural assimilation, anti-Catholic Protestant proselytizing, and the propagation of liberal thought. Nevertheless, there were hints of nascent lay anticlericalism, rooted in the Church hierarchy's backing of Canadian political centralization.

Industrialization and urbanization increasingly restructured population demographics in Lower Canada and challenged the ultramontane zeal of the late nineteenth century.[7] Canadiens faced mounting concern over the erosion of French cultural dominance through both population dilution and Anglo-assimilation. Anglophone immigration was not restricted to an English Protestant clientele but notably also included Irish Catholics, who established a minority presence—particularly in Montréal—substantial enough to cause concern among Canadien nativists.[8] Conversely, widespread French Canadian emigration to the United States—particularly New England—in the decades following the American Civil War compounded the problem, as Québécois established "Little Canadas" in Manchester, New Hampshire, and Fall River and Lowell, Massachusetts, causing great alarm among conservative politicians on both sides of the border. The arrival of non-Anglo communities of Jews, Italians, and Greeks, along with "John Chinaman," made the situation all the more traumatic to psychologically fragile Québécois xenophobes. The pressures of cultural assimilation and the loss of the traditional Canadien agrarian Catholic identity to the manifold trappings of urban vice combined with the lures of secular organized labor to threaten Catholic power and collective obedience to previously normative clerical authority.

This perceived threat to the French Catholic way of life in early twentieth-century Québec spawned a self-conscious retrenchment among traditionalist Canadiens. Most prominent among the vanguard of Laurentian revivalists was the "clerico-nationalist historian" (and sometime novelist) Lionel-Adolphe Groulx (1878–1967).[9] Groulx called for a vigorous fusion of Catholicism and Québécois nationalism and envisioned "un peuple français dans un pays français," which presupposed a direct correspondence between French ethnicity and Catholic faith.[10] The survival of French Canada depended on a cultural renaissance and the renewal of a French mystique. Groulx's separatist interpretation of Canadian political history and his vision for Francophone renewal had a profound impact on Québécois social identity and was critical in forming a pointed pedagogical mission among elite secondary schools of the 1930s. As a young student at Montréal's Collège Jean-de-Brébeuf, future Canadian prime minister Pierre Elliott Trudeau (1919–2000) was indoctrinated into a messianic francophone Catholicism of cultural salvation by Jesuit instructors—as was his eventual Parti Québécois nemesis from across the province, René Lévesque. This formation infused a generation of adolescent patricians with an Anglophobic siege mentality and instilled an ethos of revolutionary *noblesse oblige*—Groulx's *l'appel de la race* ("the call of the race")—among the ascendant political class.[11]

On a more proletarian parish level, the spirit of revival was disseminated by clerically dominated Catholic youth groups, most successfully L'Action catholique, which would be later derided by a disillusioned contemporary Lacouture for its emphasis on social activism at the expense of the spiritual.[12] Michael Gauvreau has argued that the socio-political shift that Québec experienced during the Quiet Revolution, between 1960 and 1980, was the direct result of a movement of socio-spiritual reform in the 1930s. By inspiring a sense of triumphalist revivalism among a generation of Catholic adolescents, predominantly under the auspices of Catholic Action, the Church unwittingly planted the seeds for political secularization and economic liberalism. A vigorous model of spiritual heroism infused Québécois youth with a pointed distaste for the nominal Christian mediocrity they perceived in their immediate elders.[13] Gauvreau contends that the rise of a unique blend of personalism in Québec was most influential in fostering an ethos of spiritual revolution among the youth of the day.[14] This same backdrop of spiritual renewal and dedication to Christian perfection laid the foundation for Lacouture's clerical revival.

Gauvreau's thesis is that it was, as it were, precisely the tenor of Catholic revivalism in Québec during the 1930s which laid the groundwork for the rampant secularization that renovated the socio-political climate in the 1960s, exemplified by both Pierre Elliott Trudeau and René Lévesque.[15] The vigorous sense of purpose that inspired their militant Catholicism as students would reincarnate some decades later in a massive exodus from the Church. This generation maintained a collective messianic self-awareness, however secularized, that located itself on the cusp of a great shift that would inspire socio-political renewal in Québec. Although Canadien revivalists depicted themselves as divinely ordained refugees of the French Revolution, within just three decades many would apostatize in favor of secularism and were instrumental in dismantling the Québécois Ancien Régime. What began as a rigorous adolescent catechism with millennial overtones evolved into the Quiet Revolution as this generation reached adulthood.

In his study *The Church in Quebec*, theologian and Vatican II peritus Gregory Baum applies David Martin's theory of secularization to investigate the modern development of Québécois religious life. Martin hypothesizes that Roman Catholic societies have responded to the rise of secularism in a markedly less fluid manner than their Protestant counterparts. According to Baum, the conventional model of engagement is characterized by mutual antagonism predicated on their holistic, uncompromising, and mutually exclusive natures:

> As the modernizing sector of society defined itself against Catholicism, the church identified itself with the conservative forces resisting modernization. As a result the whole of society became divided into two camps with Catholics on one side and liberals on the other. Later it was Catholics on one side and socialists on the other. The Catholic tradition discouraged cumulative legitimation. On the contrary, it tended

> to universalize conflicts in society. In the Catholic countries the conflict among economic classes and different regions easily took on the character of a total struggle.[16]

However, Martin and Baum note that there are classical exceptions to this rule, as well as mixed pattern societies that do not experience a cultural spilt as they encounter modernity (such as Germany, Holland, and Switzerland), wherein Catholics constitute a minority population within the whole. Poland and Ireland are exemplars of Catholic nations "subjugated by empire," while Belgium's particular socio-political background identifies it as something of an anomaly. In Baum's analysis, Québec actually inhabits a hybrid identity that amalgamates Martin's Polish-Irish and Belgian typologies. By doing so, the implicit presupposition is that Québec society did not, in fact, experience a cultural schism during the 1960s, as is conventionally assumed when one entertains discussion of the Quiet Revolution.

The onset of the Great Depression was interpreted by revivalists, both Catholic and Protestant, as a profoundly moral crisis. However, the Québécois Catholic response reflexively linked the calamity and aspirations for reconstruction to the vitality of the Canadien covenant.[17] It was said that modernization had precipitated the dissolution of the nuclear Catholic family and the transmission of generational values. In the ethical vacuum left by their parents—who traded for materialism and upward mobility at the expense of traditional values—youth culture adopted a strong, crusading reformist spirituality that denigrated its elders.[18] Inspired by Emmanuel Mounier and French personalism, Québécois youth rejected the bourgeois spirit of their parents in favor of a heroic Catholic social ethos.[19] Thus, Depression-era Québécois adopted a vision of novelty that varied from the stereotypical Catholic attachment to tradition.[20] Because the preceding generation had compromised itself by imbibing free-market capitalism, young Catholics rebelled by recommitting themselves to a "new Middle Ages" that was self-consciously anti-American.[21] Their rhetoric of revolution and claim of antiquity placed them in an ambiguous relationship with the past and present.

Je Me Souviens

> The sociological irony of Quebec's secularization thus came to a proper fruition: it was not at the hands of modern doubters and scoffers at religion that the core of Quebec society was evacuated of the Catholic church's once-dominant presence, but rather through the faith-filled intentions of religiously motivated and socially committed Catholic laypersons and of onetime professional operatives of the Church itself.
>
> —Kevin J. Christiano, "The Trajectory of Catholicism in Twentieth-Century Quebec," in *The Church Confronts Modernity*

The early twentieth century in Québec was a period of rapid social flux and cultural effervescence. Modernization, urbanization, ethnic diversity, and industrialization—all defining characteristics of nineteenth-century life in *La belle province*—combined to overhaul French Canadian identity—particularly among the young, who were invigorated by a vigorous spirituality of nationalist Catholicism.[22] The vertigo induced by the largely unanticipated and comprehensive dissolution of the traditional Canadien ways in Québec elicited an impassioned institutional retrenchment, furthering the already considerable socio-political consolidation of authority in the hands of Church leadership. The encroachment of Anglo-Protestant culture and economic purchasing power inspired the rise of an intentional social Catholicism that transposed clerical leadership onto a framework of labor organizing. A heightened self-awareness of Canadien Catholics resuscitated collective spiritual fervor and group consciousness. This electric environment would prove fertile soil for Onésime Lacouture's countercultural doctrine of supernaturalism, which was both a product of and rebellion against the ascendant social Catholicism in turn-of-the-century francophone Québec.

Montréal—Québec's cosmopolitan hub—served as ground zero for both French assimilation into the pan-Canadian social economy and isolationist revolt. The primary voice of militant Catholicism during this period was L'Action catholique, a collective of organizations that largely operated under the inspiration and guidance of Lionel Groulx. Groulx was instrumental in codifying, radicalizing, and popularizing Québécois patriotism, perhaps most notably through the identification of the Canadiens as an indigenous people and of Québec itself as a Catholic land toiling in a state of bondage under the oppression of Anglo-Protestantism. This militant attitude of Québécois exceptionalism amalgamated Canadien ethnicity and Roman Catholicism into a single category, intertwining maximalist spirituality and ethnic obligation.[23]

The triumphalist Canadien identity was rhetorically indebted to a mixture of cultural trauma, paranoia, anticapitalism, and binary racial essentialism that evinced a liminal cultural anxiety at the outset of the twentieth century. Roman Catholicism, French language, and Canadien provenance were juxtaposed against English Protestantism in the mind's eye of popular public intellectuals, who, perhaps not surprisingly, pushed this contrast even further toward the margins. Its testament emblazoned on the provincial license plate, historical memory plays a foundational role in Québécois identity:

> Nowhere in North America is the cult of the past stronger than in French Canada. Quebec's motto is "Je me souviens" ("I remember"), and this motto is no empty formula. French Canada has a sense of tradition unique in North America, and the French Canadians live in and on their past to a degree which it is difficult for English-speaking North Americans to appreciate. No real understanding of French Canada is possible without a realization of what its history . . . means to the French Canadian, whose most popular historian (Lionel Groulx) has made familiar the phrase "Notre maître, le passé" ("Our master, the past") and established it as a principle for action in the present.[24]

These dissonant conditions of an idealized past and a dreary cultural forecast primed Québec for the rise of a charismatic historian—an unusual pairing—such as Groulx to step into cultural celebrity. As the gravity of modernism and financial interdependence drew remote threats closer, a romanticized vision of the past provided a refuge of stability.[25] The "cult of antiquity" played a proactive, grounding role in building a container for the spirit of Canadien nationalism.[26]

In this context, the role of the historian was politicized as part of a collective social mission, inspired by ideals that deprioritized the modern understanding of professional objectivity—even if that concept itself has more generally been nuanced and problematized.[27] Lionel Groulx's historical work was its own form of evangelism, and he stoked the widespread conviction that by knowing their past the Québécois might discern a core

Lionel Groulx, 1927 (Division des archives de l'université de Montréal)

identity and thereby reconstitute themselves as (masculine) political agents with divine purpose:

> History is a moral act, consequently not free of the supreme finalities. Our ambition and our right are to write and teach as a Catholic and French Canadian should. The historian ought to work with his whole personality; if he makes it neutral and indifferent, let us say with Bossuet that he abdicates his quality as a man.[28]

While Groulx did moonlight in the world of fiction and some of his cultural anxieties pushed the boundaries of what would now be considered plausible, it was important that Groulx maintain his historian's professional credibility, which was at the root of his authority as a public intellectual. Nevertheless, "to Groulx historical impartiality was not neutrality," and he interpreted his vocation as a social responsibility to resuscitate Québécois national identity. Groulx dramatized the Canadien collective memory of a once-glorious past, contrasted against what was presented as the grip of contemporary existential malaise. In a sense, nationalist history operated as an academically respectable form of cultural group therapy and motivational speaking, which roused collective sentiment, preserved traditional values, and inspired conservative activism, based on a vigorous commitment to national purity. Purity was an enduring concern of Groulx's in terms of genetic procreation as well as cultural, literary, and linguistic preservation.

The alternate rounds of acquiescence to external temptation and insular retrenchment had considerable precedent in Québécois history. One hundred years prior, memory of an idealized past flourished in what was then Lower Canada as an integral part of the Canadien lifeworld. In Québec, nationalism and memory were coupled, which synced nicely with the customary Catholic veneration of tradition and cultural suspicion of innovation. Although the population in Québec had grown considerably more convoluted in the interim, the prevailing proximate other remained constant. An influx of diversity forged a new climate in the province and precipitated novel issues for les Canadiens. However, French Canadian identity continued to be largely defined in contrast to their Anglo compatriots. In the militantly Anglophobic Canadien discourse of the period, insofar as they themselves represented virtue, harmony, and the sacred, their English analogues manifested apostasy, hubris, and the demonic.[29]

Collective Identity and Québécois Romanticism

> In racial origin, the French-Canadian can claim to be within the circle of the elect, for his ancestors came mainly from Normandy, and he is therefore a "Nordic," but . . . a "Nordic" with a bar sinister. He is vigorous and hardy, and on the whole a better physical type than the French of old France. He has the Norman qualities of thrift and industry, all the Latin's sociability and that virtue for which the Latin is not conspicuously famous, honesty, at least honesty in the small things of life. He is medievally conservative. His is not an acquisitive or materialistic nature. He is cast in rather a small mould and is satisfied to have things as his ancestors had them.
>
> —A. R. M. Lower, "New France in New England," *The New England Quarterly*

French Canadians took pride in their collective resilience and ability to endure the onslaught of English modernism. The Québécois imagination constructed its own personal utopia in the form of *la Laurentie*—a mythical francophone land insulated against foreign invasion both physical and otherwise. The concept was adopted by the populist reactionary movement Jeune-Canada, colored as it was by a "mild strain of antisemitism" fused with a doctrinaire Catholic anticommunism.[30]

Jeune-Canada's vision of an independent, ethnically pure nation matched nicely with the aspirational ideology of Lionel Groulx, whom they courted for leadership. The promotion of the Laurentie as an alternate reality was instigated by cultural luminaries such as Groulx, along with the Jesuit Rodolphe Dubé (1905–1985; popularly known by the nom de plume François Hertel), who taught at Montréal's prestigious Collège Jean-de-Brébeuf and mentored the future political titan Pierre Trudeau.[31] The Laurentie, "a projection or development of the collectivity of the past," persisted as a rallying point for French Canadian nationalism and a distillation of Canadien ideals—in a kind of neo-conservative science fiction.[32] Even the liberally political-minded, such as sociologist Jean-Charles Falardeau, who critiqued militant nationalism, persisted in the vision of Canadien essentialism, which rested on French language, a peasant history, and Catholic religion.[33]

The nationalist Québécois narrative idealized its ancient history, often at the expense of the recent. It reached back "to a distant and presumably happy past" that was pre-Anglo and contrasted with previous generations' "weakness" and inability to hold out against invasion.[34] In this reactionary climate, upward mobility and middle-class Canadian respectability were associated with race-trading and Canadien humiliation.[35] The Treaty of Paris and concession of New France to Britain in 1763 were viewed as flashpoints for contemporary evils.[36] While historians of the Laval school tended toward a more optimistic interpretation of English-French compatibility in North America, the unabashedly nationalist historians in Montréal were more representative of popular opinion—that Canadien culture had been "decapitated" by the retreat of elites back to France in the face of British imperialism.[37] The British were a convenient and logical scapegoat for a people who saw their cherished values under attack. Canadiens cultivated an insular siege mentality that resisted novelty and sought release from the servitude that characterized their lot in modern society.[38] In the dynamic climate of nationalist politics and intransigent fixations on religious and ethnic difference, the Catholic Church became a symbol of Canadien resilience and wielded hefty social capital within the community as an outpost of traditional values—an "institution dominante d'un peuple dominé."[39] The shadow side of this capital was its capacity to be parlayed as coercive authority, reinforcing conformity among the faithful and marginalizing dissent.

Stereotypical depictions of Québec—which persisted until the dismantling of popular religious observance during the Quiet Revolution—portray the province as being dominated by a phalanx of clerical leadership which kept a stranglehold on lay activity and provided direction for battalions of dedicated and resourceful women religious.[40] In the context of an apparently hostile, foreign political structure and antagonistic national government, crucial public services were bottom-lined by numerous religious orders which swelled in urban centers to provide infrastructure that attended to practical needs and provided a layer of autonomous security from Protestant proselytism and lax morals. The parallels with modern Ireland were not lost on Canadien public intellectuals.[41] Ireland and Québec shared corresponding narratives—hearty, agrarian, peasant Catholic cultures that were devout and communitarian, had been invaded by the (Protestant) British Empire, had endured oppression at its hands, and had resisted its plans for assimilation and cultural extermination. Both the Irish and les Canadiens maintained their distinctive identities through resistance and cultural retrenchment. Seemingly benign literary and athletic associations doubled as separatist syndicates, which preserved traditional culture and fomented militant Anglophobic dissent. The preservation of language, local traditions, and religious piety took on cosmic proportions and inspired dramatic comparisons of British aggression to the Babylonian captivity. The particular ethnic and cultural iterations of Canadien and Gaelic supernaturalism were infused by the Church's overarching ultramontane antiliberalism from the 1840s through at least World War II.[42] In Québec, as in Ireland, Catholicism was characterized by outsiders as backward, superstitious, anti-intellectual, and rigorously conformist.[43]

Québécois historians and public intellectuals made industrious use of the apparent parallels between the Irish predicament and Québec's. The connection was also adopted by savvy conservative politicians and anti-Anglo agitators. It gave a sense of transcendent, pan-Catholic solidarity, which proved useful rhetorically—as it had for Ireland's "Great Liberator," Daniel O'Connell (1775–1847). Identification with Ireland reached across the political spectrum—elevated above the hallmark issues of immigration, French language in schools, and general xenophobia. As early as 1875, Wilfrid Laurier, a prominent member of the Liberal Party (which some ultramontane priests had anathematized under mortal sin) actually defended his politics by invoking O'Connell directly: "We are liberals like

O'Connell! He is a leader for us, a man that so valiantly defended religion in the English Parliament; that is where we draw our doctrine and not from the so-called liberals who seek to impose their ideas in violence and loss of blood!"[44] Laurier would go on to become Canada's first francophone prime minister. The Irish connection was, however, more easily made in terms of reactionary patriotic fire than human rights advocacy. Jeune-Canada's very name recalled that of the militant nationalist Young Ireland (whose quixotic 1848 rebellion was short-lived, and who provided a foil for O'Connell's more genteel patriotism), which itself drew inspiration from Giuseppe Mazzini's La Giovine Italia—a connection that presumably would have mortified Lionel Groulx and the Québécois ultramontanes, as it had their analogues in Ireland.[45]

As noted, Québécois identification with the Irish was based not simply on their shared mutual enemy and nominally Catholic identity. Their shared experience as "indigenous" communities whose Catholicism was steeped in the very soil they inhabited and, consequentially, whose oppression by the brute military strength of English heretics was an abomination. On an almost geologic level, Ireland—as the Laurentie—was visualized as a *Catholic* land that had been baptized by the faith of generations, and both communities depicted their bondage under Protestant rule in emphatically biblical terms. The one thing, however, that Canadien militants failed to properly acknowledge was the fact that French Canadians were not, of course, actually native to the continent, let alone the slice of land that was parceled out as the province of Québec. Cosmopolitan Québécois nationalists largely overlooked the stark fact that their bloodlines had but a handful of generations (maximum) on that land. Lionel Groulx himself went to extraordinary logical lengths in his vehement defense of Canadien blood purity—exemplified by his essentially fantastic claim that miscegenation with the First Nations was pure fabrication.[46] The French Canadian historical narrative largely overlooks relations postdating the colonial period, with the notable exception of the saga of Louis Riel (1844–1885), the late nineteenth–century biracial Métis leader, seditionist, and self-proclaimed prophet who has been called "perhaps the most prominent name in Canadian history"—although a virtual unknown in the United States.[47] However, the identification of Canadien ethnicity and culture as "native" was critical to the boundary maintenance of nationalist rhetoric and political propaganda.

Francophone Pride, Ultramontanism, and the Messianic Impulse in Québec

For Canadien apologists, there were indeed limits to the Irish connection. In Québec, particularly, that limit was cohabitation and the perceived threat of fresh-off-the-boat Irish Catholicism to French clerical power. The Irish in Ireland made for great rhetorical metaphors and abstract comrades-in-arms against Anglo-Protestant aggression. However, as in the United States, Irish immigration facilitated the ascension of politically savvy Gaels to governmental power positions, which understandably caused concern among the self-conscious guardians of francophone culture.[48] From a linguistic point of view, Irish Catholics were a threat, and as they became more prominently located in the Canadian Church they grew exponentially more dangerous to francophone stability. Things came to a head in 1910, at the twenty-first International Eucharistic Congress in Montréal (which featured appearances by the entire Canadian hierarchy, several bishops from Europe, and the notorious Americanist archbishop, John Ireland of St. Paul, Minnesota), when Francis Bourne, the British Bishop of Westminster, made the phenomenally bold, if ill-considered, declaration that the Church's future depended on the installation of English as its primary linguistic medium.[49] This set an electric stage for the bold nationalist Joseph-Napoléon-Henri Bourassa's very dramatic and public rebuttal just moments later. Bourassa (1868–1952; Ligue nationaliste canadienne political leader and founder of newspaper *Le Devoir*) defended French language as integral to the lifeworld of Canadien Catholicism and contended that the assimilation of English language would be tantamount to renouncing their racial identity and the faith itself. The implication of Bourassa's speech was that the substance of Canadien Catholic faith was wrapped up in its language and idioms and was not, in fact, entirely translatable or shared. His speech was a public, face-to-face indictment of Bourne as a cultural imperialist and drew massive applause from the nationalist press. While the primary target of this episode was a fellow Catholic, in this instance the same cultural defensiveness and linguistic Anglophobia amalgamated both Irish and English threats to francophone culture.

However implausible, the francophone nativist rendering of history filled a crucial role in the construction of Québécois nationalism. Concomitant with the rhetorical identification of French Canadians as the indigenous oppressed was an alternate and logically contradictory Québécois depiction of themselves in missionary evangelical terms. This vision embraced the community's immigrant character, with some amplification. Again, Canadiens self-identified with the biblical Israelites, but this time invoked the "sojourn in the wilderness" motif with France's revolutionary apostasy serving as the causes and conditions for their providential vocation. Their mission was dual: to protect the sacred faith from insurgent heresy and to proselytize the "heathen"—an inclusive term that applied to First Nations, British Protestants, and secular humanists alike. The fact that this characterization essentially contradicted the indigenous narrative seems to have largely escaped propagandists, who employed them interchangeably at their convenience. However, the exile/missionary narrative was more—if not completely—logically consistent, relying less on imposed cultural amnesia to correspond with "plausibility structures" of the era.[50] It may not have been seamless, but this storyline maintained continuity with the apostolic colonial era of heroic pioneering "black robes." The age of martyrdom in New France in the seventeenth century was preserved for posterity by the canonization of eight missionary saints, most prominently Jean de Brébeuf and Isaac Jogues. This era of evangelical revivalism in France left deep imprints on the religious tenor of les Canadiens that endured in Québec long after religious observance withered in France under anticlerical pressures.

The pressure cooker atmosphere of perceived British imperialism and Québec's insularity from continental trends protected Catholic culture from the mainstream influence of secularism. Turmoil within French society actually emboldened Québécois Catholic identity, fostering a superiority complex within the growing immigrant community. In Québec, the conventional intra-Catholic antagonism between ultramontane and gallican (that is, emphases on Romanism contrasted against regional expressions and allegiances) failed to take root, and to the extent that the latter persisted at all, it did so in the regionalism of francophone apologists rather than an ecclesiological philosophy. Here the traditionally competing ideologies were more cooperative than elsewhere. The imagined and real threats of Anglo Protestant invasion and persecution—coupled with Québec's unstable relationship with France—left Rome as the Canadiens' most reliable authority figure. Through the fusion of Québécois and Catholic identities, ultramontanism virtually monopolized French Canadian religious life and permeated the clerical infrastructure that controlled most of the province's public works.[51] The second bishop of Montréal, Ignace Bourget (1799–1885), is widely credited with popularizing ultramontane zeal by recruiting elite religious orders, promoting popular devotions and religious paraphernalia, and encouraging clerical involvement in local politics—reimagining the City of Saints as a "petite Rome."[52] Québécois loyalty to Rome was given an opportunity to prove itself during Pius IX's tumultuous tenure, when, in 1868, Montréal sourced 135 of their own to serve as papal Zouaves for the protection of the Vatican as an outpost against Italian unification.[53]

Even prior to the French Revolution, missionaries fostered a utopian zeal among immigrant Catholics that mimicked their Puritan counterparts to the south. The lack of government logistical support left it to the Church to provide organization and social services, which further increased their vital position within Québécois society and solidified their spiritual authority.[54] The relative isolation that early French Canadians felt abroad was radicalized by English encroachment and the eventual capitulation of New France.[55] The rise of profane modernism and ever-increasing Anglo aggression inspired panic among the francophone minority. This was periodically reinforced by supernatural retribution, such as the massive fire that decimated fully one-third of Montréal on June 7 and 8, 1852. Widely interpreted through the lens of Canadien covenant theology as cosmic retribution for lax morals, the raging fire prompted a crowd to spontaneously gather prostrate around the threatened Sulpician's Basilique Notre-Dame, petitioning (successfully, as it were) Blessed Mother's intercession—an episode dramatized by Louis Riel's commemorative poem "Incendium."[56] The end of the Seven Years' War and formal political absorption of Lower Canada into the British Empire allowed the clergy to gain further traction as custodians of the faith and cultural leaders among an orphaned Canadien populace.[57] In the supernatural imagination of *les habitants*, socio-political developments carried transcendent consequences and Church adherence flourished. This accounts for Québec's pre-1960s air of quasi-medieval immutability. For many, the looming threat of British aggression confirmed the Québécois' ordination as a divine remnant under threat of demonic infiltration through British government coercion, exogamy, proselytism, and cultural assimilation.[58] The land that had promised refuge from the infiltration of European secularism was threatened on both material and spiritual fronts. In the imagination of *les dévots*, the veil between the socio-political and supernatural was highly porous, and current events were apt to be interpreted through the dynamic light of faith.

Boundary Maintenance and the Defenders of Morality

French Canada composes what sociologist Everett Hughes calls a "culture-area" and shares many standard criteria for statehood, which composed much of the basis for Canadien patriotic secessionism.[59] However, Québécois discourse at the dawn of the twentieth century often went a step further in claiming to actually constitute a distinct race. This elevated the discourse of ethnic integration to an ear-splitting pitch and fueled francophone anxieties regarding the lure of the city:

> Cities bred standardization, homogeneity, and ultimately, they [Québécois traditionalists] suspected, assimilation. With too many people engaged in too many activities of rather dubious worth, the city could hardly nourish the values of French Canada; it might even toll their demise. . . . Sunday movies showed American melodramas with dissolute characters; the popular press aped the worst American papers by making heroes of sordid criminals; the dance halls jumped to the barbaric tones and lewd embraces of American jazz; the arenas foisted American baseball on huge crowds willing to pay for their own passivity.[60]

Morally speaking, American and Canadian social influence conspired to dilute Québécois identity, loosening the ligaments of Roman Catholic culture. Exposing francophone youth to the lure of secular entertainment, materialism, and political ambition facilitated ethnic mixing, exogamy, and the dissolution of the Canadien "race." The messianic self-image that conservative French Canadians perpetuated endowed their boundary maintenance concerns with deep significance, along with the preservation of the peculiar Québécois French dialect and agrarian lifestyle.[61]

Nationalist politics was often stereotypically patriarchal, and conservative rhetoric paired women with children as particularly susceptible targets of moral corruption. The dual specters of women's suffrage and secular employment—that is, not as women religious—were troubling for the gatekeepers of Canadien tradition. They balked at the proposition of female higher education, allegedly on moral grounds, rationalizing that, along with the rolling back of basic liberties, it would precipitate the disintegration of the Catholic family. In defense of refusing voting rights to Québécois women, which persisted until 1944 (although suffrage had been granted in federal elections in 1918), Jean-Marie-Rodrigue Cardinal Villeneuve argued it was unnatural, (again) subversive to the family, morally perilous, and rendered unnecessary on account of women's lobbying organizations.[62] Québec was the last province in Canada to concede women's voting rights. Professionally, Catholic women were discouraged from pursuing lifestyle choices that would endanger their roles as homemakers and wives—the vanguard of the Laurentie's "revenge of the cradle." The one major acceptable alternative to this was vowed religious life, and Québec was home to a multitude of women's orders that ran the province's hospitals and elementary schools and provided all manner of logistical infrastructure.[63] Additionally, more contemplative options were available for those attracted to the cloistered life of intensive prayer. Nonetheless, in 1908 a four-year women's college was established in Montréal by the Congregation of Notre Dame. While some historians have viewed these shifts in the treatment of Canadiennes throughout the first half of the twentieth century as murmurs of the impending Révolution tranquille, Québécois women's rights lagged decades behind their provincial neighbors, and ultramontane nationalist leaders such as Henri Bourassa lobbied heavily against the tides of gender equality.[64]

The Québécois self-image was based on a portable but profound sense of difference: initially relative to the indigenous First Nations, later French secularists, English Protestants, and—within the context of urbanism and increasing immigration—Irish and Italian Catholics and Jews. Their sense of mission isolated les Canadiens, and was sustained by the relative degradation of other communities as they encroached on the Québécois psyche. While Lionel Groulx formally rejected the proposition of Canadien-First Nations matrimony and procreation as even possible, French genetic distinctiveness (and supremacy) was a commonly held conviction within the transplant population. Urbanization posed a major threat to Canadien identity: it enabled racial mixing, occasions of sin, and the dissolution of traditional structures of authority—all stepping stones to spiritual apostasy. It also fostered the dismantling of the subsistence-based agrarian peasant lifestyle—although some have stipulated that French Canadians were actually not particularly prodigious as farmers in the New World—and bound the Québécois to the rise and fall of international markets outside their influence.[65] Rapid industrialization drew Quebeckers into the cities and irreparably damaged the traditional way of life that was the cornerstone of Canadien identity.[66] The rural population collapsed into Montréal and Québec City (always the more resolutely French of the two) and pegged its financial stability to that of its Anglo adoptive nation.[67] However, this draw proved unstable and, for some, the prelude to another cultural exile. When increased mechanization and the fluctuations of the urban economy could not sustain its rapidly growing population, and coupled with the myriad cultural pressures of "foreign" encroachment, French Canadians evacuated en masse.

Kerouac's Forefathers—Canadiens on the Road

The last decades of the nineteenth century saw a veritable exodus of Canadiens from the province of Québec to Louisiana, New England, and what was then known as Acadia, which comprised what is now eastern Québec, the Maritime Provinces of Nova Scotia, New Brunswick, Prince Edward Island, and northern Maine. Although a sagging economy and urban decay in Québec cities may have provided the push for emigration, American factory owners contributed considerably to the exodus through vigorous recruitment, perhaps in the hope of capitalizing on the available workforce and the Canadien reputation as docile laborers: they accepted long hours with menial pay and had little history of collective organizing, along with a stereotypically vigorous work ethic.[68] This transnational emigration was interpreted in apocalyptic terms by the French population who remained resistant to the temptation to uproot themselves from their native Catholic land. In the two decades following the United States' Civil War, the Franco-American population quintupled.[69] National ethnic parishes sprouted up throughout New England to sate the demand for francophone liturgy while mainstreaming Church movers plotted the sanding down of Canadien cultural particularities to render them suitable for the US respectability melting pot.

For those who remained, the calamity of Québécois expatriation was twofold: first off, it diluted the concentration of French within their home province, leaving the ones behind even more susceptible to encroachment from Protestant proselytism and social pressure; additionally, these émigré Canadiens were profoundly at risk without proper support and infrastructure from their native community. In both cases, francophone Catholic culture was endangered—at the very moment they were under siege, those who remained were deserted by their kin, who foolishly left the nest in search of fiscal satisfaction and unwittingly entered enemy territory. It is not remarkable that those left behind would interpret this defection pessimistically both as a logical rationalization for being abandoned and as a method of propaganda to dam the flood. This model reinforced the Québécois sense of collective supremacy and perpetuated the cosmic drama that placed them front and center. However, the émigré communities themselves viewed their story in quite different terms. While it appears that the dominant motivations were clearly flight-oriented—financial and quality of life considerations—the itinerant Québécois, not surprisingly, painted their own narrative in more brilliant colors. As emigration evolved from a threat to reality, some adopted an alternate spin on the phenomenon, more in sync with that of the exiles themselves, framing their border crossing as a heroic incursion into the heart of Puritanism.[70] The recycling of the French evangelical interpretation of colonial migration gained traction as dense settlements formed in Lowell, Massachusetts, and Plattsburgh, New York, as well as Pawtucket and Woonsocket, Rhode Island. The triumphalist pioneering spirit drew from earlier romantic visions of their colonization of the New World and acquiesced to the harsh reality that, in a sense, the French apostolic commission remained unfulfilled. This vision of rooting Canadien Catholicism in New England was temporarily successful, if somewhat short of its grandiose evangelical plans as the Québécois were themselves absorbed into the more congested matrix of American immigrant Catholicism.[71]

Jules-Paul Tardivel and Satanic Freemasons

Some of the most biting and frantic allegations regarding the appeal and influence of American culture gained a public forum in the weekly *La Vérité*, published under the direction of Canadien adopted son Jules-Paul Tardivel (1851–1905). *La Vérité* was a leading organ of reactionary conservative politics and ultramontane Catholicism and acquired an air of respectability through its association with Québec's archbishop and the first

Canadian cardinal, Elzéar-Alexandre Taschereau. Along with sharing Taschereau's anti-Masonic angst, *La Vérité* maintained the strong conviction that American culture embodied and promoted social decline: materialism, crime, divorce, immoral gender politics, secular education, and frivolity—all of which were embodied in the popular literary novel.[72] Tardivel campaigned with Taschereau against the Knights of Labor, a fraternal organization then gaining steam in Québec, and publicly scourged James Cardinal Gibbons, Archbishop of Baltimore—once seen as a close ally—whom he saw as instrumental in suspending papal censure of the Knights.[73] The controversy sparked by New York's Edward McGlynn (1837–1900) regarding the rights of personal property and collectivism further confirmed Tardivel's suspicions that American Catholicism was damaged beyond repair.[74] Although the American financial panic of 1893 and constricting US immigration policies slowed, and even reversed, the flood of French Canadians to the United States, this was only temporary.[75] The draw of material security offered by the United States left francophone immigrants susceptible to treacherous advances.

In addition to concerns—legitimate or otherwise—that Québécois culture was being oppressed and infiltrated by Anglo-Protestants, two other threats loomed large in the Canadien psyche: Jews and Freemasons. In the climate of French Canadian isolationism, they were both imaginatively linked with the phantoms of international communism (and, oddly enough, free-market capitalism) and posed a proximate threat to traditional values.[76] Francophone anti-Semitism rose considerably as the Jewish population in Québec exploded during the first decade of the twentieth century, increasing by a factor of seven.[77] The international scandal of the Dreyfus Affair reactivated an until-then latent sense of conservative French patriotism and stoked Catholic anti-Semitism in Québec as elsewhere.[78] For faithful French Catholics, this episode marked a break point in the Church's relationship to the secular world and consolidated a worldview that Stephen Schloesser has characterized as "Manichean." Alfred Dreyfus's courtroom vindication notwithstanding, Canadien nativist xenophobia combined with enduring Christian anti-Semitic prejudices and traditionalist claustrophobia precipitating a distinct form of cultural paranoia.[79] Jewish immigration in Québec was highly concentrated in Montréal, with Jews constituting six percent of the city's population by 1921.[80] As Québécois politics grew increasingly alarmist and organized, resentment over Jewish administrative control of niche industries, particularly textiles, dovetailed with familiar bigoted tropes: Judaism as alien, secretive, and individualistic—all characteristics that preyed upon the anxieties of the French Canadian imagination and lingered within the mainstream well into the later half of the twentieth century.[81]

In the rhetoric of turn-of-the-century nationalism, the Jewish and Masonic threats to Canadien society operated in cahoots.[82] Freemasonry's reputation as an international secret society made it easily scapegoated as a clearinghouse for the multitude of dark forces that seemed to be closing in on Catholic hegemony. Its rise in France was blamed for the fall of the Second Empire to Prussia (interpreted by some Québécois clergy as "the judgment of God for its sins"), and nationalist conservatives were determined to prevent history from repeating itself in Québec.[83] This was the same electrified climate that had provoked violent riots in the streets of Québec City protesting the arrival of the Salvation Army in 1887.[84] Just as the cosmic Canadien imagination supernaturalized French Catholic identity, so too did it demonize Jews and Freemasons, who were added to the litany of malicious hazards to society. Tardivel's 1895 futuristic *roman à clef*, *Pour la patrie*, portrayed the Masons as Satan's own foot soldiers whose primary political agenda was the overthrow and extermination of Catholicism.[85] Tardivel was an extremist who promoted permanently severing ties with France, which he believed to have been terminally contaminated by Freemasonry and modernism. He was also a clandestine secessionist who concealed his real heritage as a half-English Kentucky native who did not immigrate to Québec until he was eighteen. According to Tardivel, "Masonic barbarism, worse than that of Attila and Genseric," threatened to disrupt this last outpost of authentic Catholicism on political, economic, and spiritual fronts under the cloak of "progress" and "democracy."[86] While Tardivel habitually condemned fiction as a literary genre, he made an exception for his own patriotic novel, which he rationalized as subversively turning the enemy's own weapons against them. Although *Pour la patrie* was met with something less than critical acclaim—it was dubbed "unreadable" by writer and political activist André Laurendeau—it circulated widely throughout the province and was a popular read in Europe as well.[87] During its composition, Tardivel was drawn in by the revelations of Léo Taxil (1854–1907; née Gabriel Jogand), a French rehabilitated *lapsi* who published a series of books and pamphlets exposing the link between Freemasonry and a Satanic "Palladin" cult. Taxil later reviewed the whole tale of his return and subsequent publications as part of an elaborate hoax that he had concocted to unveil Catholic anti-Masonic prejudices—a very successful hoax. While the truth of this charade was a source of enormous embarrassment for Church propagandists, it did have the desired effect. Catholic apologists claimed entrapment, but the conviction that Montréal was an epicenter of Satanic Freemason conspiracy proved resilient:

> There is no longer any doubt about it: Montreal is a centre of High-Masonry, of Palladism, of neo-Manichaeism, of Luciferism—of Satanism, to call this horror by its true name. It will be denied; it will be called absurd; but the proof is there. . . . Freemasonry is clearly a unified, world-wide organization, run by High-Masonry or Palladism, which is nothing more nor less than Manichaeism or the cult of Lucifer.[88]

Anti-Palladin anxieties were raised to a frenzied pitch courtesy of an encyclopedic exposé, *Le Diable au XIX*^e^ *siècle*, penned by one Dr. Bataille, whose accusations were corroborated by the salacious autobiographical accounts of an ex-Palladin named Diana Vaughn beginning in 1895.[89] Vaughn's memoirs bolstered Bataille's claims regarding the contemporary demonic and its links to "High-Masonry," conclusively proving what many already suspected—that Freemasonry was a powerful international conspiracy whose leadership participated in an exclusive Satanic cult. According to Bataille, underneath the Rock of Gibraltar lay a laboratory operated by Protestants and British Freemasons that was responsible for the manufacture of both plague and cholera, which they intended to unleash in a plot to install an international dictatorship.[90] Bataille's study was almost a thousand pages long. It alleged that the cult had established itself in every country, on every continent on the world, and had even infiltrated the Roman Catholic clergy.[91] Unfortunately, according to the author, the modernist mentality that is so prone to liberal secularism and disbelief—even among practicing Roman Catholics—is similarly inclined to ignore the reality of the malevolent supernatural. *Le Diable au XIX*^e^ *siècle* was meant to sound the alarm, to remind the world that Evil was real and on the rise. Just as devotional writers publicized apparitions of the Blessed Mother in La Salette-Fallavaux (France), Lourdes (France), Knock (Ireland), and Marpingen (Germany), Bataille chronicled the existence of the supernatural not just in the phenomena of faith or abstraction but in physical reality—incarnate. By fabricating a genealogy of Gnosticism that began with Simon Magus and continued uninterrupted through the Freemasons' founders, Bataille attempted to frame it as part of a parallel, deformed "anti-Christianity."[92] In the modern era, the Freemasons were the elite of Satan's covert operatives, through which he attempted to consolidate temporal and spiritual power.

Dr. Bataille and Diana Vaughn became instant *causes célèbres*, and the Palladium soon found itself the target of international inquiry, with none other than Pope Leo XIII at the tip of the spear. Previous suspicions having been confirmed, Freemasonry became the subject of papal encyclicals and editorials in the pages of *La Civiltà Cattolica*, the dignified Jesuit periodical. Freemasonry had officially been on the papal watch list since Clement XII published *In eminenti* in April 1738. However, on December 8, 1892, Leo XIII actually published two anti-Masonic encyclicals—*Custodi di quella fede* and *Inimica vis*—on the same day. The pope had met with Léo Taxil in 1887 and was profoundly moved by the tale of his return to the Church. Additionally, Taxil had gained the special confidence of both Bataille and Vaughn—notoriously shy, on account of their safety—and convinced the pope that the Masonic conspiracy presented a clear and present danger, which would only multiply in the face of Catholic complacency.[93]

Taxil's descriptions of Palladin Freemasonry, coupled with Bataille and Vaughn's extensive revelations (the anti-Masonic *corpus* was supplemented by the publishing of still other revelations, such as that of Domenico Margiotta, who explicitly linked the controversial American Civil War veteran Albert Pike to Mazzini and Garibaldi), fascinated as well as horrified Roman Catholics, providing Jean-Paul Tardivel with inspiration for the futuristic *Pour la patrie*, which was set in an independent Québec in 1945 and filled with paranoid anxiety.[94] Tardivel was obsessed with the Palladin conspiracy and even traveled to Paris—despite his debilitating thalassophobia—to meet with Taxil in 1888. While their compelling testimonies had transformed the Catholic mind and galvanized support for a renewed, militant spirituality, critics and former supporters alike puzzled at the cloud of secrecy that engulfed Bataille and Vaughn, who had yet to appear publicly or, in fact, to anyone besides Léo Taxil, it seemed. In order to set minds at ease, Vaughn dramatically announced her plan to reveal herself to the world on Easter Monday, April 19, 1897, at the Société Géographique in

Paris—and inspired Tardivel to, once again, cross the Atlantic. The editor of *La Vérité*—which had made its name in Québec largely through its coverage of the Masonic-Jewish Satanic conspiracy—returned once more in the spring of 1897.[95] However, to the shock and embarrassment of many—including Tardivel—and acerbic jubilation of some others, Vaughn was a no-show. Rather, the crowd was met by Taxil, who revealed that Vaughn and Bataille had actually been two characters in his arsenal of fictitious alter egos, which he had employed in a decade-long con to bait Catholic angst and humiliate Church apologists—people like Jules-Paul Tardivel.[96] Upon returning to Québec, Tardivel composed a defensive essay on the hoax for *La Vérité* and claimed that while Taxil had fabricated Vaughn and Bataille for effect, he was confident that Taxil's revelations were mostly legitimate and well-informed by sound research. Québécois paranoia was not laid to rest with Léo Taxil's admissions. In a sense he had outdone himself: by crafting such an elaborate and convincing conspiracy, the international panic he had stirred up took on a life of its own in the absence of hard evidence.

The anti-Semitic and -Masonic scandals that rocked the Québécois community at the turn of the century were largely based on collective anxiety and an eerie hyperactive imagination, displaying many primary characteristics of Richard Hofstadter's "paranoid style."[97] Combined with the rise of nativist xenophobia and socio-economic anxieties based on Québec's somewhat late entrance into the industrial age, the atmosphere in Montréal was toxic. However, while the nationalist press, Catholic and unaffiliated alike—*La Vérité*, *Le Devoir*, *L'Action catholique*, *Le Courrier de Saint-Hyacinthe*, and *L'Action française*—was constitutionally pessimistic regarding external threats to Canadien Catholic hegemony, their remedy was often explicitly proactive. It seemed that, concomitant with the messianic supremacy complex characteristic of Québécois nationalism and ultramontane spirituality during this period, Canadien culture was resolutely optimistic in the face of what it perceived to be looming threats from Jews, Masons, feminists, Communists, secular humanists, Anglo Protestants, Irish and Italian immigrant Catholics, and Americans—groups that were often thought to operate in tandem.

This is not to say that Anglo-Protestant anti-Catholicism was a pure figment of Canadien paranoia. It was, as in the rest of the British Empire, systematically institutionalized as government policy until the

Roman Catholic Relief Act of 1829, which marked the culmination of the Catholic Emancipation movement by finalizing a gradual restitution of Catholic religious freedom and political equality.[98] Nevertheless, as one would expect, Canadian anti-Catholicism lingered well after its formal repeal, although it could be argued that Canadian institutional anti-Catholicism was not all that oppressive relative to elsewhere in the Empire. Although the Quebec Act of 1773 made provisions for Canadien religious practice—as did the Canadian Constitution of 1791—regional governments continued to suppress Catholicism locally.[99] Canadian Protestant prejudice was less a legislative than a grassroots issue, and proselytism attacked perceived institutional corruption, magical superstition, sexual perversion, and political infidelity—concluding that Roman Catholics were rabid anti-modernists, the seditious puppets of the international fascist dictatorship known as the papacy. Paralleling ultramontane Catholic paranoia, anti-Catholicism in Canada, much like in the United States and Europe, tapped into a creative cultural impulse that hatched racist comic art and bigoted exposé literature—most famously the popular *Awful Disclosures of the Hotel Dieu Monastery in Montreal* by "Maria Monk," a "deliciously salacious (and almost completely fictitious) escape account of a poor Protestant girl held captive against her will in a convent full of secret doors to priests' bedrooms, buried bodies of nuns' illegitimate children, and dark rituals in the chapel."[100] To the anti-Catholic male gaze, the convent was alternately a cultural oddity, a site of veneration, and an object of gothic fantasy. As with francophone Anglophobia, some of the anti-Catholic rhetoric was actually not—at least in reference to the conservative, reactionary margins—completely unfounded. There were, in fact, plenty of ultramontane, anti-modernist Canadiens whose only sense of kinship to their English compatriots was the result of coercive leverage and who were viewed with semi-apocalyptic resentment. Francophone Catholics were not patently wrong to think that English Canadians wanted to assimilate them, politically, linguistically, religiously, and culturally; and English Protestants were not necessarily that far off base in their suspicions that some within the Québécois community harbored insurgent tendencies. On both ends of the spectrum, extremist discourse tapped into the very real, irreconcilable differences that formed the bedrock of Anglo-French conflict.

The Rise of Catholic Labor and Seeds of the Quiet Revolution

Practically speaking, when push came to shove, the battle for the Canadien spirit was largely focused on the fate of Québécois youth in the early twentieth century. Rapid industrial development altered the province's economy, and a wave of ultramontane revivalism funneled Québec's top university graduates into either clerical or legal studies.[101] Religio-political activist groups such as the Association catholique de la jeunesse canadienne-française (ACJC) were established to retrieve francophone adolescents from the perils of modern secularism and they often framed their program as antagonistic to their parents' perceived spiritual tepidity. As Michael Gauvreau notes, there was a thick layer of irony that lay below ultramontane traditionalism in Québec, which encouraged children to reject their parents' religiosity (or perceived lack thereof) and cultural assimilation.[102] The even greater irony was the fact that this generation of reconstituted youth would grow up to preside over the virtual obliteration of the entire Canadien Catholic infrastructure.[103] As Kevin Christiano writes: "The seeds were sown for a very different type of society in francophone Quebec, one that would be revealed more fully by the 1960s, at the first opportunity for liberalization of political leadership, of basic schooling, and of the values of the workplace."[104] The poster child for La Révolution tranquille was the charismatic and fully secularized Pierre Elliott Trudeau, whose election to the position of Canadian prime minister was symptomatic of the triumph of French Canadian assimilation and liberalism. While Trudeau's public persona—the charismatic playboy diplomat—has been well-chronicled and still fascinates, new research has revealed that he was, in many ways, also a prototypical success story of ultramontane Catholic formation gone askew.[105] Trudeau is—among many other things—a case study in Gauvreau's revisionist thesis and a symbol of the rigorous spirit of energetic, crusading Catholicism that was chronic among the Canadien elite during the early 1900s.

Trudeau (whose complete forename was Joseph Philippe Pierre Yves Elliott) was born into an aristocratic, "biracial" (that is, Anglo-French), bilingual, and cosmopolitan Montréal family. There has been some speculation among Trudeau biographers that, on account of his mixed bloodline, he was "psychologically dislocated," corresponding to Lionel Groulx's hypothesis in *L'Appel de la race*.[106] If nothing else, this historiographic bias shows how enduring Groulx's influence has been on the French Canadian imagination. Trudeau entered the prestigious Jesuit-operated Collège Jean-de-Brébeuf in 1932, just before his thirteenth birthday. Brébeuf, which drew students from the francophone elite, Canadian and international, was a breeding ground for future leaders in a Québécois world, and education there was an exercise in the cultivation of *noblesse oblige*, of molding fortunate young men into cultural and political leaders for the next generation. The ministry of education had been dismantled in 1875 in acquiescence to the Catholic educational monopoly to accompany its oversight of hospitals, orphanages, trade unions, and cultural censorship.[107] It was the kind of society that would have turned the famously autocratic Archbishop of Boston, Cardinal William H. O'Connell, green with envy.

The clericalized academic funnel in French Québec helps to clarify how a high school teacher like Rodolphe Dubé ("François Hertel") could be said to have "influenced a whole generation of students, outside as well as within Brébeuf."[108] While the stereotypical Canadien nationalist was a peculiar blend of ultramontane and Gallican conservatisms, Hertel attempted to promote a more progressive spirituality among Québécois youth that appealed to their sense of vitality.[109] Drawing on the philosophical synthesis of French personalist philosophers—particularly Emmanuel Mounier—Hertel and his cohort encouraged Catholic social reform as an alternative middle path between communism and free-market capitalism, one that emphasized both the individual and collective, material and spiritual. They rejected their stereotyped view of the modern trend toward individualism and mutual estrangement, bolstered by a supremacist vision of Christianity as the sole spiritual mechanism for communitarian liberation, based on its unique recognition of the fullness of the human person.[110] Québécois personalism challenged some of the clerical presuppositions of mainstream nationalism and flirted with the possibilities of philosophical dissent. However, the movement never really got off the ground, as membership was largely restricted to a collective of young, cosmopolitan intellectuals who subscribed to the journal *La Relève*, and members of the short-lived Bloc Populaire Canadien party—which sought to adapt Catholic social teaching to the Québécois context. Personalism's enduring contribution to Canadien society was to inspire a generation of progressive lay *dévots* to political service in the interest of social reform—this utopian idealism would mature, if in somewhat mutated form, by the

Quiet Revolution. In the more immediate future, however, the prevailing climate in postwar Québec was characterized by staunch retrenchment, which catapulted Maurice Duplessis (1890–1959) and the conservative Union Nationale party back into power.[111]

Following the Québécois World War I "Conscription Crisis" of 1917, the province retreated into a deepening insularity that contrasted with Canada's growing immersion in international politics. This came to a head following Canada's declaration of war against Germany in 1939—its first as an independent nation.[112] For francophone noninterventionists, at the heart of the matter was the ethics of French Canadians being drafted into military service under the auspices of the British Empire. This was a hot-button issue not confined to secessionist extremists, and memory of the conscription fiasco twenty years earlier, along with frank Catholic sympathies toward Mussolini's Italy and Franco's Spain, resuscitated old anxieties about the reinstatement of the draft in Québec.[113] The Canadian armed forces were not particularly inviting to francophones, as English language was normative in all but one regiment and Canadien officers were virtually nonexistent.[114] As in its predecessor, French Canadians were highly underrepresented in the military during World War II (Québécois men served at about half the rate of the provincial average), both among the working class and the bourgeois elite who populated institutions like Brébeuf.

While Hertel was an unassuming awakener of conscience who formed close bonds with his students and adolescent compatriots, Lionel Groulx's resilient shadow carried considerably more heft. He did not parse words, had little time for nuance and subtlety, and was, at least tactically, himself a "philosopher of the hammer." In the political sector, Groulx's militant conservatism was institutionalized during Maurice Duplessis's reign as premier—divided into two stints bookending World War II, which leftists nicknamed *La Grande Noirceur* ("The Great Darkness"). Groulx's vision of history had a profound influence on Canadien Jesuit educational pedagogy, and his writing was featured heavily in Canadian history syllabi at Brébeuf, which approached the subject from the presupposition of Québec as an illegally occupied nation, coupled with francophone Catholic manifest destiny. Groulx never budged from his messianic view of the francophone vocation, which he believed required a re-enchantment of the Québécois mentality to reverse the mongrelizing effects of modernism and immigration.[115] The revival of the Québécois mystique that Groulx fantasized about had practical fallout—economic, social, and political. Provincial, francophone isolationism was encapsulated in Groulx's catchphrase "l'achat chez nous," which was directed toward the restoration of a collectivist Canadien economy—that is, one that boycotted Anglo, Jewish, and minority merchants and goods. Groulx's strong insularity also required perpetual border policing, for which he enlisted the support of the nationalist organization Action française and its affiliated journal of the same name, which he directed.[116] Groulx fostered a militant sensibility among adolescent members of Jeune-Canada, whose *Manifeste de la jeune generation*—published in 1932—was essentially a proclamation of generational superiority at the grave expense of conventional authorities (parents and the provincial government), who they denounced as race traitors teetering at the edge of "the abyss."[117]

Increased industrial proletarianization among the Canadien working class guaranteed that the mainstream Church would be drawn into organized labor disputes in much the same way as was characteristic in the United States. In Québec, the clergy's general policy of non-intervention, and emphasis on harmonious relations between labor and management, led many to conclude that their bias fell on the side of the petite bourgeoisie.[118] Québec's natural resources, particularly in the hydroelectric sector, proved a welcome wellspring of income and job stability.[119] However, while this encouraged foreign investment, it also became a source of grave concern among Canadien nationalists, who resented their lack of authority in administration and collective bargaining, and with the Knights of Labor.[120] As in the United States and elsewhere, organized labor was stereotypically associated with socialism, and the Catholic hierarchy felt compelled to intervene—both out of genuine concern for workers and as a strategic pre-emptive strike against lapsism. In 1900, the Archbishop of Québec, Louis-Nazaire Bégin, intervened in a footwear industry strike, which drew the attention of Samuel Gompers and the American Federation of Labor, which came to exert a strong influence within Canadian labor politics. The cause of Catholic syndicalism was arrested somewhat during the interwar years and appeared to be dealt a deathblow with the ascension of Duplessis, who was notoriously antagonistic toward organized labor and incredibly popular among the rank and file of parish priests.[121] In time, the American Federation of Labor (AFL) and Congress of Industrial Organizations (CIO) would come to be seen as allies of Catholic labor in Québec rather than ideological threats.[122] The Duplessis regime's contempt for strong labor contributed to a tense atmosphere that finally erupted in 1949 in the aptly named mining community of Asbestos, virtually equidistant between Montréal and Québec City.[123] On February 14 of that year, workers walked off the job sites of four mines. All four were either English Canadian—or American-owned, the largest being operated by the Johns-Manville Company.

The fact that Johns-Manville had a reputation for relatively high workplace quality and fair play caused a bit of confusion for some onlookers: one of the miners' stipulations was the removal of layers of slowly accumulating asbestos dust from mill grounds, which seems pretty reasonable by contemporary standards.[124] Nevertheless, as things progressed and strikers found themselves financially crippled, they clashed with both police and scabs. Lionel Groulx and the majority of clergy called for a national movement to support the union, and the dispute morphed into a crusade. The strike drew francophone attention throughout the nation and attracted many of the Canadien bourgeois—including Trudeau—to the cause of labor rights for the first time. It became a symbol of Québécois bondage at the hands of Anglo tyranny and inspired revolutionary sentiments that breached traditional lines. That year, the typically conservative then-Coadjutor Bishop of Sherbrooke, Philippe Desranleau, with "social encyclicals" in hand, made a rather uncharacteristic Labor Day Sunday speech at a syndicate rally:

> Capitalism is the cause of all our miseries. We must work against it—not to transform it, for it cannot be transformed; not to correct it, for it is incorrigible; but to replace it. The reform of our socio-economic structure will be made through Catholic syndicalism, or through revolution, blood and death . . . .
>
> Men over 60 have seen two world wars and will perhaps see a third, even more unjust, more destructive, between two totalitarian camps—that of the concentration camp, and that of the American dollar. It is our task to change this situation by implanting the doctrines of the Church . . . .
>
> But we cannot succeed by the practice of virtue alone, for this is no longer a personal but a social evil. We must have reforms of the socio-economic structure, and no one has the right to dissociate himself from these reforms.[125]

Archbishop Joseph Charbonneau of Montréal, more conventionally liberal, attempted something of an end around (albeit a presumably sincere one) by claiming that the Church was the sole legitimate champion of labor, and rallied his constituency to the material aid of miners' families. Most of the Canadian hierarchy supported Duplessis's repressive measures, and the premier successfully petitioned the Vatican to force Charbonneau into early retirement.[126] Nevertheless, the strike was reconstituted as a "holy war, a battle for the faith" against heretics, and Catholic syndicalism became a bulwark of Québécois racial preservation.[127] While the Asbestos Strike ushered in a new alliance between the Canadien clergy and proletarian laity, it also marked the beginning of the erosion of the old guard theocracy in Québec[128]—"the social question" struck a new balance as priests joined manual laborers in the resistance.[129]

Seeds of the coming tectonic shift in Québécois culture that would bear fruit in the Quiet Revolution of the 1960s were sown in the sharp messianic climate of the '30s and '40s. The spirit of Catholic exceptionalism and ultramontane ascendancy witnessed the profound appeal of Lionel Groulx and François Hertel—in many ways on opposite sides of the clerical spectrum but nonetheless generational classmates who fostered an elevated cultural tenor. Of substantially less popular acclaim during this period, but of much consequence among the vowed religious of this generation in the province, was a revival of spiritual rigor initiated by the evangelical footwork of a young Jesuit named Onésime Lacouture. His mystical revelations in the Alaskan wilderness inspired him to delve back into the Catholic contemplative tradition and evangelize the Canadien clergy, giving breath to a movement that was short-lived within Québec but had legs well beyond the confines of the province. Lacouture's move toward interiority was radically opposed to the socially engaged Catholicism then on the rise in Québécois society but also harnessed the reinvigorated maximalist spiritual climate pervading the Canadien atmosphere. His scrupulous attention to ascetic discipline was in many ways an internalization of the muscular Catholicism that roused Canadien nationalist identity and political fervor. The charismatic sense of supernatural purpose that saturated Québec at the crest of this period of renewal proved fertile ground for Lacouture's maximalist doctrine.

2 Onésime Lacouture and Conversion in the White Desert

Let the good Lord do as He likes with His earth . . . with these "pagans"! The insomnia, the fire, the heat, and the ugliness were but samples, perhaps, of what awaited me in the North! God could burn me with His cold as well as fire: when it freezes they say it burns! Maybe God wanted to detach me from my desires to see the great earthly things. After all, how great are these magnificent worldly beauties, compared to those in Heaven? Nature couldn't satisfy my desires, but faith would show me grandeurs even more splendid than those visible to the naked eye. Doubtless, God summoned me by frustrating my desires for worldly greatness. Let Him be blessed!!!

—Onésime Lacouture, *Mon séjour en Alaska, 1910–1913*

He was engulfed in flames. Lacouture's first thought was that this was probably Purgatory. He awoke with a start, gasping for air, in a dark room that felt like an oven. It was sweltering, and all he could do was lie in his top bunk, dripping in his own sweat, and panic. Lacouture quickly came to his senses, which did not help clarify things—but at least he was able to deduce that he remained among the living, if for an indeterminate amount of time, given the heat and smoke that permeated the sleeper car he was trapped in as his cross-continental train sped westward through the Canadian boreal forest. At the age of twenty-nine, Lacouture had entered the Society of Jesus—more commonly known as the Jesuits—and was still six years away from his ordination to the priesthood. With no more than a couple of hours' notice, his rector at St. Mary's College in Montréal, where he had been teaching for a year as part of his seminary formation, had sent him on a great adventure: Lacouture would spend the remainder of his regency at the Holy Cross Mission along the Yukon River, some four-hundred twenty miles southwest of Fairbanks. For the enthusiastic budding cleric, this was the opportunity he had been waiting his entire life for: to follow in the footsteps of the iconic missionary Saint Francis Xavier and the North American Martyrs. He wanted to save souls, to evangelize indigenous communities in the desolate, frozen wilderness. But his expedition seemed to be off to a tragic start: Lacouture felt like he was being cooked alive.

A lot of people, probably most people, would have tried to take evasive action of some sort. Onésime Lacouture thought about God, Purgatory, and sin. In the analogical imagination that would characterize his theological doctrine of samples, his mind instinctively turned toward the supernatural. The next day, he realized that a forest fire had decimated the landscape. In the light of day, Lacouture looked out upon the scorched earth and meditated on the missionaries and martyrs who have brought the Gospel to these lands generations before—of Saint Isaac Jogues, SJ (1607–1646), and how he drove pagan demons from the land and was repeatedly called to the ultimate sacrifice of Christlike imitation through his capture, torture, and Passion. Lacouture prepared for a similar fate and steeled himself against overwhelming waves of self-doubt and trepidation. The charred carcass of the recently vibrant forest gave him a foretaste of the penitential life of a missionary in the frigid land the he would later call the White Desert. However, the nature of the desolation he would experience would be radically different than his expectations: it was he who would be converted, not in some stereotypical *Dances with Wolves* kind of neocolonial "White-Savior-gone-Native" narrative, but rather to a deeper, more intensely ascetic, mystical, and anti-intellectual prophetic Christianity. The White Desert became an incubator for his radical revivalist spirituality, and Lacouture would emerge convinced that it was mainstreaming moderate Catholics who were the true pagans.

Young Lacouture

At least according to his own autobiographical account, Onésime Lacouture was essentially born to be a priest—his vocation was providentially sealed. Throughout his youth, there is little evidence that he experienced any cognitive dissonance or anxiety whatsoever. Even later points of radical interior transformation seem integrated into natural, linear progression—though that may be a natural function of retrospective sanitization. Although his later trials and radicalization marked a profound transformation, in many ways it was a matter of degree and not kind, but this may not have been how he understood it. But there was no "sinning unto grace." In his memoir, *Mon séjour en Alaska* (*My Sojourn in Alaska*)—composed as an extended confessional letter to his mother—Lacouture chronicles his childhood and early life as a Jesuit. The text records his time at the Holy Cross Mission—the White Desert—beginning in the summer of 1910, where he had a series of unmediated, mystical revelations from God, which sowed the seeds for his future career as a revivalist and ascetic barnstormer. Critically, this experience destabilized his fixation on social respectability and intellectual prestige. Lacouture's experiences in Alaska occasioned a dramatic conversion from the personal ambition that been the hallmark of his time in Jesuit formation, which he came to see as infected by a deformed pagan Christianity. This profound turning point informed his fresh vision of himself as a prophetic iconoclast, which necessarily pushed Lacouture somewhat to the margins of Church life—although from his perspective the margin was the center.

As he saw it, secular modernism was invasive and permeated traditional outposts of Canadien ultramontanism, a situation that demanded vigorous spiritual renewal to circumvent compromised institutions—which, in Lacouture's case, were embodied by his Jesuit and archdiocesan superiors. His cycle of solitary illuminations was critical to forming an austere aesthetic vision of Church renewal. In the context of a rapidly accelerating social climate back east, the bracing stillness he found in coastal Alaska proved fertile soil for cultivating his new vocation as a "sign of contradiction." This liminal environment rooted Lacouture's visceral sense of cultural dislocation—being out of step with prevailing tides—and his consequent self-righteous evangelical mission. Lacouture's fortress-like family life seemed to insulate him from the existential turmoil that infected much of Québécois society—both in Canada and the United States. It was not until later in life that he realized the depths to which "pagan" influence had penetrated, even down to his own spirit.[1]

Onésime Lacouture was born on Holy Wednesday, April 13, 1881, in Saint-Ours-sur-le-Richelieu, forty-five miles northeast of Montréal. His father, Xavier, was a widower who married twice and had twenty-one children in total—of which Onésime was the second youngest.[2] Taken at his word, family life at the Lacouture household was idyllic—a pious, working-class family infused with love of God and charity for one another. When Onésime was six years old, the entire brood immigrated to the United States—first to Woonsocket, Rhode Island.[3] Incidentally, Woonsocket would shortly gain some notoriety as the adopted home of a Canadienne stigmatic named Marie Rose Ferron (1902–1936). The cult of the "Little Rose" was promoted vigorously by none other than Lionel Groulx and once aspired to usurp the popular devotional appeal of Saint Thérèse of Lisieux. It proved largely unsustainable in the long run and, as Paula Kane notes, now "endures mostly on the Internet." However, devotees credited Ferron's cosmic mediation with defusing the toxic Sentinelle Affair (1924–1929), which saw radical Canadien resistance to the homogenizing program of Irish Church authorities in Woonsocket escalate to the level of mass excommunications by Pope Pius XI—all eventually lifted following the offending parties' repentance.[4]

The Lacoutures' tenure in Woonsocket was short-lived, as they relocated to Ashland after just a year. There, Onésime became fluent in English and was afforded a rare occasion to craft his own classical curriculum, which may have had the side effect of isolating him somewhat from his peers. Although he did not indicate any sense of being a lonely adolescent, his social life appears to have been somewhat sterile and isolating, which future devotees would interpret as providential insulation from the corruption of US secularism.[5] During this time, even though he was positively smothered by his enormous family, Onésime managed to cultivate a deep and abiding affection for solitude and the outdoors, which would later color his spiritual development. Time spent playing in the forest and lake in Cochituate (now part of Wayland), Massachusetts—a Boston suburb where Onésime attended high school—seems to have formed Lacouture's analogical association between God and the natural world as a locus of providential insight, where the veil between the sacred and profane was particularly porous.[6] It was during this period that Lacouture's interior life began to deepen and he had his first inklings of a vocation to the priesthood. Although he had been raised in a devout family, he hadn't previously contemplated vowed religious life. It was a Redemptorist priest named Father Rheaume who seems to have exerted some influence on the entire Lacouture family and who first prompted Onésime to some early discernment. Subsequently, he became enraptured by the imagined heroism of missionary life, fantasizing about conversions he would win in remote, exotic—even harrowing—regions, winning souls "by the dozens and the hundreds."[7] This early romantic fixation on missionary conversions would alternately contract and expand throughout the next years.

Dreaming Big in the Society

Onésime Lacouture's eventual articulation of a "doctrine of samples" received its first glimmers of life during his adolescence. His high school insights regarding the relative goodness of the natural world and its divine referent, the ultimate source of Goodness, parallels Augustine's (354–430) own practical theology of ordered affect and encountering God through creation—that the natural world was a sort of refracting prism of divinity.[8] Nevertheless, Lacouture's rendering of his doctrine of samples formed the bedrock of his opponents' allegations of Jansenist tendencies. Lacouture's vision of creation as "good" but fundamentally hollow—not intrinsically valuable in and of itself—demanded that adherents guard against attachments to base pleasures and, ultimately, to even more abstract obstacles such as personal reputation. Herein lay the origins of the seemingly bizarre focus of Lacouturites against cigarettes.[9] Renunciation of material goods and finally of one's very self, for the greater love of God, was a core feature of Lacouture's spiritual vision. Holiness required painful sacrifice, but this was only experienced *as* sacrifice in proportion to our defective affect. The existential conversion that Lacouture's retreats would attempt to inspire, however, aimed to reconfigure the soul's disposition toward God—what he called the "supreme dominion of God"—to the relative devaluation of the created world.

Midway through high school, Lacouture's dreams of higher education were crushed by the realization that his family was too poor to afford college. This precipitated an adolescent crisis of faith for Onésime, but the Spirit consoled him and he emerged with renewed confidence in divine providence. With the help of two sisters, Élise and Philomène, Onésime managed to cajole his family into consolidating funds to put him through college. He had decided that one of the Catholic schools in Québec would suit him best, although it did promise some logistical difficulties, since Onésime had received all of his recent education in the English language and had become somewhat deficient in French. Despairing—a bit melodramatically—Onésime believed that his high school years were time wasted but pledged to redouble his efforts to bring himself back up to speed. However, his close family ties presented another obstacle: his father became emotionally distraught at the prospect of losing his youngest son and dramatically threatened to die of grief.[10] Onésime capitulated, but only a couple of weeks later—on September 18, 1898—disaster struck, and his father Xavier Lacouture died unexpectedly. The family was crushed, and when the dust settled it was Onésime's mother—Catherine Allaire—who implored him to stay. Again, he deferred his plans and graduated from Wayland High in 1900. After some time, he finally extracted himself from the Lacouture microcosm and entered the Collège de l'Assomption, outside of Montréal. However, a strong sense of guilt for dishonoring his father's wishes and abandoning his lonely mother remained potent—although one might speculate that Onésime's ten full biological siblings (from the Lacouture-Allaire marriage) may have provided an ample security blanket.

If the immediate preamble to Lacouture's entrance into higher education had been somewhat tumultuous, his objectives remained unshaken, and he seemed to find an amenable home in the world of academia. One of his classmates at the Collège, Joseph Sénécal, introduced Lacouture to the Society of Jesus, and Onésime would enter their novitiate at Sault-au-Récollet à la Saint-Ignace in 1902.[11] The combination of the Jesuit commitment to intellectual rigor and the order's history of activism seemed a perfect fit for Lacouture's romantic aspirations.[12] As with the decision to return to Québec for his studies, the prospect of his joining the Society seems to have been a great trial for his mother. Throughout the memoir, Lacouture repeatedly invokes Catherine Allaire as an exemplar of devout, voluntary self-sacrifice—an *alter* Abraham and Blessed Mother. This is perhaps not surprising, given that she is at least the nominal target audience of the work (even if it was baldly meant for public consumption), but even so, the text's maternal veneration is extreme. Lacouture viewed his decision to accept his vocation as viscerally traumatic for his mother and read her eventual acquiescence through a biblical interpretive lens. Just as Abraham was obedient—and the Virgin Mary watched her son offer himself to the authorities to be tortured, publicly humiliated, and crucified—Lacouture's mother accepted his calling and, therefore, in a sense, her own: a vocation to suffering, quiet forbearance, and endurance in obscurity that would enable her son's radical mission.[13] Lacouture's romantic depiction of his mother paralleled his perception of entrance into vowed religious life and, eventually, the priesthood. Lacouture viewed his life, like that of his mother, in terms of self-sacrifice for the sake of God's will—although his vocation located him as a more central protagonist. Insofar as he saw his childhood, missionary activity, prayerful sojourn in the wilderness, and later evangelism as an imitation of the life of Christ, so too did his mother's stoic suffering as a bystander to her son's "Passion" re-enact that of the Virgin Mary.

Two years after entering the novitiate, Lacouture returned to the United States to enter the scholasticate at the amalgamated Maryland and New York Provinces' St. Andrew-on-Hudson, in Poughkeepsie—now more properly known as the campus of the Culinary Institute of America and a pilgrimage destination for devotees of Pierre Teilhard de Chardin, SJ.[14] For his regency—a period of intensive apostolic work and contemplative service during Jesuit seminary formation—Lacouture initially took a position as a Latin instructor at St. Mary's in Montréal.[15] However, his mind was elsewhere: The Society had recently opened a university in Tokyo, and Lacouture seized the opportunity to apply for a position, believing it would fit nicely with his aspirations for advanced scholarship with a tinge of missionary drama. To his disappointment, his application was denied. Instead, he returned to St. Mary's on July 9, 1910, after his summer leave—a week of hiking, swimming in the Lac des Deux-Montagnes, and lounging about in Vaudreuil-Dorion (southwest of Montréal)—to learn that his provincial superior had volunteered Lacouture for the Jesuit Canadian Province's mission in a remote corner of Alaska. He would leave that night.

Conversion and Spiritual Autobiography

> The classic religious autobiography speaks to those readers whose faith and hope lies in stability of character and to those whose optimism depends on the possibility of basic transformations of character. Such an autobiography appeals strongly to the Western religious consciousness—to our deep desire for a finally complete self, based on the ideal of the unified self and the idea of the soul. Such a work appeals, as well, to our modern anxieties about the self, and to our awareness of the realities of character change, role-playing, and self-deception.
>
> —John D. Barbour, "Character and Characterization in Religious Autobiography"

In terms of literature and the genre of Christian spiritual memoir, Augustine of Hippo's *Confessions* remains the undisputed paradigm, essentially uncontested for the past sixteen hundred years. The argument has even been proffered (albeit hyperbolically) that Augustine virtually invented the first-person pronoun, so comprehensive has been the North African's influence on autobiographical thought.[16] In grossly abridged form: through God's gracious, unmerited intervention, Augustine abandons his philandering, egomaniacal pursuit of fame, intellectual superiority, and base satisfaction for one of chaste discipline, charity, self-detachment, humility, and community service. He is granted the gift of clarity—to see his own delusion—as well as an exit strategy, which is to give himself over to God's providence and renounce his previous life—to "put off the old man, and put on Christ," in the words of Saint Paul. Augustine's progression of depravity, short-circuited by conversion and a renewed life in faith—the "once lost, but now found" model, drawing heavily on Paul—has become a blueprint for Christian conversion narratives and has maintained an almost totalitarian hold on the Christian imagination. Even a millennium and a half later, American Catholicism's two most acclaimed contributions to the genre—Dorothy Day's *The Long Loneliness* and Thomas Merton's *The Seven Storey Mountain*—cling tightly to the Augustinian template, which Dorothy Day—referencing Baudelaire—called the "downward path that leads to salvation."[17] Augustine's model is characterized by intense psychological bifurcation and inner turmoil followed by release, which framed his imagination of the beatific vision in terms of tranquility—the oft-quoted "our hearts are restless until they rest in You [God]."[18]

At the heart of William James's theories of religious experience is a useful tool for analyzing the process of destabilization and reunification that Onésime Lacouture underwent during his sojourn in the "White Desert." As a bit of foreshadowing, James's Gifford Lectures at the University of Edinburgh (1901–1902), published as *The Varieties of Religious Experience*, would play an important role in Dorothy Day's interpretation of her heart's movements as she gravitated toward Catholicism. James attempted to analyze human conversion in psychological terms, based on a category of person—adopted from Francis W. Newman—that he labels the "twice-born."[19] Fundamentally, James reduces human personality into either the once- or the twice-born types.[20] In the most simplified terms, and as the name implies, only the twice-born are capable of conversion (to be "born again")—although the diagnosis is purely retrospective; if the distinctive feature of a twice-born is that one has had an experience of rebirth, then it is, at its core, a designation that can only be applied after the fact. There is no really practical way of distinguishing the once-born from the potential but as-yet unactivated twice-born. In James's typology, the once-born are characteristically optimistic and impervious to prolonged psychological discomfort. They have subconsciously—although sometimes intentionally—either insulated themselves against empathic responses to human frailty or have willfully blocked it from their stream of consciousness. They appear to float through life casually, untouched by existential crises or angst. The once-born type has no *real* understanding of personal sin and similarly "no element of morbid compunction or crisis."[21] This can either result from an involuntary personality predisposition or a more deliberate, systematic form that holds "good as the essential and universal aspect of being"—don't worry, be happy.[22] To the person thus disposed, the real problem is simply the melancholic temperament itself. It begins with the premise—self-aware or not—that happiness or contentment is life's paramount objective, refusing to recognize the presence of facts, emotions, or existential states to the contrary. Such people appear constitutionally incapable of developing the requisite cognitive dissonance necessary to precipitate a radical personal transformation.

More complex and, in the end for James, more compelling is the twice-born. They begin as "sick souls"—James uses the seventeenth-century English preacher (and author of *The Pilgrim's Progress*) John Bunyan, Leo Tolstoy, and himself (anonymously) as examples—whose experience of reality is infused with a painful unrest that precipitates profound existential crises. This eventually triggers a fundamental recalibration of self-identity. As a side note, James does not speculate on the consequences for the soul in crisis that does not eventually "unify." His basic premise is that the personality of the twice-born is initially disordered ("sick," in his language) but meanders toward a final state of "unification" or interior homeostasis. While there are numerous variations of the twice-born (or heterogenous personality) type, James considers them to be more mature than those characterized by patrons of the "religion of healthy-mindedness" (or what is commonly referred to as therapeutic religion) because of their more candid acknowledgment of human suffering and pain—although the threat of irreversible melancholia derailing the soul's progress toward wholeness is ever-present.[23]

William James's project has mostly diagnostic preoccupations, and although he clearly believes that conversion forms a more well-acclimated and complete person, James's project is primarily concerned with describing theoretical mental states. He did not compose an apologetic or construct a religious program; nevertheless, his abstract insights into the phenomena of religious experience and conversion may be helpful in thinking through Onésime Lacouture's Catholic revivalism. What Lacouture and (later) Hugo alleged—at least implicitly—was that the revival of a robust Christianity demanded nothing less than collective, radical conversion. The tragedy of contemporary Christianity, in their eyes, was that we are lulled into a complacent once-born mentality, drowning ourselves in materialism, and are therefore resistant to the pull of interior transformation. The Lacouturite doctrine of Original Sin hinged on a belief that, objectively, human nature *is* fundamentally "sick"—that is, incomplete, finite, and damaged. The rivals to Lacouturite rebirth were gross materialism, modernism, "Americanism."[24] Many who returned to the retreat and became avid supporters of Lacouturism did have such an experience—a profound reunification of the self that was precipitated by this teaching. Lacouture, Hugo, and the apostolic inner circle of their movement were convinced that conversion was an imperative prerequisite for holiness in contemporary society.

Les Déserts de Neige!

> I felt like I was dying to this world only to be revived in another. Something told me that I was beginning a new existence: I had been living more or less on the moon, by absorbing the doctrine of Jesus Christ intellectually: I had studied the spiritual life, I had heard it and knew all the great lines; I would live them now, sacrificing creatures and myself. If God forced me to experience something of Tabor, it was because my Calvary is not far!
>
> —Onésime Lacouture, *Mon séjour en Alaska, 1910–1913*

Lacouture was profoundly deflated at his appointment to the Holy Cross Mission, which seemed to terminate his aspirations for a career in academia; Lacouture's early dreams of evolving into a renowned scholar and making his mark on the Catholic intellectual tradition were dashed. He would not be another Aquinas, Bonaventure, or Bellarmine.

Rather, he would be sent into an arctic wasteland, spending what was left of his regency in the most hostile environment North America had to offer, amid a "primitive" people with sparse opportunities for intellectual development. The post seemed utterly cataclysmic for the frustrated aspiring scholar, as despair engulfed his spirit. However, Lacouture's considerable psychological resilience rapidly kicked in and fundamentally reconstituted his identity and sense of religious vocation. With the idealistic, somewhat overly dramatic (given that the term of his deployment was meant to be, in truth, relatively short) excitement that would be expected of an adolescent missionary, Lacouture encouraged his distraught mother to embrace a "redemptive suffering" interpretation of the family's collective sacrifice at his absence.[25]

It is not in itself peculiar that a young seminarian at any point in history—but particularly during an effervescent period of spiritual renewal, such as Canadien Catholicism was experiencing at this time—would view his narrative in dramatic terms that recycled mythical Christian plot lines and fixed himself at the epicenter of a transcendent supernatural conflict. While this could legitimately be interpreted as elements of a burgeoning messianic complex, and might appear a tad egomaniacal in retrospect, it is not, it seems, uncommon among the devout of any stripe. Lacouture was probably not the first Jesuit scholastic missionary to envision himself as another Saint Francis Xavier, boldly leaving comfort and worldly ambition to do God's work among the "heathen":

> I admired Saint Francis Xavier for sleeping under the beautiful stars . . . he was just like me: no bed sheets! . . . I must die to my pagan life in order to live that of Jesus, which is a life of renunciation, and deprivation, and suffering of all kinds. All this is nice enough to say, but I sensed that God would make me perform it, to show me that the service of God does not consist in words, beautiful and sincere as they may be.[26]

As it was, Lacouture's particular circumstances actually fit quite well into his newfound Xaverian mold, as the young missionary who had forsaken a life of academic comfort and prestige in favor of evangelical itinerancy in uncharted and ostensibly malevolent foreign lands.[27]

Onésime Lacouture's spiritual imagination already showed a strong affinity with Knox's "enthusiast"—which may, at least partly, be chalked up to youthful excitability and an unusually permeable supernatural worldview. Much like anyone—not just the young—may fantasize about glory and a truly meaningful life, Lacouture surveyed his future and realigned his self-image according to a missionary strain of Catholic tradition he had assimilated into his own narrative. Francis Xavier was the prototype for this muscular, adventuresome, Indiana Jones–style Christian evangelism, which eschewed safety and stability in favor of the wild. Lacouture fortified his new sense of vocation by reading the lives of his Jesuit predecessors and other missionaries—such as the North American Martyrs—in addition to that of Xavier himself.[28] These would steady his resolve in the period leading up to—as well as throughout—his time in Alaska. However, while he now reveled in his newfound calling as a missionary on the arctic frontier, he could not have anticipated that his life's signature contribution would be the re-evangelization of his own people upon returning east. At this point, there is also none of the dark, anti-intellectual, anti-Jesuit cynicism that would mark his later antagonism to the mainstream Church.

In Montréal, as he boarded the train that would take him across the continent to Seattle—where he would transfer onto a boat named the *Saint Joseph*—Lacouture was filled with nervous excitement mixed with a healthy dose of pure dread. He was conflicted about leaving the comforts of civilization for the frozen tundra. His messianic fantasies alternated with disastrous visions of terror. Lacouture viewed his sojourn in the wilderness as a spiritual battlefront, not only for Native souls but for his own. Additionally, his enduring sense of guilt for abandoning his mother was debilitating. If his relocation to Montréal had been trying, he could barely stand to think of how she would suffer as he ventured into such a distant, hostile environment. However, he soldiered on, surrendering their shared sacrifice to the greater glory.

Lacouture was primed for action. His spiritual enthusiasm piqued an already-heightened allegorical worldview and receptivity to religious experience. The world was pregnant with potential sources of divine illumination, and apparently mundane phenomena contained existential truths and inspiration, requiring only the proper discernment. While the "manifestation and likeness of God within nature" was on exhibit, it simultaneously revealed the "radical disjunction or unlikeness" between the created and Creator.[29] Lacouture's own imagination was vigorously dialectical—interpreting phenomena as alternately disclosive of God's proximity and radical ontological difference.[30] Additionally, Lacouture read Catholic metaphors into everyday occurrences. Otherwise mundane life events provoked reflections on the lives (and deaths) of previous Jesuit missionaries and Christ himself.[31]

Lacouture routinely contemplated what it would be like for himself to follow in Christ's footsteps. Like the young Thérèse of Lisieux, he imaginatively inserted himself into the lives of missionary saints, although his own vocation lacked the ironic juxtaposition that marked that of the strictly enclosed Discalced Carmelite. It did not, however, lack some of the same saccharine rhetoric that was characteristic of the Little Flower. As his train journeyed westward, Lacouture could not help but reflect on the supernatural majesty of creation and his missionary predecessors who sacrificed all:

> These men were made of flesh and bone, just like me. . . . They had to feel some natural repugnance and terrible fear as they left for these enormous forests where they would encounter tribes hostile to missionaries who might kill them, as, in fact, several were. God supported them so well that they ended up loving their painful apostolate, and returned as often as possible, even when they knew martyrdom awaited.
>
> These thoughts brought me more courage to face the coming miseries among the Eskimos. God could do the same for me, if I remain true to Him in my mission which was entrusted to me in Alaska. He gives His graces in proportion to the sacrifices that He asks. Moreover, I greatly needed to learn the science of suffering, following the example of my Savior, in order to follow Him later in His glory![32]

As the terrain turned rockier, Lacouture grimaced and puzzled why such a magnificent God would have created something so unattractive—although he decided to interpret it as a lesson in detachment. Lacouture's indignation at God for the unimpressive scenery aside, this passage reflects the pervasiveness of his supernatural interpretive reference point. Joyous experiences were occasions for reflection on divine goodness, while depression and spiritual desolation gave pause for acknowledging the relative depravity of temporal concerns. Throughout, there is also a self-centered (in a non-pejorative sense) focus on his personal vocation and mission to evangelize both heathen and Catholic *lapsi*—a category that would, in Lacouture's estimation, eventually expand to include the vast majority of mainline Catholics. Lacouture imagined himself recapitulating the lives of Christ and the saints—particular Hebrew Bible protagonists too—viewing history as a series of conical revolutions, wherein patterns repeated but were differentiated by time and—sometimes—space. The young Jesuit who would, in his maturity, be likened to Savonarola showed a cyclical historical eye of the sort most explicitly articulated by the visionary twelfth-century monk Joachim of Fiore in his concept of three *stati* of history, derived from the visions of John of Patmos (Rev. 14:6) and codified in the Calabrian abbot's Venn diagram–like illustration.[33] Without Joachim's explicit apocalypticism, Lacouture allotted himself a critical role at this decisive juncture in salvation history, which reiterated the spiritual warfare waged by his evangelist predecessors.[34]

The Slow Grind of the White Desert

Lacouture left for the Holy Cross Mission full of devotional fervor and expectations of missionary heroics but was unprepared for the more subtle internal transformation that would come to pass in this White Desert.[35] While he rapidly reconstructed his ambitious autobiographical narrative to compensate for his lackluster placement, Lacouture maintained a triumphalist tint but showed little anticipation of—or, frankly, openness to—the idea that he would himself undergo a radical religious conversion. To his initial dismay, rather than the evangelical fireworks that he had braced himself for, Lacouture's obedience to his calling was rewarded with loneliness, depression, and squalor.[36] This marked a decisive evolutionary phase in Lacouture's spiritual orientation:

> After the first weeks of profound *ennui* that brought out unexpected gushes of tears and pushed me to the edge of despair, the good Lord never ceased to give me practical lessons in the spirit of faith. Often, with a heart full of sadness, I went into the woods, first to frolic, and then to cry and pray. I asked the good God to let me know his reasons for having created beings as wretched as those who lived with me.
>
> Little by little a light dawned in my soul, and I began to see the divine side of human affairs. I understood that the evil was only in my twisted pagan spirit which judged everything solely from the point of view of this world, while God does all in view of the next.[37]

Lacouture had anticipated that his greatest challenge would be suffering through the austere conditions of the Alaskan wilderness and the loneliness of his isolation from civilization. He had arrived with dreams of saving pagan souls but teetered on the precipice of his own conversion. Again, it was the solitude of the natural world that served as the catalyst for Lacouture's religious experience, a spiritual breakthrough that rescued him from the throes of a psycho-spiritual meltdown, although any crises during this period regarded the nature of his vocation, not doubts that he did, in fact, have one. The question was not whether he believed in God or would be a priest but rather whether he could detach himself completely from the pagan Catholicism that he saw pervading the Church and his own spirit. Through a series of interior revelations, Lacouture came to "know many things"—which he would later interpret as analogues to Saint Ignatius's experiences at Manresa.[38] He suddenly found himself living on the supernatural plane in which he had previously professed belief on a conceptual level but had yet to experience directly. It was this sequence of transmissions that he later credited as his primary formation in the Christian spiritual life, superseding any formal training he received from his order. Future disciple John Hugo's semi-hagiographical account of Lacouture's regency does little to diffuse Lacouture's own theatrical account of his experiences in Alaska: "Onesimus was a *new creature*. The passionate desire for secular learning—for the curiosities of philosophers—had gone. A new passion began to rule his soul."[39]

Lacouture's illumination fundamentally altered his religious worldview, which—according to Hugo—only "broadened, although scarcely deepened," in following years.[40] As Hugo notes in the passage above, Lacouture believed that his revelations manifested spiritual truths that he had previously studied intellectually as a scholastic but had yet to fully internalize or encounter in any direct fashion. This marked a distinct evolution in his consideration of the limits of speculative philosophy—and discursive thought in general—in favor of personal, "unmediated" experience. His recently enhanced ultra-supernaturalism was expressed in a contemplative shift, accompanied by a concomitant anti-intellectual revolt that would become a signature feature of Lacouturism and a source of enduring confrontation with the movement's various critics. Lacouture's interior illumination and newfound dedication to Christian perfection created immediate difficulties with his Jesuit superiors, which would endure

Holy Cross Mission, early 1900s (Photo credit: Frank G. and Frances Carpenter Collection, Library of Congress)

for more or less the rest of his life. Along with his new vision came his relentless outrage toward the perceived worldliness and spiritual mediocrity of conventional Catholicism, including that of his fellow Jesuits, "clearly lacking *the mind of Christ*," regardless of good intentions. The gulf he witnessed between the supernatural life and pagan Christianity was so broad that they might as well have been different species of faiths altogether.[41] The trappings of paganism were particularly concentrated, he believed, in his incompetent Jesuit superiors and the wider Church authority, which sought to maintain or extend power at the expense of spiritual integrity. Lacouture eventually returned to Montréal for his preordination studies in theology. He seems to have suffered through it—on account of his professors' incessant philosophical abstraction—and never overcame his disenchantment with academia, which he saw as infatuated with the production of erudite scholars but not saints. Even more dramatic, Lacouture came to believe that intellectual sophistication and personal holiness were all but mutually exclusive.

Holy Cross occupies an area known as Anilukhtakpak in precolonial times, which persisted until the mid-nineteenth century when the Jesuit missionary Aloysius Robaut established the mission in 1888. The Jesuits and Sisters of Saint Anne operated a day and boarding school, along with an orphanage, primarily targeting the Deg Hit'an Athabaskan people indigenous to the lower Yukon River. The last vestige of the mission—the boarding school—was closed in 1956, although its legacy of infrastructure and public works subsist alongside a history of child abuse (corporal, labor, and sexual) and cultural trauma.[42] For his part, Onésime Lacouture's account of his time at Holy Cross tells us very little of the day-to-day activity of the place or of what actual work his assignments consisted. We do know, however, that he grew quite fond of his adoptive indigenous community. As one might expect, though, his account of the period is also stereotypically romantic, infantilizing, and primitivist in his treatment of the Arctic people: their simplicity, chipper worldview, discipline, and industrious nature—all common colonial tropes of the "noble savage." However, Lacouture's appropriation of indigenous "simplicity" profoundly affected his understanding of the good life and animated whatever anti-intellectual skepticism might have been lurking dormant in his newfound missionary identity; which is not to say that the Deg Hit'an's lack of refinement, typical western amenities, overt displays of affection, or "culture" did not shock and disturb him and perhaps even fostered his romanticized sense of reverence. Much like Francis Xavier himself, Lacouture admired his hosts' integrity and puzzled over the fate of their souls. Somewhat surprisingly—given his rigorist scrupulosity, Christian perfectionism, and theological conservatism—Lacouture experienced substantial internal conflict regarding the eternal destiny of the unconverted Athabaskans.[43] While by contemporary post-Vatican II standards, his hopes that God might deign to grant the souls of unconverted Deg Hit'ans an eternity in limbo might not seem an especially charitable concession, in Lacouture's particular case it truly was, given his dour speculation later on about the fate of his self-professedly Christian contemporaries. The genuine, albeit deeply romanticized, fondness that he developed for his indigenous hosts made his tenure along the Yukon River somewhat more bearable and proved instructive for his developing appreciation for austere simplicity.

The physical mortification of Lacouture's isolation in Alaska was now paralleled by an interior, spiritual analogue of absolute receptivity to the will of God: "I was conscious of renouncing all, more perfectly than ever: I had left civilization, the comfort of my friends, to live with possibly the most poor and most primitive people in the world."[44] The purgative effects of these revelations cleansed him of pagan attachments, which he retrospectively viewed as infecting his prior spiritual life—a point Lacouture reiterates constantly throughout his memoir with intentionally violent imagery ("massacre") to describe this process.[45] Later, he explicitly identifies spiritual development as "cette guerre contre notre mentalité païenne" ("this war against our pagan mentality").[46] Nevertheless, his retrospective gratitude for the purgation he endured ought not obscure Lacouture's emphasis on the proactive effects of suffering: "In any case, God wanted me to learn His wisdom through pain and sorrow."[47]

The autobiographical nature of Lacouture's account does not lend itself to the wholesale conclusion that he saw suffering as an objective necessity on the spiritual path. However, it did hold a central position in his understanding of the soul's ascent to God, and the refinement of Christian faith. In fact, Lacouture believed that the "life of Jesus"—the ultimate model—was "a life of renunciation and privations and all kinds of suffering."[48] Lacouture's meditations on the Passion played a fundamental role in cultivating his devotion to the Sacred Heart and fostered a deep sense of the redemptive effects of asceticism and voluntary suffering, in both dissolving one's attachment to temporal goods and also by participating in the divine life of Christ:

> I understood that, to penetrate the Sacred Heart, it is necessary to make sacrifices: in the same proportion He is opened to us. A note to those who find the life of Jesus arid in their meditations: they would do well to sacrifice more.[49]

As popular support among the lay clergy drew increased scrutiny, and theological criticism evolved into disciplinary restrictions and eventually exile, suffering would endure as a central characteristic of Lacouture's spiritual ideology; it played a critical formative role in his conversion from pagan Catholicism to authentic Christianity and continued to perfect him throughout his life by detaching him from things of the world. However, in many ways, Lacouture saw suffering as also an experience appropriate for the true Christian, who lives in this world as a sign of contradiction conforming himself to the code of the Folly of the Cross.

During his time in Alaska, Lacouture experienced both interior and exterior forms of deprivations and varieties of what Kallistos Ware has called "natural asceticism"—the withdrawal of trivialities rather than the imposition of direct forms of self-injury, which he views as pathological and violent (Ware uses the example of wearing simple clothing, as opposed to piercing oneself with spiked fetters).[50] This condition was, of course, all voluntarily entered into, although Lacouture (and later, Hugo) would make much of his diligent obedience in accepting the post against his will, without any apparent awareness of irony concerning what may fairly objectively be described as profound disobedience to his superiors in mature adulthood. Although it is fair to assume that he failed to recognize it at the time, the purgative effects of Lacouture's suffering during his regency—physical, psychological, and emotional—laid the spiritual foundations for his illuminations and empowered him to incorporate them into his path of formation. Lacouture's understanding of suffering as a method for cultivating detachment would display a strong thematic affinity with the affective darkness mysticism of Saint John of the Cross, one of his favorite ascetic theologians in later life.[51] John of the Cross delves more deeply than most into the different variations of suffering, which nevertheless all have a similar purpose: purifying the soul from attachments—to sensory objects, spiritual consolations, and finally to itself—so that it may desire God alone. The austerity of the Alaskan White Desert mimicked the internal aridity that Lacouture felt in his relative isolation.[52] While it may be argued that Lacouture's conditions compared quite favorably to those of traditional ascetic icons and his pioneering missionary predecessors, the salient point for understanding Lacouture's *mentalité* is his interpretation of events and how they fit into maximalist imagination. While Lacouture never self-flagellated, perched himself atop a pillar, or even fasted excessively, asceticism—as a means of spiritual formation—played a central role in his practical theology from a very early age.

In his exposition of "The Dark Night"—a poem which may have been partly composed during a stint in a Toledo prison, where he was incarcerated by "conventual" members of his own order—John of the Cross employs two different allegorical motifs to explain God's purgation and purification of the contemplative's soul: that of the loving mother who must wean her child as he matures and that of an all-consuming fire.[53]

In order for the soul to progress in the spiritual life, it must experience growing pains. The two "dark nights" that John highlights are actually signs of progress and thus, from the perspective of the soul's development, should be celebrated. However, as John carefully explains, the darkness is experienced primarily as pain, loss, boredom, and spiritual aridity. It is the paradox of the spiritual life that as the Christian grows in holiness and draws closer to God, he, in fact, experiences this as suffering.[54] John goes so far as to say that in the very depths of the second, more vigorous "dark night" that purifies the soul, the contemplative loses even hope and feels utterly destitute, so that it seems to be only momentum that keeps him from total despair, even to the point of suicide. At this stage, there is virtually no sense of self at all or spiritual consolation available to reinforce ego-identity—not even the self-assurance that one is actually progressing on the path. All the signs and inspiration that God had previously bestowed to encourage the soul further are now withdrawn, lest they become mistaken for ends in themselves.[55] Our attachment to sensory and spiritual consolations conditions us to experience their withdrawal as painful suffering. However, the soul's perseverance in faith confirms that faith as authentic, while simultaneously purifying it further by that suffering; and in this sense, the occasion of suffering provides the opportunity to express, while further deepening, faith.[56] The purifying and perfecting self-abnegation that John of the Cross prescribes would become hallmarks of Lacouture's spiritual posture.

Divine Illumination in the Tundra

> During these two retreats God was pleased to enlighten Onesimus on all these matters. One day he understood, in a practical manner, the use of creatures; another day, the contempt for creatures, the folly of the cross (i.e., the renunciation of our love of creatures, to gain the love of God), the reason for such trials as he had been undergoing, and for trials in general, and how God uses men, especially superiors, as blind instruments in detaching us from this world and our own wills. These truths were imprinted so deeply on his soul that the impression never faded; they became the foundation of his whole life.
>
> —John Hugo, *Your Ways Are Not My Ways*

Onésime Lacouture's account of his Alaskan sojourn does not dwell extensively—or much at all—on the actual subjective experience of his revelations, although these were the catalysts for his spiritual radicalization. He does not talk of sensory visions, of lights, the feeling of divine presence, or ecstasies.[57] We do, however, know something of the preamble—Lacouture was unable to participate in his annually scheduled summer retreat, because of his work commitments, and received permission for a solitary retreat. Although he would return to his normal residence in the evenings, Lacouture spent days isolated in the forest wilderness, uninterrupted by missionary labor or social obligations. Armed with high spiritual expectations, a romantic ascetical imagination, and a copy of Ignatius's *Exercises*, Lacouture was inspired and invigorated by these days spent in prayer and meditation under the open sky, huddled under some natural shelter, or even in bare snowdrifts along the banks of a nearby lake. The hostile environment gave him pause but also excited his flair for the dramatic, much like his Alaskan adventure had in the very beginning. The conditions were intimidating, and Lacouture suspected that malevolent forces might be conspiring to derail his progress in prayer. And as had been characteristic of his missionary experience, Lacouture's initial enthusiasm was again soon overcome by tremendous doubt and depression, bordering on complete despair.[58]

Lacouture's anxiety and frustration during his retreats became so unbearable that at one point he actually threw in the towel, turned right around, and started home in defeat. However, he checked himself and resolved to slog through the full term of his planned retreat. That evening he gained his first insight into the faults of his previously indulgent piety, which had persisted at the expense of a more humble, deocentric orientation; he saw the vanity of his prior concerns, hitherto having been governed by self-absorption and ambition, coupled with a need for comfort and approval. God's gracious intervention illumined his mind and gave meaning to his experience of suffering. Once more, Lacouture received comfort from the natural world and interpreted the eerie shimmer of the Northern Lights above him as a providential sign that he was back on track. The next day, he found a fresh delight in his asceticism and experienced the conformity of his will to God's own. His doubts, spiritual laziness, and inertia had all been laid to rest, and he experienced a delight in his asceticism that was previously lacking.

While Lacouture remained tight-lipped on the descriptive end of his mystical experiences, he was substantially less so regarding their substance. His silence on the former could be explained by a host of legitimate reasons: perhaps his sense of privacy dictated that he keep it to himself; perhaps he was anxious at the prospect of suspicion that might be aroused, and the fear of being discredited as a mentally unsteady quack; perhaps he did not want the accounts of mystical fireworks to obscure their more fundamental theological essence; perhaps he simply found himself unable to translate a nonconceptual encounter with ultimate reality into neat, comprehensible prose—like Saint John of the Cross's ecstatic "stammering" at the point of mystical union, when words fail, when the intellect fails.[59] There is certainly historical precedent and a legitimate rationale for Lacouture to keep mum about the subject—although one might not necessarily presume self-deprecation to be the most likely suspect.[60]

Everything in Its Proper Place: Asceticism and Ordered Affections

The practical theological insights on the love of God and proper ordering of affections that he received from his revelations would drive Lacouture's vocation as a reformist spiritual director and retreat leader for the rest of his life.[61] All manner of seemingly everyday occurrences now informed and reinforced his vision. Even his unholy and incompetent religious superiors could be unwitting tools for divine instructions on spiritual detachment and would serve him well in a future that would be characterized by perpetual conflict. Also integral to the development of his practical theology were the teachings on renunciation, asceticism, and the hierarchy of affections—the relative priority of the divine to the temporal, the ordered enjoyment of creation, and the dangers of attachment to what is provisional at the expense of the eternal. The hard environment in Alaska and the stark conditions of his wilderness retreat mirrored the interior scrupulosity developing in Lacouture's thought.

Lacouture's insights into detachment and affect pair nicely with those of traditional Catholic authorities. Augustine of Hippo, the Catholic orthodoxy trump card—at least until the elevation of Thomas Aquinas in Leo XIII's encyclical *Aeterni Patris*—wrote prolifically on the subjects of ordered affections and the proper use of temporal objects. Augustine's explicit distinction between *uti* and *frui* (use and enjoyment) in *On Christian Teaching* helped form the Christian philosophical hierarchy of "goods."[62] Augustine riffs off of Scripture by proposing that God is not just good but is actually "Goodness itself."[63] He contends that God is the very standard of "goodness" through which we evaluate creation, and it is God as the source of all goodness who imparts relative goodness to created "things." Classical Christian mystical texts often structured themselves around the progression from love of the temporal world to love of God and using our love of Creation as a reflective lens to reinvigorate love of Creator. Conversely, a habitually reinforced disordered love of things as ends in and of themselves represents the self's descent into idolatry. Properly formed, our affection for transient phenomena fosters but is ultimately inferior to our love for God.[64]

The twelfth-century mystical luminary, reformer, and cheerleader for the ill-conceived and ill-fated Second Crusade Bernard of Clairvaux also wrote prolifically on the subject of ordered affect. Saint Bernard's treatise *On Loving God* catalogs four developmental stages of love that the Christian experiences as the soul progresses in conforming itself to God's will. The soul begins with the most mundane forms of self-interested love, which are eventually transmuted into a more purified form so that one's affect is synchronized with God's.[65] Only at Bernard's fourth stage does our love become completely self-disinterested, and he is careful to note the improbability that this is even possible in this life, given its conditions. The main body of the system is concerned with renovating our affect, away from pure self-interest and "mercenarial" love that measures value in terms of potential benefit.[66] Bernard's treatment of the four degrees of love addresses the purgation of conventional egocentric love and its development in holiness, which is the restoration of appropriate order to our affect. Rather than loving God and others for itself, the soul comes to love itself and others in God as it ascends.[67]

The American medievalist Bernard McGinn has written of the "Mellifluous Doctor": "But whether we judge him right or wrong on particular issues, we cannot accuse Bernard of tepidity, indifference, or of failure to shoulder what he conceived to be his responsibility."[68] While Bernard of Clairvaux is a few hundred years too old to make the list, McGinn's words could very accurately be applied to Ronald Knox's litany of enthusiasts—and certainly to Onésime Lacouture as well. As his apologists, John Hugo foremost among them, would make in defending his orthodoxy, the pith of Lacouture's revelations did not depart dramatically from conventional treatments of affective mysticism and holiness. His unmediated communion with God, the core of Lacouture's later defense was that his teachings on the contemplative life added nothing to the extant canon of Catholic theology. At the heart of the Lacouturite call to renewal was the conviction that the illuminations given to Lacouture during his missionary retreats were of the very same substance as that which the Church had faithfully taught for two millennia, and contributed nothing new or remarkable in terms of essential content.

The Long Road Home

> Farewell to my dear Tabor, where I lived so close to God, and where I would have happily pitched my tent forever. It was so beautiful . . . but it would be crazy to spend one's life simply enraptured by these samples of God. Just as Jesus brought his apostles there [Mount Tabor] to strengthen them for the trials of his approaching Passion, I descended from my Tabor to EARN THROUGH SACRIFICE the splendors of which God gave me a glimpse in the wilds of Alaska. Now I was ready for anything!
>
> —Onésime Lacouture, *Mon séjour en Alaska*

Lacouture's Alaskan revelations were foundational both in the development of his characteristic spiritual rigor—founded on a principle of radical conversion with no remainder—and anti-intellectual antagonism to conventional institutional mediation and protocol.[69] Throughout his memoir, in addition to the White Desert motif—recalling Christ's forty days of fasting and prayer in preparation for public ministry—Lacouture envisioned the Holy Cross Mission as a recapitulation of Mount Tabor, the site of Christ's Transfiguration both foreshadowing his anticipated "Passion" at the hands of clerical superiors and the mainline, tepid, Catholic intelligentsia. Lacouture's direct experience of God, which occurred outside the hierarchical Church infrastructure, also inspired the vigorous iconoclasm that would thereafter be characteristic of his ultra-supernaturalist rhetoric. Outside the intellectual binds of the academy, Lacouture had traveled to the ends of the earth and the sparse, desolate wilds of Alaska had accomplished what his schooling and devout upbringing had failed to achieve. This period marked a pivot point in the trajectory of the scholastic's life, which diverted him from what could have been a more generic life as an academic, parish priest, or perhaps even a socially-conscious public intellectual—which was becoming an increasingly influential role in Québécois society at the time.[70] His vocation as a renegade spiritual director was actualized by the profound transformation he underwent at the Holy Cross Mission—quite separate from his formal missionary activity. The practical experience of Christ that he believed he had acquired now superseded the abstraction and theory that had played heavily in his formation studies and persisted among his brothers religious.[71]

Lacouture was now consumed with living the life of Christ, and whispers of his later anti-institutionalism murmured to the surface as the young scholastic reflected on his revelations and furthered his vocational discernment. His prophetic embrace of the Cross anticipated the Lacouturite revolt as a sign of contradiction, which sometimes seemed tailored to render his theology of suffering into a feedback loop, virtually courting institutional hostility:

> It is in the solitude of exile that one appreciates our station as pilgrims on earth. God does not want us to attach ourselves to the things of the world, so he takes away worldly pleasures so as to keep our heart for Himself alone! He came to life as Jesus in the midst of strangers for us to remember that we are also strangers on this earth; that we are seeking our homeland in the other world and will merit it by paying for it with this world. One cannot give his heart to both: it's one or the other! So, when God detaches us from the world, it is because He wants to give us Heaven in exchange. God sent His chosen people into exile for years to punish them for deserting the true God and so that in the privations of the exile, they would learn to put their heart only in God.[72]

Throughout the solitary days of recollection, meditations on the Passion of Christ had the most enduring impact on Lacouture, a feature that would factor heavily into his pedagogy as a retreat leader in the future. In Lacouture's mind, rather than humbly imitating the life of Christ, the vast majority of priests conformed Christ to their own standards of worldly ambition and ethical mediocrity.[73] Suddenly, there was a theological hermeneutic that incorporated his dissatisfaction with not simply an abstract mainstream clerical status quo but even his own immediate superiors at the Alaskan mission. Although he admitted they were good men, even good priests, they blatantly lacked an evolved supernatural orientation. Lacouture's developing self-image as a spiritual revolutionary was divinely sanctioned—an "authorization through personal experience rather than official credentials."[74]

When his three years of regency at Holy Cross came to a close, Lacouture's thoughts turned to his return to proper civilization. Although his missionary term had technically run its course, there was some question of whether he would be asked to stay on another year to orient the replacement of a brother Jesuit named Sigouin, who had seniority and had previously scheduled his departure from Alaska for that spring. For all of his reflective romanticizing of the Alaskan wilderness and his muscular conditions living with the Eskimos, he bucked at the suggestion that he remain at the mission to help support Sigouin's substitute and when given the opportunity skipped town at—almost literally—a moment's notice.[75] Late that July, when the *Saint Joseph* prepared to leave port for the mainland, Lacouture's superior, Father Luchesi—apparently somewhat offhandedly—offered to let him hop aboard at the last minute if he could pull his belongings together before the vessel shoved off. Little did he know that Lacouture had actually packed his bags already in the hope of serendipitous divine intervention. He quickly retrieved them, paused in the mission's chapel for a moment of reflection punctuated by several *mea culpas* for lapses of faith during his residency, and then—by his own admission—quickly stowed himself away on the *Saint Joseph* before Luchesi had the opportunity to rescind the proposal. The young seminarian who now dubbed himself "God's scalpel" suddenly found his Alaskan sojourn at an end and returned to his Jesuit community in Montréal convinced of a divine commission—although not before making a short detour to Massachusetts for a triumphant and tear-filled reunion with his mother and siblings.

> I felt like I was in between two worlds: Alaska, which was disappearing; and my return to civilization. In truth, my heart was surely with the world that I left: my soul was indelibly filled to the brim with

souvenirs of all that God gave me in His immense solitude—that dear country where I had suffered so much and where I had so much joy, where my "pagan" self was massacred, but where my soul received the grace to better understand the divine plan for us with Him in Heaven.[76]

3 Onésime Lacouture and the "Return to the Gospel"

Many do not realize the gravity of this conflict which is in reality a struggle "*in coelestibus*," between the good and the bad angels.

Because of the immense number of Christians who are gently slipping in the direction of paganism and damnation, through the appeal of comfort, of well-being and of "legitimate" pleasures, certain priests have begun to reject this state of affairs and have begun to preach the Sermon on the Mount once more.

—D. L. Crenier, OSB, English translation of "Grâce et Nature"

By the fall of 1941, Onésime Lacouture had emerged front and center in a vicious, and often unbecoming, intra-clerical scuffle that threatened to consume the Québécois clergy but, in the end, produced only one notable casualty—that of Lacouture himself, who was eventually stripped of his priestly faculties and shuffled around North American Jesuit provinces until his death in 1951. Given the iconoclastic and decidedly disobedient tenor of his rhetoric and countercultural posture, one wonders what other outcome Lacouture might have legitimately envisioned. The meteoric success of his Ignatius-inspired retreat among Canadien religious precipitated a firm response by more moderate skeptics—the pool of Lacouture's antagonists was not relegated to tepid secularists. Lacouture and other "preachers of the Sermon on the Mount," such as the Benedictine Dom Léonce Crenier of the monastery Saint-Benoît-du-Lac, further escalated matters until a critical mass was reached, and Lacouture's notes were taken to Rome and formally vetted by his Jesuit superiors, resulting in an unfavorable verdict. Lacouture's censorship signaled the end of his formal retreat ministry but not his evangelical influence; he persevered for the remainder of his life to gain satisfaction for his brand of maximalist moral theology and vindication for himself on the allegations of heterodoxy. While Lacouture was fortified by local support in Québec, the saga of the retreat was relatively short-lived in French Canada, as the lion's share of his legacy would play out south of the border.

Following his regency in the White Desert of Alaska, Lacouture the scholastic returned to Montréal profoundly transformed. He had been cleansed of all aspirations toward the academic life that had once been so alluring. In fact, at this point, Onésime Lacouture had already adopted a passionate anti-intellectualism, which must have made his four years of theology training at L'Immaculée-Conception somewhat daunting—however euphoric his enthusiasm as he sailed along the Pacific, back to civilization.[1] But the fideist hyperbole that would characterize much of his material—throughout his retreat notes but even more so in his public writings, which were few but memorable—was sharpened by his abysmal experience re-entering seminary life and the world of speculative theology ungrounded in experience.[2] The passionless formalism and meaningless intellectual complexities that had once enticed him now elicited only boredom and scorn. Lacouture did not even deem his instructors worthy of the title of theologian, pointedly referring to them instead as "philosophers of religion." The ongoing clarification of his calling as a sign of contradiction contributed to his habitual obstinacy to the norms and basic propriety of his order, which would later bloom into full-on—albeit surreptitious—insubordination. Following his third year of formal theological studies, Onésime Lacouture was ordained to the priesthood in 1916, on the Feast of Saint Ignatius—July 31. He was thirty-five years old. This momentous occasion did little to temper Lacouture's ultra-supernaturalist spirit, and it seems that his final years of academic training only exacerbated his already fierce opposition to mainline academia.

With World War I well underway, the newly minted Lacouture jumped into clerical life with both feet and characteristic zeal. After some work at the Jesuit novitiate in Sault-aux-Récollet—which he himself had attended—he entered the military chaplaincy. Lacouture traveled to England, France, and finally India, once combat had subsided.[3] These posts appealed to his missionary sense of adventure and came to a dramatic climax when Lacouture had the opportunity to serve Mass in Goa, at the tomb of his idol Saint Francis Xavier. He left the service in 1919 and completed his tertianship in Belgium, along with expatriate Jesuits from France. In Florennes, Lacouture received personal encouragement from his director,

Raoul Plus, SJ, but did not feel that he had gained markedly from his training—he received some spiritual nourishment and reinforcement of his already fully formed and intractable ascetic program, but nothing new in terms of substance. At the end of this period, Lacouture had been initially scheduled to set sail for China but was rerouted back to Canada by his provincial, who appointed him to the position of prefect at St. Boniface College, in Manitoba, where he would remain for three years.[4] His next stop was a post at the Mohawk First Nations' Mission in Kahnawake, just across the Saint Lawrence River from Montréal. There Lacouture gave his first spiritual conferences to the Sisters of Saint Anne, whom he had first worked with in Alaska.[5] These were apparently so well-received that word got out, and Lacouture generated a sufficiently high demand to warrant being placed on the province's missionary circuit as a professional itinerant preacher. With Sault-aux-Récollet again serving as his primary residence between 1927 and 1931, Lacouture used its facilities as a home base for his retreats, which were now primarily directed toward members of the clergy.

A relatively late bloomer, Onésime Lacouture did not actually give his soon-to-be-hallmark retreat in its final iteration until his fiftieth birthday, April 13, 1931, at "The Sault."[6] It was humbly enough received, with a grand total of four participants. Nonetheless, as Lacouture continued to plug away, his numbers began to swell—although he never had more than thirteen participants at any one retreat in its first year on the market, by 1937 his clientele had grown considerably to 1,116 annually, at an average of forty-eight per retreat.[7] This same year saw Lacouture expand his reach outside the world of French Canada, giving his first retreat in the United States—in his semi-native English language—to priests at the Sulpician Seminary in Washington, DC. The substantial headway that the Lacouture retreat made during these years, while perhaps not quite meteoric, was nonetheless impressive, given its humble beginnings and otherwise mercurial leader. As it began to make its name, Lacouture's "Sermon on the Mount" doctrine—as proponents dubbed it—also became a magnet for skeptics who looked with increasing suspicion on his aggressive, maximalist brand of Christianity, "so plainly lacking in *finish*."[8] By 1939, Lacouture had preached to almost three thousand retreatants (2,932), many of whom returned for repeat performances (5,400 cumulative participants).[9] This was also the year that the controversy came to a head, through the interces-

Onésime Lacouture as a military chaplain, ca. 1918 (*Archives des Jésuites au Canada*/Archive of the Jesuits in Canada)

sion of Lacouture's provincial, Emile Papillon, SJ. By the time his notes were formally censured in 1941, Lacouture had already been cast out into "the desert" once again—although this time his exile came in the form of the considerably more temperate Santa Barbara, California. Things certainly could have been worse in terms of punishment, but nevertheless, this marked the end of the first phase of Lacouturite history, which forced the movement more or less underground in Canada. Lacouture was relegated to minor tasks, while his adoptive provincial, Francis J. Seeliger, racked his brain trying to find him something useful to do with his time. Eventually, Santa Barbara was swapped out for Los Angeles, then Edmonton, and finally the St. Régis Mission in upstate New York, where he lived out the remainder of his years in relative obscurity as a bursar in the financially strapped community—punctuated by scattered visits from enthusiastic disciples, who made the pilgrimage to seek spiritual counsel. During this period, Lacouture largely followed orders and kept mute—with the very notable exception of two "anonymously leaked" rants that circulated widely among interested parties in the North American clergy and caused no small amount of trouble for his regional administrators. Although he claimed to have acquiesced quietly in submission—which he reliably narrated in dramatic biblical terms—Onésime Lacouture never ceased to angle for public endorsement and official remission of his censure. Lacouture was unable to resist the dream of mainstream acceptance and respectability to which his own prophetic doctrine was so ostensibly opposed.

Lacouture's Rise and the Doctrine of the Sermon on the Mount

> It is the intentions that form the scene of the battle between good and evil angels, between grace and nature, between God and man. . . . It is quite ignored by priests, sparsely employed, as one can see by the absolute ignorance of the faithful on the topic of difference between natural and supernatural motives. Above all, they have never heard of their radical opposition in the work of salvation.
>
> . . .
>
> To conquer ourselves, therefore, is to slaughter something of our little god on a daily basis; it's to wage a war to the death with him EVERY DAY!
>
> —Onésime Lacouture, SJ, *Mes retraites, première série*

Onésime Lacouture's Canadien arch-apologist and trusted correspondence custodian Anselme Longpré has written of his dear friend and spiritual director that he was, first and foremost, a disciple of Saint Ignatius.[10] Longpré is careful to distinguish, as did Lacouture, between this identity (Ignatian) and Jesuit—although in Lacouture's case, he was, of course, both. However, his spiritual affiliation with the Basque saint and his early companions superseded institutional vows as a religious, as Lacouture increasingly saw the Jesuits as emblematic of bourgeois ecclesiastical hegemony, unworthy of its founders. Lacouture's retreat was modeled on Ignatius's *Exercises* but was divided into three sections, rather than the more conventional four—corresponding thematically to meditations on sin, the life of Christ, the Passion, and the Resurrection. Lacouture's lesson plan was organized somewhat differently, reflecting his pedagogical idiosyncrasies and personal taste. Essentially, he compacted the second and third weeks of the *Exercises* into his second "*série*," calling it "la marche à la suite du Christ" ("following Christ") and repackaged Ignatius's fourth week as "l'Activité du Saint-Esprit" ("the work of the Holy Spirit"). However, this process was rendered essentially moot on account of Lacouture's extreme reliance on the first series of spiritual direction, to the almost complete exclusion of the last two. In fact, according to Longpré, Lacouture became so absorbed in his meditations on detachment and purification that he very rarely even touched on the second series and never once actually made it to the third during a retreat.[11] Longpré was confident that this imbalance was the source of the theological controversy that swirled around the Lacouture retreat, which was only exacerbated as former retreatants refashioned themselves as self-proclaimed spiritual directors; although they had only received a third of Lacouture's insights, they took it to be the complete package, thereby misrepresenting the fullness of his thought. That being said, there is no evidence that Lacouture ever attempted to amend his retreat structure once he became aware of the increased scrutiny, and actually doubled down on his preexisting bedrock issues: the relative opposition between natural and the supernatural, the properly ordered affect, voluntary suffering, God's supreme dominion over creation, and the radical rejection of secular norms.

Lacouture's inability to condense the full range of his program into any one retreat becomes somewhat less opaque when one takes into account that each of his three retreat texts—which he codified and surreptitiously distributed in 1948 on a very limited basis—clock in at over four hundred pages apiece. The first series, subtitled *Supernatural Doctrine: To Defeat All Pagan Mentality*—which made up essentially all of what was actually preached during the retreats—is subdivided into thirty-four sections with stark, severe titles such as "Jesus Condemns the Pagan Mentality," "The Folly of the Cross," "Hell," and—without any apparent implication of irony—"Obedience and the Sovereign Domain of God among Superiors." His extremely detailed texts make for somewhat repetitious reading, presumably in part because they were meant to outline or model conference preaching, and Lacouture saw fit to return to basic principle repeatedly throughout. From the very outset, Lacouture got to the point and illuminated the central themes of his preaching:

> By nature, man has two loves: the love of creatures and love of self. By grace, he is able to transfer unto God alone all his capacity for love, according to the First Commandment: You shall love the Lord, your God, with all your heart, all your soul, and all your mind. Man must be like Attila [the Hun] to his two natural loves, to follow the divine plan, the Christian must fight to the death against them, because Jesus says that we cannot love both God and the world, and that it is necessary to renounce oneself to follow Him.[12]

In a nutshell, the fundamental purpose of the Lacouture retreat was the conversion of participants toward a maximalist spirituality that radically internalized the Sermon on the Mount; as a mandate to wage unrelenting war against attachment to all that is not God: to created things—material objects, sensory pleasures—but also intangible objects, and eventually oneself altogether. The program was self-admittedly ambitious, if in the somewhat intransigent way that extreme forms of spirituality tend, accepting nothing less than complete self-renunciation. Although at this point the retreat was only prescribed for vowed religious and secular clergy, the fundamental principle underlying Lacouture's teaching was that the call to holiness is universal—a point that later apologists would implausibly attempt to spin as evidence that he was a progressive forerunner of Vatican II.[13] Lacouture was nauseated by the bourgeois convention of settling for the bare ethical minimum—calculating what we can get away with while still technically avoiding sin—and he railed against the misguided impulse to prioritize self-care, stoking the habits that lead down the path to sin. Extramarital flirting was a favorite analogy.

Although the retreat was never formally restricted to priests, they certainly were Lacouture's target audience. His mission was the rehabilitation of the clergy—to rescue them from the mediocrity that infected their ethical standards. From Lacouture's perspective, the modern clergy had abdicated its moral authority and pastoral leadership in favor of avarice and ethical laxity. In his estimation, the comfort, sophistry, wealth, and yearning for power that had permeated the clerical worldview made it impossible for them to effectively minister to their flock and were—in this manner—responsible for the degradation of Canadien Catholic culture. The loss of a pious, rural, agrarian lifestyle among the native Québécois—their secularization—was rooted in clerical corruption, which left the laity ill-equipped to resist the onslaught of Anglo-industrialist values. This was evinced by the sanction of "frivolous" activities on church grounds, such as youth sports and social gatherings, including bingo.[14] The assault on Canadien Catholic life that roused the passions of traditional patriots such as Lionel Groulx was at its root directed against the supernatural vocation of its people. While Groulx projected much of his ire onto the Anglo threat, Lacouture's critique was largely internal to Canadien Catholic life. It was a matter of language, education, and labor rights, yes; but even more critically, it was a question of Catholic values and God's dominion over creation. This critique even extended into the realm of social Catholicism—Lacouture was a staunch critic of L'Action Catholique—which he believed was too often compromised by financial greed and a thirst for power; an attempt to beat the Anglo-Protestant invaders at their own game, yes, but still playing their game. Lacouture's vision of renewal was to produce better priests, who would then make better preachers—and, thereby, to divert the Canadiens from their course of self-destruction.[15]

Making All Things New: Inside the Retreat

> This renunciation of one's whole self is repugnant to any rational being; it is ludicrous to him from the "natural" point of view, and just as men generally judge from this point of view alone, one may say that it is foolish when looked at from the perspective of man. St. Paul says that God chose what is crazy in the eyes of men, and condescended to speak like them, although he later said that this madness is God's wisdom, from the point of view of the supernatural. . . . One could say that this is the Folly of the Cross.
>
> —Onésime Lacouture, SJ, *Mes retraites, première série*

In his history of the movement's early years, Anselme Longpré isolates three basic principles of Lacouture's preaching: the Christian's supernatural ends, detachment from all created things, and the love of God.[16] This last point is subdivided further, as Longpré clarifies the fundamental expression of Lacouture's theology: conformity of one's will to God; giving oneself over to the Folly of the Cross; the imitation of Christ; the practice of perfect charity in the apostolic life. The theme of the "Folly of the Cross," pulled from Saint Paul's First Letter to the Corinthians, distilled Lacouture's basic principles highlighting the profound antinomy between the world and the supernatural—illustrated in the apparent absurdity of a God that would become fully human, let alone crucified on a cross. Lacouture juxtaposed authentic Christian values with those of a secular—in his own terminology, "pagan"—worldview, categorizing them as mutually unintelligible and irreconcilable.[17] This contrast points to a basic binary division that frames his practical theology: Catholic spirituality and secular values are, for all intents and purposes, fundamentally incompatible. In the Christian's soul, there is no compromising between the two, and any capitulation toward mainstream culture is, in fact, apostasy. The middle ground most Catholics attempt to inhabit is no middle ground at all—it is a disavowal of the divine and corruption of the soul. Lacouture was very much a "Christ *against* culture" purist, bolting from H. R. Niebuhr's general association of Catholicism with his "Christ above culture" model—although this might also be more broadly symptomatic of the diasporic "Immigrant Church," wherein pre-assimilation Catholicism found itself in unfamiliarly marginal positions.[18] In Lacouture's simple, uncompromising, even fundamentalist, terms, there is not partial or nuanced illness for the soul: it is either sick or it is healthy. Thus Ronald Knox's characterization of the prototypical enthusiast—she does nothing by halves.[19] In Lacouture's maximalist ideology, any compromise is a complete abdication, and those who preach moderation are counseling heresy.

In his study of the Folly of the Cross in Lacouture's theology, Karl Strauch notes that it was grounded in his view of the relative opposition between the natural and supernatural worlds.[20] The difference was stark: the supernatural world is, in a nutshell, God, and the natural world is everything else. It is by virtue of humanity's imaging of God, as well as its redemption through the Incarnation, that souls serve as the locus of the cosmic conflict between Good and Evil. Insofar as we are disposed toward what is low—the things of this world—Satan gains a foothold. Because of inherited Original Sin and the persistent tactical operation of malignant supernatural forces, thorough conversion is necessary in order to safeguard against backsliding.[21] The life of Christ provides an example of the absolute renunciation of the natural world in favor of the supernatural. In Lacouture's maximalist vision the Christian is called to perfection. An inverse proportional relationship subsists between our two ends: to the extent that we maintain and cultivate our attachments to the natural world, we alienate ourselves from God. Perhaps more important, the converse holds true: the only enduring means of growing closer to God is through renunciation and asceticism. Lacouture equates base moral instincts with paganism but also an overreliance on the intellect, which he sees exemplified by "*les philosophes*"—which echoed the Jansenist apologetics of Blaise Pascal.[22]

Lacouture was at pains to disclaim any heterodox statements regarding the objective opposition between faith and the intellect. In the abstract, he supported the traditional assertion that the intellect supports faith and is, in fact, a critical component of a healthy, homeostatic Christian life. Lacouture denounced abstraction as the purview of *les philosophes*, devoting more effort to examining how the natural and supernatural are, in fact, often opposed in the realm of practical spirituality. On this matter, Lacouture did not equivocate: "From the perspective of LIFE, the supernatural must entirely destroy our natural love for created things—and for ourselves—in order to safeguard our capacity to love God alone, as required by the First Commandment."[23] Theoretically, the natural supports the supernatural—reason illuminates and informs faith; philosophy undergirds theology; love of created, provisional goods are used to redirect our affections toward God, the supreme Good, and root of all goodness. It is not as if Lacouture is categorically opposed to philosophy—or parochial intramural sports, for that matter. They are all part of the inherent goodness of the created world; however, as provisional, they are not really goods in and of themselves but only insofar as they somehow lift the soul up toward the love of God.[24] However, human finitude dictates that this is rarely how things pan out. The soul gets caught up in its love of things—material objects, but also intangibles such as fame, reputation, even subtly manipulative erotic (in contrast to agapic) love—at the expense of love of God. Thus, rather than serving as vehicles that bolster our love for God, our attachments inhibit this growth and actually compete for our affection. And if the proper definition of freedom is the ability to choose what is proportionately superior—to be elevated above compulsion toward inferior objects—then humans rarely exercise free will, properly speaking, on account of our clouded perceptions.[25]

Renunciation is at the heart of the doctrine of the Folly of the Cross. With the aid of God's grace pious souls enter into the spiritual combat to reform their habitual attachments. The transformation is experienced as intensely painful, for the soul is not conditioned to love God alone and still clings to objects it has formally renounced, potentially long into the future. This recalibrating process of purification and aligning one's affect and intellect—of doing the good that one wishes to do—makes up much of John of the Cross's "dark nights"—particularly the first cycle, the "night of the spirit."[26] For Lacouture, austerity was not something optional on the path to sanctification, but a requirement:[27]

> Mortification deprives the affect of bodily and spiritual goods. . . . This is the reason for these meditations on the Folly of the Cross, from the practical point of view.
>
> Mortification consists in voluntarily depriving oneself of a satisfaction that one could legitimately take, or imposing some physical discomfort on oneself in order to expiate one's sins, or merit some further grace.[28]

Along with John of the Cross, the Desert Fathers, and other contemplative adepts, Lacouture echoed Christ's counsel to vigorously safeguard humility and repel alternative motivations associated with the spiritual life, and thus emphasized the interiority of self-mortification—its secrecy.[29] In Lacouture's system of thought, self-mortification is a process that one undergoes for the purpose of annihilating one's "pagan." "Pagan" is a term that Lacouture used liberally as code for base sensuality and materialism. Very rarely, if ever, is Lacouture talking about actual pagans—he uses it as a purely pejorative term. In Lacouture nomenclature, "the pagan"—natural man—remains attached to things of the flesh. Lacouture was not implying that there is actually some sort of possession occurring—although he did claim exactly this regarding some of his enemies as polemics heated up. Rather, he talked of "the pagan in us" as that part of the soul that delights in the world—and that was the pagan that Lacouture believes must be stifled, indeed, eradicated.

Throughout his writing, not just in his retreat notes, but really his entire corpus (including the anonymously leaked essays in the guise of private letters), nothing drew Lacouture's ire more predictably than academic speculative ethics. For Lacouture, they were the pagans par excellence and, therefore, his mortal enemies. Showing remarkable consistency throughout virtually his entire adult life, Lacouture cultivated a profound, obsessive hatred for the phrase "*in se*," which makes frequent cameos throughout his work. At every opportunity, Lacouture made a point of discussing the profound difference of a moral theology approached from the perspective of "*in se*," as opposed to "*in nobis*": it is in the space between the *in se* and *in nobis* that contemporary ethicists compromised their craft and otherwise well-intentioned Christians lost themselves in pursuit of goals that are not intrinsically evil but nevertheless distract from the soul's ascent to God.[30] Candy, money, baseball, dancing, and the ever-present Lacouturite leviathan—cigarettes—are not malicious, *in se*, but from the perspective of Lacouture's practical theology, they are dangerous. They are dangerous because we are easily tricked into seeing relative goods as objective, and this is habit-forming. It easily becomes obsessive and what is permissible *in se* has become idolatrous *in nobis*. As Saint Augustine observed at the very beginning of his *Confessions*, when narrating his hypothetical infancy—a passage that earned him a somewhat bizarre reputation for hating children—there really is no point at which we were free of self-absorption.[31] We come into life with this inclination fully formed, and it is only through grace, coupled with strenuous effort, that we may right ourselves and set our interior life in order.

Pagan philosophers mislead us by focusing on generalized abstract acts and calling them harmless, when they are the seed of addiction and obstacles to the spiritual life. The Folly of the Cross calls on Christians to renounce not just what is evil *in se* but *all* things insofar as they distract from our focus on the divine. Things that are "good," or even morally neutral, become treacherous for the Christian on the road to perfection. Christians are not called to renounce simply those things that are intrinsically evil; and it is not enough to simply not murder, cheat, lie, or steal. Lacouture's rigorist moral theology demanded that we mortify ourselves to all things. Lacouture's Sermon on the Mount retreat did not counsel asceticism as a penance but as a means of perfecting the soul. Thus, Lacouture makes it explicitly clear that the need for renunciation is not dependent on Original Sin but is embedded in our very creation.[32] Indeed, even the angels must practice self-mortification, which includes the practice of obedience—conforming one's own will to that of another. And, again, with Lacouture, there is no middle ground:

> Saint Michael's team gives itself completely to God; Lucifer's is completely self-absorbed. . . . How Christians imitate them! They act like

> true pagans, solely according to their own judgment and their own will, saying: "this is not evil *in se*." Lucifer is their patron, and where are the priests to challenge them?[33]

Lacouture employed Michael's and Lucifer's entourages as prototypes for self-renunciation and attachment, respectively. Although it was not in any way out of character for Lacouture to polemically draw an analogy between *in se* moral theologians—those who preach a doctrine of moderate, permissive Christian ethics—and Satan, in this sense he really meant it. Insofar as Church leaders, secular priests, religious, and laypeople are unwilling to renounce all creation, themselves included, for the love of God, they really *are* Lucifer. Similarly, Lacouture viewed Adam and Eve as "ideal types" for human sinfulness and harbored a palpable resentment toward the couple for torpedoing the Garden of Eden for humanity.[34]

The extent to which we are able to detach ourselves from the world determines how intimately we will abide with God in the beatific vision. Even more, Onésime Lacouture counseled vigilant Christians to cultivate "disgust" for sensory, temporal pleasure.[35] Lacouture envisions a directly causal, almost karmic, relationship between our life on earth and supernatural ends; even his understanding of the beatific vision appears hierarchical, although this is not, in truth, a topic he dwells on in great detail. If we are attached to God in this life, so we shall be in the next, and in direct proportion. Thus, the need for self-mortification predates and persists—in one sense—independent of the question of Original Sin.[36] Lacouture went so far as to describe this life as the *real* purgatory, in which we are called to imitate Christ's own "mystical death" so that we might enjoy eternal life with him in heaven.[37] Lacouture draws on the imagery of the seed that bears much fruit—our fruit being the fullness of the beatific vision. We sow good seeds by dying to ourselves daily and cultivating a one-pointed focus on the supernatural—and as it was on earth, so it will be in Heaven.

This vision of relative sanctification dependent on one's detachment from worldly life, while evincing the kind of moral scrupulosity and antipathy for "the world" that might be expected from an allegedly Jansenist movement, does not exactly bear a stereotypically robust Augustinian doctrine of grace. There is no doubt that Lacouture's extreme belief in the absolute supremacy of God would preclude any claims that grace is not absolutely critical to the soul's initial turn toward the supernatural and its support throughout the journey. However, the substance of the retreat was more focused on building a response to animating grace and seemed to take it for granted that holiness is ultimately a matter of our doing, predicated upon our own actions. This muscular spirituality—its Norman Vincent Peale "pick yourself up by your bootstraps" approach to the religious life—accounts for the very un-Jansenist charges of Pelagianism that were also levied against the movement. His is not a spiritual world where we do the best we can and God swoops down to save us, or—in a more Sanjuanist articulation—perfect us at the end. Lacouture's emphasis on *fuga mundi*, withdrawal, and vigorous spiritual activity evokes strong tones of traditional monastic theology, whose eschatological communitarianism has, if pejoratively, been linked to Pelagian inclinations toward self-mastery.[38] One spiritually controversial inclination with which Lacouture was never charged was excessive passivity. Although some of the heterodoxy charges directed at Lacouture and his followers took the form of very specific textual criticism, their reputation as theologically problematic and suspicious was based largely on tone: they were labeled "Jansenists" because of their dour, gloomy, moral scrupulosity and "Pelagian" because of their uncompromising Christian perfectionism.

Lacouture's doctrine of samples, which he first began to develop during his regency in Alaska, forms the basis for his understanding of the proper order of created "goods" in relation to the supernatural. The supernatural vision that he tried to instill throughout his retreats was fairly simple: all joys that we experience in life are but samples of the supreme happiness that we find in God, and they should be treated accordingly—that is, as strictly provisional and therefore somewhat hollow. Our fundamental error is to view them as static and indispensable. Lacouture drew on Saint Ignatius to illustrate his doctrine of samples, the proper "use" of creatures "to aid us in praising, revering, and serving God."[39] God has provided creation as a sample of Heaven so that we might merit contemplating Him directly for eternity. To this end, Lacouture describes God as a traveling salesman who displays samples of his wares in order to entice prospective buyers. Because we inhabit the temporal sphere, God meets us where we are and is reflected throughout creation. Creation's role in our spiritual life is to redirect our affections skyward and in doing so give us a foretaste of Heaven. In this sense, our interior lives may be transfigured from an earthly purgatory to an immediate vision of God.[40]

Lacouture located the morality of discrete actions squarely in the individual's motivation; thus his antipathy to any discussion whatsoever of things *in se*. As rosy as the doctrine of samples sounds, Lacouture cautions of the practical stumbling blocks that are inherent in lived reality, our fallibility and natural self-absorption. Lacouture deemed it virtually irrelevant that particular actions may be considered harmless in and of themselves; our motivations render all temporal pleasures potentially hazardous. Our interior disposition and our underlying existential motivations are the determining factors when it comes to moral judgment. This is not to imply that Lacouture disbelieved in the existence of intrinsic evil. For his purposes, that was not really an issue; and actually, engaging in that kind of speculation is exactly what he disdained about his corrupt strawmen moral philosophers. The root of our moral failings is concupiscence, which infects human motivations and deforms all our actions in respect to their proper order in the supernatural scheme of things:

> Concupiscence is the sensible attraction to pleasures. It is the great underlying source of our natural motives, because it easily infects all our approaches and actions, so that we revel in the creatures we encounter.[41]

Lacouture proceeds to use the example of alcohol dependency as illustrative. He treats our attachment to all things in terms similar to substance abuse—he does not argue that a glass of wine at dinner is an obstacle to holiness. However, alcoholism and drug abuse are predicated on some initial consumption; there is some progression of cultivating an addiction. The major difference here is that we all carry a predisposition toward self-absorption, in a manner that does not apply as universally to alcohol or narcotics. Our inheritance of Original Sin prescribes that we are, as it were, born into a state of temporal attachment. It is only divine gift—most fully expressed through the Incarnation and Passion—that empowers us to rise out of the muck, so to speak. While radical detachment, *apatheia*, may be the final goal of the ascetic, most practitioners must take baby steps. Although tedious, it is more practical to instruct discipline and restrict participation in specific activities, thereby transforming oneself on a more existential level, which will, in turn, extend to all activities. External ascetic practices are valuable precisely because they facilitate interior conversion.[42]

The experience of suffering is a necessary aspect of the life of renunciation, a kind of spiritual growing pains, as the soul tears itself from—and is torn from—its habitual attachments.[43] As the Christian soul begins on the road to perfection, it needs to recondition its loves, initially through deprivation, while keeping its supernatural vocation squarely in view. This is experienced as suffering and persists in varied levels as the vigilant soul progresses in holiness. However, this is only one form of suffering that Lacouture touched upon throughout his retreat program. Drawing inspiration from the letters of Saint Paul, Lacouture delineates three causes of the suffering that the pious soul should expect to endure as it becomes increasingly sanctified—our sins, the imitation of Christ, and our participation in the divine life.[44] While in many ways suffering is a side effect of the soul's ongoing conversion, it is also the spiritual flesh wound doled out by malevolent forces—whose endurance itself serves a redemptive function and further speeds progress toward sanctification:

> According to Saint Paul, God truly slaughters us! For the body, He sends all sorts of illnesses and infirmities; by the deprivation of poverty, and the avarice and ambition of others. Those big businesses that destroy smaller ones! Those giant industries that exploit their employees! Like the governments who oppress the world through excessive abuses and debilitating taxes for the common people! . . .
>
> Then plagues ruin the earth: fire, flood, earthquakes, drought, torrential downpours, frost, etc.[45]

Natural disasters and "bad luck" present us with an opportunity for detachment and, in so doing, to imitate Christ's activity and thereby participate in the divine life. He even goes so far as to imply that certain instances of this form of suffering may actually be sent by God in order to purge and perfect us—although it is impossible to determine if he meant this literally or if he is capitalizing on a pedagogical opportunity. It is one thing to say that God sends us trials and tribulations as part of our spiritual development. It is quite another to believe that specific events—an earthquake or a loved one's tragic death, for instance—are penances that God has employed for instructive purposes. Lacouture does not dwell on the subject long enough to clarify a position one way or the other. His agenda is spiritual development, and to this end he suggests one incorporate suffering onto the spiritual path. Among other forms of suffering that are inevitable for the Christian progressing in holiness are those imposed by antagonism—from loved ones, those we leave behind in "the world," even religious superiors (with which Lacouture grew very familiar). The maximalist Christian must prepare to be mocked, rebuked, attacked, and—verbally, physically, and psychologically—persecuted, as Jesus was. The interior stumbling blocks we may encounter find their exterior, macro-scale counterparts in the trials that are sure to come, even within the Christian fold, when one renounces the pagan worldview in favor of the Sermon on the Mount's inversion of the natural order.[46] The antidote for suffering is detachment, which is achieved through the practice of self-mortification. In doing so, we steel ourselves to the pain that results from fighting habits, inspire further aggression from critics, and, in turn, develop increased fortitude to persevere. In Lacouture's system, again echoing John of the Cross's "dark night of the spirit," persecution is itself a sign of progress, and we may take consolation in that assurance during times of anxiety and doubt. In fact, Lacouture goes one step further by alleging that one cannot achieve true holiness without being hated, reviled, and oppressed by those who uphold pagan hegemony and Christian mediocrity—a claim that has extreme countercultural implications if taken to its logical conclusion. Moreover, the drama that plays out in the renunciate's interior life—her struggle against her own attachments—is simultaneously paralleled on the supernatural plane in the battle for souls. The individual committed to a life of renunciation enters into a cosmic battle or, rather, picks a side in that battle; and the closer she draws to holiness, the more powerful and subtle the assaults against her will be, in order to derail her progress.

The Cavalry: Demons and Saints in Lacoutourite Cosmology

> Humans must be annihilated before the divine. How contrary to our nature! . . .
>
> This is why the demons do their utmost to prevent us from understanding the Folly of the Cross and preaching it to the faithful: to deprive God of all His glory.
>
> —Onésime Lacouture, SJ, *Mes retraites, première série*

One major feature of Lacouture's retreat notes and later polemics that may seem bizarre to modern readers—as perhaps they did to some contemporaries—is his frequent and candid references to demons and their role in derailing spiritual progress. Lacouture's worldview was immanently supernatural: he did not believe in angels and demons in a kind of hypothetical, competing-forces-in-the-universe way; he believed that they were real: sentient, invisible beings who inhabit our world and war with one another. Demons, like angels, are immaterial but may engage physical reality; they can influence human inclinations and behavior, inhabit bodies, and even incarnate as humans. Lacouture's cosmology was teeming with supernatural enemies who prey on human weakness and use the allure of paganism to coerce vulnerable Christians. Put bluntly, Lacouture talked about demons *a lot*.

In his study of demonology and early monasticism in fourth- and fifth-century Egypt, David Brakke highlights the monk's role in replacing the martyr by, as it were, amplifying and supercharging assaults on the early Church. As anticipation of the imminent end of the world waned, along with the "prospect of *actual* martyrdom" for the Christian majority, steadfast fortitude in the face of violent persecution was internalized and reconceptualized through an emphasis on the moral life and cultivating a resistance to temptations.[47] In this context, desert ascetics came to be viewed—in no small part thanks to Saint Athanasius's then-voguish *Life of St. Antony*—as God's infantry, spiritual warriors who vanquished demons through the interior combat.[48] On the micro level, the monk's ability to withstand an onslaught of demons in the desert—and he ventured out into the desert specifically to confront them—was a personal victory. The monk himself grew in holiness, being spiritually fortified throughout the process. From a macro perspective, however, this personal victory had wide-ranging fallout on ecclesiastical and supernatural levels. Although monasticism has been polemically criticized as profoundly negative—representing an antisocial, navel-gazing impulse—in the Christian context, it came to be viewed as a critical service to both the larger community of believers and God. The cultivation of individual holiness served a vital and profound social function.

In Onésime Lacouture's schema, the demons' primary role is to sabotage the Christian soul's progress toward perfection.[49] It does this using any means at its disposal—the full range of its considerable resources including the ability to manipulate our affections or confront us through more direct means. In the context of his retreat and the spiritual combat more generally, demons prey upon insecurities, constitutional weaknesses, and our ignorance—to draw us back into our addiction to the natural world and sever our attachment to God.[50] Moreover, they manifest in human form through *les philosophes*—morally bankrupt theological inquisitors, heretical preachers, and ecclesiastical authorities—who are simultaneously victims and agents of demonic aggression. They will stop at nothing to interrupt the soul's focus on God; thus, participating in the Lacouture retreat carried potentially grave consequences for the precise reason that it was itself massively threatening to the forces of evil.[51] Even spiritual jealousy and competition for holiness (or a reputation for holiness, more properly speaking) might well be the subtle tugs of demons attempting to sabotage God's work.[52] Lacouture's sense of diabolic opportunism—in this he was very Ignatian—perceived psychological defects based on "progress," such as spiritual pride, to be a Trojan horse for demonic assault.[53]

Conspicuous among the ascetic's special cache of ammunition for the spiritual combat is the communion of saints. With the exception of Michael, discourse on angels is virtually absent from Lacouture's retreat notes. However, the intercession and lives of the saints are invoked repeatedly throughout. Their very example of triumph makes them instructive texts in their own right, and, thankfully, they have bequeathed a wealth of material to support their fellow travelers. Their lives are blueprints for the spiritual combat and contain inspiration as well as practical instructions and guidelines for success. Not surprisingly, Lacouture's favorite saints are those who specialized in subjects nearest and dearest to his heart: contemplative techniques, God's absolute supremacy, and theological anthropology. There are appearances by the typical honor roll of Catholic spiritual writers: Saint Paul dominates, as one might expect—Lacouture seems to quote him as much as possible without simply transcribing his entire corpus verbatim. John of the Cross stands head and shoulders above the rest of the noncanonical authors, "the one who best explains a system of renunciation."[54] Lacouture was especially drawn to the ascetic bent of "The Ascent of Mount Carmel" and "The Dark Night," while less so the affective romantic mysticism that one finds in "The Living Flame of Love."[55] He considered John of the Cross the most "practical" of spiritual writers, because of his scrupulous focus on purifying intent and "natural affections," and unrelenting advocacy of self-scrutiny as one progresses—always wary of pride and surreptitious backsliding.[56] Other favorites who make repeat appearances are Francis de Sales, Alphonsus Liguori, Catherine of Siena, John Chrysostom, and Gregory the Great. Two uncanonized but authoritative bona fides who Lacouture cites repeatedly are Thomas à Kempis and Lorenzo Scupoli—the latter a once-popular but now commonly overlooked sixteenth-century spiritual author.[57] À Kempis's *Imitation of Christ* and Scupoli's *The Spiritual Combat* both make cameos with some regularity in Lacouture's notes.[58]

Ignatius of Loyola is referenced throughout the notes—particularly on affect and supernatural intent—which is exactly what one would expect, given the central position of the *Exercises* in framing Lacouture's retreat.[59] Whatever problems Lacouture had with the Society, he never seems to have flinched in his devotion to his Jesuit Fathers. Francis Xavier, Lacouture's original archetypal saint from his days as an aspiring missionary, continued to be a model of the heroic Christian life.[60] Lacouture's regular citation of Thomas Aquinas—the great theological trump card of the modern era—lent an air of doctrinal orthodoxy to his teaching. For someone accused of Jansenism, one would expect that Augustine would warrant a greater presence in Lacouture's footnotes. In truth, his name occurs only five times in the entire trilogy of retreat texts: twice in his first and second series, and just once in the third.[61] However, the tenor of Lacouture's theology is Augustinian through and through: his vision of the use of creatures, the interest in affect and proper order, the moral scrupulosity, the emphasis on conversion, and his assimilation of Saint Paul. Nevertheless, the absence of direct reference to the *Doctor Gratiae* is curious. On the other hand, Aquinas looms large. Along with their pedagogical utility, Lacouture's arsenal of certified, vetted authorities on Catholic spirituality presumed to insulate him from charges of heterodoxy; claiming doctrinal antiquity might have blunted some of the criticism his retreat courted. However, in the end, even adopting this litany of contemplative adepts proved insufficient for those purposes.

Grace and Nature

> We intentionally use the very jarring words "Manichaeism" or "Catharism." The comparison would not hold up except from the point of view of ethical behavior. Manichaeism affirms that this world—and all it

> contains—comes from the devil: matter and the world are works of evil, and thus all attachment to worldly goods, all voluntary contact with matter, is bad. It is the result of an extreme rigorism—abusive, pessimistic, and anti-social.
>
> —Roland Fournier, PSS, "Grâce et Nature"

By the time Roland Fournier, a Sulpician theologian at Montréal's Grand Séminaire, published his article "Grâce et Nature" in the seminary's academic journal, Onésime Lacouture's exile was already well underway, and the controversy surrounding his retreat movement—at least in Canada—was more or less a closed case. Lacouture was no longer giving his retreats; he could not preach openly or publish and had been formally censured by Wlodimir Ledóchowski, Superior General of the Society of Jesus. As described in a letter to one of his nieces, the "Blitzkrieg" had already come and gone.[62] However, in what amounted to a widespread insubordination among the Canadien clergy, Lacouture's teaching continued to circulate well after he had relocated to sunnier environs. Rumors spread that Jean-Marie-Rodrigue Cardinal Villeneuve, the archbishop of Québec and a one-time retreat supporter turned apostate, had compared Lacouture to Saint Paul.[63] It seemed that the disciplinary measures leveled against the Jesuit preacher only solidified his constituents' anti-institutional suspicions, confirming what was taught in the retreats themselves: that the powers of evil would conspire to attack this revival of the true Gospel through the machinations of the enemy within—Church authorities and academics.

For all his popularity among blue collar priests and religious in the trenches, love for the doctrine of the Sermon on the Mount was not at all universal. Lacouture's austerity—the absolute silence that he mandated throughout the retreat—coupled with the obsessive perfectionism and apparent devaluation of happiness, along with what many perceived to be an arrogant messianic complex, earned him a reputation as something of a Savonarola-esque fundamentalist.[64] His attacks on bourgeois mediocrity struck many as utterly void of basic compassion for human frailty, the hallmark of the unsympathetic Pelagian. On November 9, 1931, the new provincial of Lower Canada, Adélard Dugré, composed a tactful but inquisitive letter to Lacouture, proclaiming his support for the retreat's emergent social traction but advising caution on matters of doctrine and unseemly trash talk:

> My dear Father,
>
> P.C. [*Pacem Christi*]
>
> I was delighted, a few days ago, to allow you to circulate your letter to the priests, inviting them to make an eight-day closed retreat.
>
> I want to take this opportunity to ask you to follow, as much as possible, the Exercises of our Holy Father Ignatius in your meditations. It is our treasure, and if—as we have reason to believe—he was inspired by the Holy Virgin, then we will never discover a better method for converting sinners and leading the righteous to holiness. It is our family inheritance: we must utilize it, not abandon it to the others. . . .
>
> One might think that your theology sometimes borders on error. Dirty word! You damn too easily those who have not yet laid their poor human nature to waste.[65]

Dugré remarks that his correspondence was occasioned by a letter he had received just days earlier from a concerned brother priest, notifying him of rumors circulating that Lacouture's redaction of the retreat was incomplete and theologically distorted. Dugré also suggested that Lacouture show a little discretion and tone down the public scourging of those with divergent moral opinions. Before closing out the letter with an affected formalism that presumably made Lacouture's eyes burn ("I have written this letter in all simplicity . . ."), Dugré attempted a sympathetic clarification, reiterating his support for Lacouture's creative remix of the *Exercises* but warning him not to mutilate its substance. While the letter smacks of sincerity and tact, one can imagine Lacouture fuming at its perceived condescension and spineless "anonymous paganism." Dugré was now suspect.

Among his many other responsibilities, Dugré tactfully spent the next several years compiling a dossier on Lacouturisme in the province. Lacouture sympathizers and allies lobbied with rather lengthy testimonies, speaking to his sound character, gifts as a retreat leader, theological orthodoxy, even holiness. One fellow Jesuit described him to Wlodimir Ledóchowski as "a supernatural man, disciplined, and very zealous" and assured Dugré that Lacouture would welcome the provincial's constructive criticism and adjust the retreat likewise—which, in truth, could not have been further from reality.[66] Another acknowledged the disgruntled criticism of those who considered the retreat overly harsh and arrogant, but reassured Dugré that much of the controversy was rooted in a lack of charity among a minority caucus of retreatants, coupled with their disorientation at the unfamiliar structure of the conferences.[67] He chalked up reports of melodrama and severity to Lacouture's poor facility with the French language—having spent the majority of his youth in the United States—coupled with his excitable nature and religious enthusiasm, which left him vulnerable to misinterpretation. Some claimed it was the greatest thing that had happened to them since their Long Retreat during the novitiate: "This retreat did me a great good, above all, by its basic concept—abandonment to the will of God."[68]

There is no indication that Dugré ever did more than gently nudge Lacouture in the direction of temperance, while fielding letters from across the spectrum of the retreat sympathizers and enemies. During the mid-1930s, the retreat went viral among the clergy and religious in Lower Canada. As Longpré's earlier statistics indicate, Lacouture's doctrine piqued a latent Canadien spiritual curiosity and certainly drew a crowd—and a brigade of understudy preachers.[69] The downside of all this popularity was an increasingly alarmed bevy of skeptics, precipitating a vicious backlash. Two years after his initial outreach, Dugré followed up with Lacouture, suggesting a few specific points of improvement.[70] Tactful as ever, Dugré remarked that he had waited until the end of the retreat season, so as to not cause undue embarrassment, and allow the leisure to give these points some thought. Essentially, they amount to: tone down the rhetoric, do not be so lopsided in your focus on the first series of teachings, and stay on message (the Ignatian message). Yet again, there is no indication that Lacouture received these recommendations in the spirit that they claimed to have been given, or implemented any of Dugré's suggestions; in fact, he does not seem to have modified his retreat at all, ever. To whatever extent Dugré attempted to impose his will more aggressively, he failed. With Dugré moving on to greener pastures, it would be left to his successor, Emile Papillon, former rector of L'Immaculée-Conception, to manage this increasingly unmanageable priest.

Papillon took a decidedly less permissive tone. When word came that Lacouture had been touting Villeneuve's one-time support for his retreat, a clearly exasperated Papillon sent a blistering letter to the enthusiastic preacher, scolding him for impropriety and advising considerably more discretion than he had shown thus far by tangling the Church hierarchy up in his personal issues:

> My dear Father, you are deluding yourself if you believe that these remarks are just the doing of priests who find the supernatural too demanding, and are not suited to the austere demands of Christianity. . . . This anxiety and disaffection is much more widespread than you think.[71]

Presumably to Lacouture's great dismay, Papillon let him in on some behind-the-scenes dealing, in which Villeneuve had actually requested that Lacouture be given a six-month leave from his preaching duties, a Judas-like betrayal in Lacouture's eyes. Papillon puzzled over Lacouture's condemnations of tobacco, which seemed to him so bizarre they delegitimated his ascetic theology's fundamental substance: "Tobacco is something whose use is legitimate '*tantum quantum*,' even '*ad honestam recreationem*.'"[72] He finished by imploring Lacouture not to allow himself to get wrapped up in the self-fulfilling prophecy of antagonism and "persecution"—he astutely worried that his disciplinary measures might actually have the opposite effect, convincing Lacouture even further of his divine mandate. Rather, he hoped Lacouture would interpret his warning as God's use of creatures as a medium to instruct and correct, reminding him of his vows to obedience and docility to Society authority.

A month later, in October 1937, Papillon received a letter from an anonymous Jesuit confrere, who—with much hesitation but dutifully under obedience—reported that Lacouture had ignored his directive and persisted in giving retreats.[73] Moreover, he was still denouncing tobacco, implying—according to participants—that mortal sin might be involved because of its completely non-instrumental character, outside of base pleasure. Lacouture had caused great scandal by routinely criticizing Jesuit house masters in his conference sessions—sowing dissension and insubordination among participants. Lacouture completely disregarded Papillon's initial instruction to desist, and the provincial had to resort to deporting him to the Holy Land for a six-month "pilgrimage."[74] Lacouture returned to North America undeterred in his mission, as by early June of 1938—having just touched down on Canadien soil—he took no time in circulating a letter to the entire body of Canadian bishops, inviting them to participate in the newly reinstated retreat, which he had scheduled for the end of the month. In his letter to Émile Yelle, PSS, the coadjutor bishop of St. Boniface, Manitoba, Lacouture's unwieldy enthusiasm morphed into a rant that demanded *all* clergy make this retreat as soon as possible, on account of the imminent consolidation of malicious demonic forces.[75]

By late September, Lacouture seems to have mellowed considerably and, perhaps sensing that his days were numbered, wrote Papillon an uncharacteristically deferential letter, taking full responsibility for past indiscretions and vowing to submit his teaching to whatever revisions the authorities deemed necessary. His gesture was too little, too late: in Papillon's reply the next day, the provincial notified Lacouture that he had received word that the retreat had been submitted to the Sacred Congregation of Religious in Rome, and ordered Lacouture to suspend his work until a formal verdict was given.[76] Papillon recommended that Lacouture take some consolation in knowing that the subject had not made its way further up the chain of command to the Holy Office, which would have caused even greater embarrassment, not to mention the collateral damage the controversy would have inflicted on younger participants. With typical decorum, Papillon thanked Lacouture for submitting himself to the authorities, while touting the superior objective judgment of external review: "Believe that we are better situated than you to judge the overall impression [of excessive rigor]."[77] He also reiterated once more his plea for Lacouture to please leave the whole topic of smoking alone, as it not only ran counter to the prevailing wisdom and standard discipline but seemed to disorient the younger Jesuits within the province. Understandably, Papillon seems to have harbored suspicions regarding Lacouture's sincerity and contrition, given their history.

On November 11, Adélard Dugré got back into the fray, offering Lacouture a few words of advice from his new residence in Rome. His more patient disposition, augmented by the fact that he no longer found himself in the midst of all the bureaucratic haggling over the retreat, belied his rather stern opening words: "There can be no more discussion, nor explanation, only obedience."[78] Dugré had acquired a copy of Lacouture's retreat notes—the same ones that had been forwarded to the authorities for review—and offered up some line-by-line theological editing and more thematic points of wisdom:

> It is not necessary to go overboard. . . . Nothing can do you more harm than your own insistence that what you say is unique. . . . There is always a great risk in desiring to introduce new theology, as there is in seeking to "rediscover" teachings of the primitive Church, after intervening centuries. One usually only succeeds in being clumsy and incapable of nuance.
>
> Bravely—heroically—commit yourself to an act of great selflessness, as you yourself so often recommend, and renounce your own judgments by relying on our superiors.[79]

Dugré, ever the diplomat, was—like Lacouture's nominal submission to Papillon's authority—late to the game. Less than a month following Dugré's peppy, if didactic, letter, Papillon sent Lacouture a notice that his notes had been formally reviewed and that he was in grave danger of being stripped not simply of his right to preach conferences but of *all* his priestly faculties.[80] Papillon did not mince words and raised the specter of Savonarola, telling Lacouture candidly that his reputation was bringing dishonor to the Society and that his narcissistic self-depiction as a "great ascetic," on par with Ignatius and the rest, was naïve and frankly undeserved. Papillon closed out this scolding by reminding Lacouture that he was being watched closely by Ledóchowski and a shadowy anonymous inquisitor known only as "Censor," and that this was his last shot.

By March, four months later, it had all been settled. Papillon wrote Lacouture, informing him that he had been ordered by their superior general to suppress Lacouture's teaching in order to pre-empt an intervention by the Holy Office and thereby save him and the Society from further disgrace.[81] Apparently, the powers that be were concerned—not unreasonably, given the personality cult surrounding Lacouture—the movement was beginning to take on characteristics of a schismatic sect:

> It is becoming more apparent that there is a danger that some kind of sect is forming among your disciples. The only effective remedy is your absence.
>
> If we do not act, the ecclesiastical authority will do so vigorously, and you would wear—and we shall carry it with you—the responsibility for the disorder being cast into souls.

> There is only one way to proceed in order to avoid scandal; that is for you to request to be sent, for example, to China or Alaska, so that your request can be made public, and given as the cause of your departure.[82]

Papillon goes on to suggest that, since Lacouture always had such fond memories of Alaska, maybe it would suit him to return there, since his classmate in theology, Walter Fitzgerald, SJ, had just been appointed auxiliary bishop—a comment that, sincerely intended or not, was quite likely interpreted by Lacouture as the provincial's gloating sarcasm. Attempting a bit of heartstring tugging, Papillon lamented his role as ecclesiastical hatchet man, claimed to sympathize with Lacouture's sacrifice, and reassured him that nobody in the Society second-guessed his supernatural passion. Nevertheless, he finished by reminding Lacouture that he was sworn to secrecy and that the restrictions on promoting "his" doctrine extended to personal letters and informal conversation.

Papillon's platitudes did not, it seems, have the desired effect. Lacouture apparently solicited support from friends and sympathetic bishops by very publicly divulging the intimate details of his censorship. This annoyed Papillon to no end, precipitating a scalding letter from the provincial that autumn, ordering him, in no uncertain terms, to cease and desist—to get on with life and take his lumps with some modicum of dignity: "You are mistaken if you think that it is God's Spirit that animates you in this. . . . Actually, it is you yourself who is responsible for all these difficulties, your long-standing resistance to your superiors."[83] There was to be more where this came from, as Lacouture proved to be rather immune to directives "under holy obedience." By that winter, he had received the official kibosh on his preaching and relocated to Santa Barbara, California.[84] Thus began his exile, and Lacouture was thrust back into a semi-itinerant lifestyle, sojourning in foreign provinces without any real role or audience to indulge his messianic vocation. Meanwhile, back in Québec, whispers of Lacouturisme continued to hover about the archdiocese. However, its public moratorium rendered it something of an in-house matter. That bubble burst with Roland Fournier's publication in *Le Séminaire*, which was allegedly egged on by Apostolic Delegate Ildebrando Antoniutti as the movement's death knell.[85] In fact, it had rather the opposite effect and only aggravated the simmering resentment of the Lacouturites, who responded swiftly, if with potentially disproportionate aggression that further stirred the hornets' nest—although as Abraham Joshua Heschel and Walter Brueggemann have noted, tact has never been a stereotypical hallmark of the prophetic temperament.[86]

Exile

> We did not find in Lacouture the respect, deference, and submission that would demonstrate in him to be a man animated by the spirit of God. He was resistant, and spread sharp, contemptuous, and unedifying criticism against his superiors—not excepting the Very Rev. Fr. General, nor the ecclesiastical authorities which did not fully approve of his teaching. . . . If he had known to humbly accept the comments and recommendations of his superiors, he would have avoided the debates that his teaching and presentation raised, and would not be responsible for the interruption of an apostolate that could have been much more successful.
>
> —Emile Papillon to Ildebrando Antoniutti, 29 March 1940

John Hugo's later narration of the controversy depicts the opposition largely in terms of corrupt outsiders—represented by Rome and the Jesuit hierarchy—intoxicated with power and intent on dismantling Lacouture's eschatological grassroots movement—positioned against a supportive local magisterium such as Joseph-Alfred Langlois of Valleyfield and Archbishop Philippe Desranleau of Sherbrooke (both in the province of Québec). Along with Antoniutti, the turncoat Villeneuve, and "Censor," pride of place among the great villains of the "inquisition" is given to Zacheus J. Maher, SJ—the Poughkeepsie-based North American assistant to Wlodimir Ledóchowski.[87] Although Hugo was confident he played a part behind the scenes long before, in early 1941 Maher showed up, testily grumbling to Papillon about the mimeographed retreat notes that were being passed around the US clergy.[88] Papillon's speedy reply dutifully professes ignorance of the notes' publication and promises that a full investigation would be carried out and justice swiftly applied. Perhaps it was concern over the widespread circulation of these notes that inspired Antoniutti to enlist the theological polemics of Roland Fournier, if Hugo's hypothesis can be trusted.

By the time "Grâce et Nature" hit the press, Lacouture had been neatly tucked away at the Church of Our Lady of Sorrows in Santa Barbara for almost a year and a half—under the supervision of Joseph R. Stack, SJ. During that time, there was a flurry of correspondence between Émile Papillon and Francis J. Seeliger, SJ—the California provincial—trying to sort out the logistics of Lacouture's condition, while commiserating with one another about all the drudgery wrapped up in the conflict.[89] During Zacheus Maher's California visitation late in the summer of 1940, the father assistant had decreed that Lacouture be forbidden from *all* preaching, after what appears to have been a rather unpleasant personal exchange.[90] This left Seeliger in the somewhat precarious position of trying to find some sort of work with which Lacouture might pass his time, as apparently he was not very much inclined toward parish ministry. The bewildered provincial inquired of Papillon as to the possibility of relocating him to Edmonton. Although Lacouture did eventually make the move to Alberta, it was not for some time and involved considerable effort on Papillon's part—coupled with Seeliger's despondency, which did not improve once he was notified of Lacouture's restriction not just from preaching but from all regular forms of ministry.[91] Eventually, Seeliger did find a position at Loyola University in Los Angeles that seemed to suit him temporarily, at least until it was deemed safe for him to return to Canada. Furthermore, Maher instructed Seeliger, via Papillon, to monitor Lacouture's written correspondence in order to ensure he did not promote his doctrine on the sly.

Apparently, Seeliger was not well-suited to the task of fraternal spycraft. If the Jesuit hierarchy had been fixated on the idea of settling the affair as quietly as possible, those dreams were sent packing by Roland Fournier.[92] By this time, it seemed clear that nobody actually bought the cover story about Lacouture's supposed request for an international missionary post. However, save the underground circulation of Lacouture's retreat notes, the issue had been successfully kept out of the public domain, and the Canadian authorities could plausibly comfort themselves in knowing that the worst was behind. That all came crumbling down with Fournier's publication, or, more accurately, the retaliation it provoked. In truth (as its own critics acknowledged), the article itself seemed quite temperate and somewhat understated—if the true intention behind it was to squash Lacouturisme once and for all. Conversely, it could be considered an exercise in theological passive aggression. In fact, the name "Lacouture" is not even mentioned in the article. Fournier made no specific charges against any person or group, and an unsuspecting reader would not likely have even interpreted this as a direct assault. In his September 1941 rebuttal essay, D. L. Crenier acknowledged that, on the face of things, Fournier seems rather impressive and theologically sound. However, "after a more attentive reading . . . we definitely catch the ill-smelling odor of a very ancient heresy: the denial of original sin."[93] While Fournier's article depicts itself as an orthodox philosophical treatment of the unified identity of the human person—as opposed to a Manichaean bifurcated dualism—Crenier suspected a more insidious motive. Anselme Longpré's identification of Fournier's essay as the real flashpoint of the "Lacouture Affair" seems logically implausible, taking the article at face value. This does not, however, mean that Longpré was necessarily mistaken and, regardless, it indicated that some measure of collective outrage had been bubbling below the surface among Lacouture supporters—"Grâce et Nature" being the last straw and convenient scapegoat. At this stage, it is difficult to gauge how much of the controversy was grounded in truth—on either side of the coin—as opposed to paranoid speculation.

If Papillon, Seeliger, and Maher had harbored hopes of keeping Lacouture mum during his exile years, they were quickly laid to waste. In mid-October, Lacouture circulated a response to Fournier, colorfully titled "Are Creatures Dung . . . . . . or Dessert?"[94] Or, rather, he claimed—preserving himself from charges of disobedience to his moratorium on publishing—he innocently wrote a private letter to "a friend," who leaked it to the public without his consent. Its English-language translation was made available in late November. Thinly veiled as a personal consultation on the distinction between speculative and practical theology, Lacouture pulled no punches. After the initial pleasantries, he quickly riled himself up and launched into an invective against the state of contemporary Church authority: "How many theologians and priests enjoy of all the riches of our time: who feast daily and are dressed in fine linen . . . and are very glad to be invited to their rich dinners, to enjoy turkey, nice cigars and costly wines and while lounging in magnificent easy chairs and marveling over all the vanities of the world!"[95] The letter quickly morphed into a somewhat manic indictment of academic theology and mainline Catholicism:

> St. Paul says that he rejects all for the love of Jesus; the theologians say: enjoy as much as possible up to sin. For St. Paul, creatures are DUNG . . . for those theologians of the Pharisaic type . . . their DESSERT! DUNG . . . DESSERT! DUNG . . . DESSERT! DUNG . . . DESSERT! A wonderful summary of their respective mentality! All the saints have followed St. Paul in preaching the contempt of that DUNG . . . and that is the reason all have been persecuted by the theologians and priests of the DESSERT theology![96]

Drawing inspiration from Philippians 3:8, Lacouture's letter ushered in a new phase of pugilistic rhetoric, punctuated by scatological imagery. The underlying message was vintage Lacouture—anti-intellectual, stressing the role of supernatural motives, decrying all forms of secular habits (but singling out smoking at every opportunity), primitivist, substituting theatrics for nuance.

In a "confidential" letter, marked November 4, 1941, Zacheus Maher notified Émile Papillon and Francis Seeliger that Lacouture was to be prohibited—"in virtue *sanctae obedientiae*"—from all priestly ministry and spiritual direction.[97] That same day, he also wrote Lacouture directly, informing him of his silencing.[98] It appears, at this time, that the verdict was brought on largely by the dissemination of Lacouture's retreat notes, as Maher still had not gotten word of the "Are Creatures Dung . . ." essay, which was being distributed among sympathetic clergy in both the United States and Canada at that very moment. With Lacouture stripped of all ministerial prerogatives, the question was again raised of returning him to Canada, and the related wariness that this might be perceived by his devotees to overturn his exile, as some sort of latent exoneration of his doctrine.[99] It was not until the next February (1942) when—courtesy of Ildebrando Antoniutti—Émile Papillon was forced to deal with Lacouture's intransigent response to Roland Fournier.[100] Antoniutti scolded Papillon for dragging his heels, while the provincial defended himself by claiming that he had been waiting to obtain a copy for himself, so as to avoid acting on hearsay.[101] Papillon quickly sent out letters to local officials, including Cardinal Villeneuve and Guido Leclaire, SJ (the rector of Montréal's house, L'Immaculée-Conception), notifying them of Lacouture's silencing and warning them to be on the lookout for his retreat notes and the "Are Creatures Dung . . ." manifesto.[102] Furthermore, Papillon noted that since the "letter" was dated October 17 and his formal suppression had not been carried out until November 4, Lacouture, while imprudent, was not in violation of holy obedience.[103]

While it appeared that Papillon was willing to give Lacouture the benefit of the doubt, Maher was not so inclined. He interpreted Papillon's reluctance to condemn the publication as a sign of equivocation and weak leadership—considering that Lacouture had already been given some measure of formal censure: "A more obedient man would not have sent such a letter without first showing it to his Provincial under the conditions then obtaining."[104] It is difficult to imagine a scenario in which Lacouture would have considered this option seriously, but Maher's point was made. Furthermore, Maher had gotten word that Lacouture planned to send his retreat notes directly to the superior general for his personal review, and urged Papillon to impress upon him the futility of such an endeavor. And finally, one more indignity: all Lacouture's subsequent communications would be subject to review, in order to "induce him to obey as a genuine son of the Society, submitting his judgment to that of the Society and keeping not only the letter, but the spirit of the injunctions placed upon him."[105] This put Papillon in a tight spot, and while the provincial appears to have been less inclined toward the authoritarian measures that Maher suggested, he was, nevertheless, profoundly exasperated by the whole conflict he now found himself mediating. To get to the bottom of things, Papillon sent Lacouture a curt note that simply contained six yes-or-no questions—all intended to determine if Lacouture participated, in any way, with the text's English translation.[106]

Lacouture's explanation to Papillon was as glib as it was unconvincing.[107] To summarize briefly, he claimed to have been solicited to write the essay as a response to Fournier's article and admitted to composing the English translation himself, but rejected any allegations that he was acting outside his rights, because "it was not a theological treatise, nor spiritual direction," but simply a historical account of a long-standing dispute.[108] He did not run it by Seeliger, or any other authority, because his personal correspondence was, frankly, none of their business. Furthermore, he went on, how was it his fault if other priests decided to duplicate and distribute copies of letters he intended to be private? Papillon appears to have forwarded Lacouture's reply to Maher, who, unsurprisingly, was furious:

> Father Lacouture's explanation is most unsatisfactory, yet naught would be gained by further dealing with him on the matter. Our concern is for the future. My suggestion, therefore, is . . . that superiors, both local and provincial, strictly enjoin Father Lacouture from *writing anything* and communicating the same in any way to externs without previous censorship by one on whose judgment Your Reverence can fully rely.
>
> There should be no quibbling, no subterfuge, on Father Lacouture's part in obeying this injunction.[109]

The climate surrounding Lacouture did not improve over the summer, on account of yet another "letter" surfacing that bore Lacouture's name, dated July 4, 1942—a clear violation.[110] "Philosophe ou Théologien?" was composed as a treatise to clarify certain points in "Are Creatures . . . . Dung or Dessert?" but largely reiterated his signature go-to points of doctrine. Again, Antoniutti sounded the cry and compelled Papillon to investigate.[111] Again, Lacouture—now writing from his new residence in Edmonton—claimed ignorance of the whole enterprise and vowed that he had written innocently enough, with no intention of his anything going public.[112] Lacouture surrendered—not, however, before making a few choice remarks about the hallowed tradition of saints and prophets being persecuted by ecclesiastical authorities.[113] He promised no further correspondence of this sort, pledged fidelity to Papillon's authority, and apologized for any damage he might have caused along the way—albeit with ambiguous sincerity.

It Is Finished

> People call me crazy, nobody wants to believe me, but I tell you this, even though I know this may be the last time I speak publicly: your churches are filled now—in twenty-five years, they will be empty and serve as bingo halls! The seminaries and novitiates overflow with students; in twenty-five years, they will all be closed! Because of you priests, through your laziness and negligence; you who'd rather smoke your pipes on the balcony, and ride around in Chryslers than teach the Catechism in schools: in twenty-five years, all the doors to these schools will be shut because of you religious; instead of living evangelically, you live "like the pagans!" . . . In twenty-five years, you will be expelled from the schools and hospitals!
>
> —Onésime Lacouture quoted in Anselme Longpré, *Un mouvement spirituel au Québec*[114]

Although Onésime Lacouture was good to his word and never published anything for the remainder of his life or spoke publicly on any subject regarding asceticism or spirituality, he persisted in the hope that he would, in the end, be vindicated. For a preacher who made his name as an iconoclast, and purportedly expected nothing but antagonism from Church authorities, he was uncannily persistent in pressing for formal recognition and acceptance. He also proved exceedingly resilient, and by the time he finally received word that his retreat notes had been deemed theologically deficient by the Father General's anonymous censor, Lacouture had outlasted his third provincial. Anthony Dragon, SJ, had succeeded Émile Papillon in Montréal and was tasked with the grim responsibility of disabusing the aging Lacouture of his tragic optimism. Lacouture himself admitted that this was the knockout blow and resigned himself to living out the rest of his days in relative obscurity.[115] Lacouture was now in St. Régis, along the south side of the Saint Lawrence River in upstate New York—his terminal destination as it were. He worked as a bursar at the indigent parish mission, performed minor, ineffectual duties for the local Kanienkehaka (Mohawk), and received occasional clandestine visits from his more prolific American disciples—such as John Hugo, Pacifique Roy, and Hugo's faithful colleague, Louis Farina.

This would have been the end of the Onésime Lacouture era of the retreat, if not for one last peculiar twist. Following the deaths of Wlodimir Ledóchowski and his interim successor, Alessio Magni, SJ, Norbert de Boynes, SJ, was elected temporary vicar general of the Society in the spring of 1944. Lacouture must have interpreted this as some sort of serendipitous new opportunity, because within weeks he had sent de Boynes an uncharacteristically polite appeal for reconsideration of his retreat doctrine, ostensibly not out of vanity but rather the salvation of souls and posterity of the Church.[116] From the very first sentence, Lacouture's note exuded a quixotic scent: "Now that the Allies have entered Rome and we can contact you, I hasten to write you about a matter which is already quite old, but which remains important for myself and many others"—apparently assuming that this might be a good time to bring up his own travails.[117] The letter is saturated with earnest platitudes coupled with a palpable sense of urgency. He blames his censorship on the viral spread of "paganism" within the Church authority, without, it seems, any obvious awareness that his new vicar general might consider this offensive.[118] Lacouture proceeded to employ a conspicuous variation of the Matthew 7:16 "you will know them by their fruits" dictum—essentially claiming that the retreat's popularity should override the Censor's personal verdict. He depicted himself as an *Alter Ignatius*, interspliced with a resurrection of his "persecuted prophet" theme: "If I was an ignorant heretic, the demons would never have mobilized their ecclesiastical army, throughout the rungs of the hierarchy, in order to silence me."[119] At this point, Lacouture seems to have fully lost his grip on the diplomatic tone his letter initially sought and succumbed to his apocalyptic spiritual impulses. While it may have made for a dynamic narrative, it seems an odd tack when requesting special reconsideration from the vicar general of the Society of Jesus, a mere two days after the liberation of Rome from Axis control.

There is no indication that Norbert de Boynes ever responded to Lacouture's request for a second opinion. Presumably, the vicar general had plenty on his plate that was more pressing than tending to personal requests from a convicted and constitutionally belligerent "country prelate" who was repeatedly disobedient to his authorities and made vague allegations that they were, in fact, possessed by demons. While it is not shocking that in his very animated demonology, Lacouture would view opponents as steered by the hand of Satan, or actually *being* demons in the guise of powerful Church officials, one suspects that this is not something that would endear him to his new vicar general. From his initial sequence of revelations as a scholastic in the White Desert of Alaska until the very end, Lacouture remained unbowed and supremely confident of both his divine commission and that his doctrine was—absolutely and without equivocation—identical with God's own truth. His rhetoric was polarizing and did not elicit nuance or, frankly, sympathy. Lacouture did not abide constructive criticism, only conformity; and while many found him positively magnetic, his lifeworld and personality cult depended heavily on a vision of cosmic crusade that located him prominently among the litany of saints, on the side of righteousness.[120]

Onésime Lacouture died rather suddenly on November 15, 1951. Alfred Langlois, the bishop of Valleyfield who had been his staunch advocate in an otherwise mercurial and finally unsupportive regional hierarchy, presided over his funeral Mass. Dorothy Day made the pilgrimage to Québec for the service—the only American to do so, as none of his clerical disciples from the United States were granted permission to travel.

Some interpreted Day's presence as auspicious, considering—at least retrospectively—she played a lead role among Lacouture's spiritual progeny. And this was most important, for Lacouture was all but scrubbed from Canadien memory and would be relegated to a footnote in the province's historical record—an insult that struck loyalists as clearly conspiratorial. John Hugo's secondhand rendition of the event wistfully captures the movement's dual sense of prophetic mission coupled with suspicions of antagonistic collusion—as well as his teacher's own cantankerous spirit, which Hugo inherited and smuggled across the border, along with the retreat curriculum itself:

> At the time of his funeral I had been refused the few days of leave needed to go to St. Regis. The very request was construed as evidence of conspiracy. Yes, we were charged, at least by persisting innuendo, of conspiracy against the Church and were described by our colleagues, with vipery humor, as "Lacoutermites" and "Hugonuts." The Inquisition would not release its compassionless grip even at the graveside. Meanwhile, Dorothy Day, who had written his epitaph . . . closed her obituary with the scripture that had become central to her life . . . : "Unless the grain of wheat falls into the ground and dies, itself remains alone. But if it dies, it bears much fruit [Jn. 12:34]."[121]

Lacouture's recipe for spiritual renewal was fiercely antagonistic to the secular impulse he perceived invading Canadien society. Along with the loss of the traditional Québécois lifestyle to urbanization and industrialization, Lacouture's anti-Americanism and Anglophobia was symptomatic of a much more comprehensive suspicion of the modern Church and respectable Catholicism. His message was rigorously countercultural, and his combative demeanor almost guaranteed suppression. The tone of his rhetoric occasionally verged on being outright seditious, and although he never ceased to hope that the hierarchy would be won over, it would be hard to imagine what the logistics of such a concession would actually look like. Rather, while Lacouture was charged with just about every heresy in the book, he was certainly guilty of disobedience and making promises to his superiors in bad faith; however, it is likely that he would excuse such conduct on account of his superseding obligation to a higher power, or the invalidation of vows made to morally bankrupt institutions. Although he counseled obedience as a characteristic of humility within the retreat itself, this evidently did not extend to those he deemed to be apostates, or worse. If anything, the well-over-a-decade of persecution deepened his righteous sense of vocation—and while the institutional recognition he sought eluded him, Lacouture was able to bear witness to his retreat's transplantation across borders, largely under the stewardship of John Hugo.

4 Mackerel Snappers in the US Industrial Era

> The real danger for the established system is not the abolition of labor but the possibility of nonalienated labor as the basis of the reproduction of society. Not that people are no longer compelled to work, but that they might be compelled to work for a very different life and in very different relations, that they might be given very different goals and values, that they might have to live with a very different morality—this is the "definite negation" of the established system, the liberating alternative.
>
> —Herbert Marcuse, "Aggressiveness in Advanced Industrial Society," in *Negations: Essays in Critical Theory*

Onésime Lacouture's ascetic, mystical antimodernism found a receptive audience among enthusiastic vowed religious whose dormant restlessness at Catholic accommodation to secularism was primed. Lacouturite theology was intentionally countercultural and carried a strong indictment of secular proliferation, based on an extreme distinction between sacred and profane spheres of existence.[1] Although Lacouturisme was stamped out in its home province of Québec, it migrated southward and enculturated its analysis to mirror its new host. While Lacouturite rhetoric spilled a disproportionate amount of ink condemning particular secular practices, like smoking, its root focus was the holistic conversion of souls to the Sermon on the Mount's inverted theology.[2] During the interwar period, the collective trauma of World War I and the Great Depression gutted the once-ascendant liberal Protestant confidence in progress and threw an at least temporary monkey wrench into the American affliction of resilient positivity that conditions a belief that structural inequality may simply be overcome by a positive attitude and sufficient elbow grease.[3] American cultural disillusionment was met by Christian fundamentalism and the hard "realism" of Reinhold Niebuhr but also opened space for Catholic philosophical exceptionalism to assert itself as a perennial antidote to the instability of juvenile, unbridled optimism. Lacouturisme presented an alternate muscular Catholic critique of the fundamental underpinnings of American culture—not from the perspective of sober, methodical Neo-Scholasticism but the radically un-American paradigm of the Folly of the Cross. But unlike its foundational insularity, Lacouturism in the United States would integrate some of the bite of contemporary social analysis of the production of social inequality into its vision of the Christian vocation. Lacouturite theology embraced suffering as an antidote to pagan America's "cruel optimism" that quixotically promised a peaceful utopian future accelerated through the reproduction of violence.[4]

The Gilded Age and Second Industrial Revolution

The rise of industrial mechanization and attendant consolidation of wealth in the United States at the turn of the century created a vacuum that was filled by radicalized, proletarian-minded clergy—such as Charles Owen Rice—who set the stage for John Hugo's socially engaged permutation of Lacouture's anti-triumphalist retreat theology. Although the volatility of American life may have lacked some of the cosmic paranoia that marked its Québécois counterpart, the socio-economic instability of the era was brutal. Following the collective trauma of the Civil War, America's Gilded Age witnessed a tremendous expansion of the industrial complex, along with the migration of labor to urban centers and aggregation of capital in the hands of a powerful elite. Sydney Ahlstrom has argued that this period of "economic dislocation," which shrunk the number of corporations by tenfold around the turn of the century, empowered Americans—for the first time since the founding of the Republic—to critically assess the hegemony of US socio-economic policy and civil religion.[5]

In Pittsburgh, U. S. Steel—a conglomerate of Andrew Carnegie's Carnegie Steel Company and William Henry ("Judge") Moore's National Steel Company—was a prime example of the mammoth scope of the new corporate America.[6] Primarily backed by J. P. Morgan, it was the first corporation in history to break the billion-dollar mark.[7] The Carnegies, Morgans, and Vanderbilts had deep hooks in the Pittsburgh economy and their manipulation of lax workplace regulations fostered egregious practices, which in turn inspired workers' mobilization—most notably among the American Federation of Labor (AFL) in 1886, an umbrella group that sought to build solidarity among disparate unions and coordinate opposition to workforce exploitation. The Panic of 1893 propelled the US economy into a four-year economic recession and signaled the end of this chapter of the Second Industrial Revolution, although the transition was far from seamless and it was not until 1913 that the creation of the Federal Reserve Board began to address the financial and ethical concerns raised by industrial monopolies.[8] Literary public intellectuals also got in on the social reform, and Upton Sinclair's 1905 exposé novel *The Jungle* stimulated a drastic overhaul of the meatpacking industry, laying the groundwork for the modern FDA.[9] The Progressive Era emerged in its wake and promised a tightening of national financial, governmental, and individual morals.

Many Progressives looked to Scripture for inspiration and drew fortitude from Christian ethics and postmillennial eschatology. This theological leaven had a long history of vying with a more divine-interventionist rupture apocalypticism and gained traction among Protestant liberals "who anticipated the gradual diffusion of Christianity until the Millennium almost imperceptibly became a reality."[10] Although the upstate New York–born German-American Baptist Walter Rauschenbusch—a figurehead of the Social Gospel Movement—attempted to navigate a middle course between pre- and post-millennialist Evangelical camps, liberal Protestants tended toward a more activist identification of American progress with the gradual unfolding of God's Kingdom.[11] Nevertheless, even he—perhaps especially he—succumbed to the occasional millenarian fantasy, such was his enthusiasm for the transformative power of the Social Gospel:

> The men who have worked out the new social Christianity in their own thinking and living constitute a new type of Christian. . . . Their horizon is wider; their sympathy more catholic; their faith more daring. . . . The men of natural ability and idealism are most receptive to the prophetic ideas now dawning, and in turn these ideas enlarge and lift the mind that harbors them, so that even those who do not think that way pay the tribute of attention when they speak.[12]

Rauschenbusch's social criticism included a sober assessment of contemporary industrial corruption and labor abuses, but along with his progressive compatriots, he believed that the faithful Christian was duty bound to carry his personal experience of salvation into the socio-political sphere.[13] Socialism was, for the time, a somewhat intellectually respectable and undemonized political philosophy, and Eugene Debs—Industrial Workers of the World (IWW) founder and former locomotive union man (although he only worked briefly on the rail itself)—launched a handful of newsworthy but self-evidently doomed presidential election campaigns beginning in 1900, frequently employing Evangelical motifs, while remaining constitutionally indisposed to organized religion.[14] While Debs recognized that the election of any Socialist candidate was a practical impossibility, progressives did see a viable candidate in William Jennings Bryan (Democratic nominee in 1896, 1900, and 1908), "The Great Commoner," who was solidly populist, if also something less than a trailblazer of racial equality.[15]

American Innocence and the Illusion of Progress

The consolidation of wealth and economic power in the United States inspired a socially conscious reaction among liberals and the working class that enabled the expansion of federal regulatory authority and unification of organized labor espousing Social Gospel-like principles. Political reform was perceived by many progressives as a divine mandate and eschatological imperative. Although they were called to vigilantly recollect that the fullness of life lay in the world to come, many liberal Protestants could not resist the temptation to view their civic participation in messianic terms. The presupposition that progress was inevitable—on both the macro-social and micro-individual levels—persisted resolutely. Personal conversion was a hot priority as well, and the temperance movement, punctuated by thirteen years of Prohibition beginning in 1920, highlighted the deep interpenetration between the individual and public spheres—although Catholics, as often as not, interpreted the Eighteenth Amendment as an aggressively racist Anglo-Protestant conspiracy, depriving them of cultural rights.[16] The discipline of the Protestant ethic was matched by a measure of labor self-empowerment and a wider rejection of the instrumentalization of workers by industrial tycoons. The revival of social consciousness was not limited to workers and the higher-educated intelligentsia, and government restructuring was matched by an upsurge of philanthropy on behalf of upper class elites—in many instances spearheaded by precisely those individuals whose companies were being monitored by the Fed for exploitative and immoral labor practices.

"The War to End All Wars" struck a crushing blow to the psyche of mainline Protestant America. The religious optimism that reached its zenith in Walter Rauschenbusch's conflation of the personal and political crumbled in the wake of the prospect of human self-annihilation and the evident resilience of evil.[17] Until then, American Manifest Destiny sensibilities had evolved from a chiliastic ethic of sojourning exiles to an internationally dominant, largely postmillennial, evangelicalism that was synonymous with democracy and free-market capitalism:

> Americans have long experienced and articulated a sense of urgency, of hanging on the precipice of great change, of living in the "fifth act" of history. . . . They have fallen easily into the Manichean habit of dividing the world into darkness and light, Evil and Good, past and future, Satan and Christ. They have seen themselves as a progressive, redemptive force, waging war in the ranks of Christ's army, or have imagined themselves even as Christ Himself, liberating those in bondage and healing the afflicted.[18]

This collective, self-confident faith in national destiny is symptomatic of what Henri de Lubac gloomily dubbed "*Joachimisme*"—the sense of living on the precipice of a new, perfected plane of existence.[19] De Lubac traced this tradition of millennial expectation back to Joachim of Fiore, whose influence he witnessed across an extremely variant swath of religious and secularized ideologues—from the thirteenth-century *Fraticelli* to the Soviet Union.[20] An optimistic vision of human nature, a vigorous bootstrapping ethic, and "the belief in a rational and predictable cosmos" were characteristic features of pre-war liberal Protestantism, with the perky confidence that, with the proper motivation and persistence, social ills could be ameliorated efficiently and harmoniously—that the soft coercion of hegemony was a delusion and personal disposition a greater obstacle than tectonic forces such as racism, misogyny, class exploitation, and institutionalized violence.[21] The Protestant ideals that anticipated an imminent unfolding of the Kingdom of God on earth were largely dismantled—at least that was the interpretation of Catholics waiting eagerly on the sidelines.

The psychological vertigo among mainline progressives of this period opened up a cultural gap that was filled in by Christian fundamentalism, along with a minority strain of Niebuhrian realism more amenable to the disillusioned intellectual elite. For the so-called Christian Realists, the old confidence in cultural progress as inevitable was antiquated and, in fact, logically untenable: "The reality is that human nature is perverse and that society tends toward evil. Science, sanitation, and education cannot, will not, produce a perfect world, Niebuhr asserted; neither will a sentimental Protestantism that refuses to confront the undeniable realities of war, greed, exploitation, prejudice, poverty, cruelty, injustice, and lust."[22] A more fiery brand of "hot religion" swept through working-class America and Fundamentalism, which had been combatting the dangers of modernist accommodation and adopted an even more confrontational countercultural position than its earlier incarnations.[23] Satan became a more imminent threat; it was not just individual souls that were the cosmic battlefield, the socio-political arena was now at risk. The demonic offensive that manifested in World War I and the immediately following years drew Christians further out into the public: "In the face of this threat, the political battle to defend God's kingdom could not be entirely postponed until a coming era."[24] Both neo-orthodox and fundamentalist Protestants believed that mainline Christianity had failed them and, in rather different ways, reimposed strong boundaries between the secular and the spiritual. Whether it was a question of evolution, biblical criticism, free-market capitalism, or federal government, both communities drew inspiration from their profound disillusionment with conventional religiosity and their fusion of national and supernatural interests.

William Halsey notes three common features of nineteenth-century thought that were critically destabilized during the interwar period: the belief in progress, the conviction that objective reality was discernible (a kind of natural law, although it was not described in these terms), and the idea that culture was a legitimate and valuable expression of these beliefs.[25] Although the binary distinction between Protestant fundamentalists and modernists—further complicated by the rise of realism and various permutations of millennialism—is not as clean as the narrative historian might like, the bubbling ferment of countercultural positions expanded during the first decades of the twentieth century as a response to the corrosive effects of modernity:

> The time and special character of the prewar rebellion were, I believe, determined in part by the very surface placidity of the Progressive Era. Traditional American beliefs in moral certainty and inevitable progress had for some time been subjected to inner strain and external attack, yet in the prewar decade, for the last time, the official custodians of culture were able to maintain and defend a common front.[26]

Old progressives' assumptions about the structural integrity of their worldview began to wither as the dawn of the 1900s brought a complex set of new approaches, leaving them in the lurch, disoriented and anxious. Scholars seem to differ considerably regarding the timeline of this dissolution of confident American Protestantism or, truly, if there was ever such an idealized homeostatic era in the first place.[27] Similarly, other questions linger in the debate: whether World War I was a distinct catalyst for the unraveling of mainline Protestant optimism, or simply represented a traumatic peak occurring primarily as a result of its trauma; and if the collapse of the Social Gospel was really as stark and definitive during this period—only to be resurrected decades later in the form of the Civil Rights Movement—as has typically been depicted.

Papists to the Rescue

> Above and before all, he ["the capitalist"] must cultivate and strengthen within his mind the truth which many of his class have begun to grasp for the first time during the present war; namely, that the laborer is a human being, not merely an instrument of production; and that the laborer's right to a decent livelihood is the first moral charge upon industry. The employer has a right to get a reasonable living out of his business, but he has no right to interest on his investment until his employees have obtained at least living wages. This is the human and Christian, in contrast to the purely commercial and pagan, ethics of industry.
>
> —John A. Ryan, *Bishops' Program of Social Reconstruction: A General Review of the Problems and Survey of Remedies*[28]

On February 12, 1919, the US Catholic hierarchy published a twenty-one-page pamphlet outlining their "Program of Social Reconstruction" as an attempt to translate the somewhat nascent field of

Catholic Social Teaching—first given explicit form in Pope Leo XIII's 1891 groundbreaking encyclical *Rerum Novarum*—into American idioms, to speak to contemporary industrial concerns.[29] While the publishing body—the fledgling National Catholic War Council (NCWC), a predecessor of the United States Conference of Catholic Bishops—had no official canonical status and there was substantial dissent among the American hierarchy about the document's content, this represented a seismic shift in participation in political evolution.[30] Although the American bishops had made pronouncements on moral issues—notably in the painstaking debates regarding parochial education and the employ of the King James Bible in public schools—this represented their first foray into the realm of socio-economic critique, demonstrating a development in collective self-confidence, insofar as the bishops believed that they had something worth saying on the subject of structural economic justice and similarly had an audience who might listen. The document was ghostwritten by John A. Ryan, a priest of the Archdiocese of St. Paul residing in Washington, DC—where he taught at the Catholic University of America. Ryan was an economist and moral theologian whose expertise on the ethical implications of the modern industrial complex poised him to contribute mightily to the field of American Catholic social thought, which he, in large part, created.[31] As a codirector of the NCWC's newly formed Social Action Department, John Ryan—dubbed the "Right Reverend New Dealer" by the radio-celebrity-turned-rabid-anti-Semite Charles Coughlin—would shape the American Church's social mission for decades to come, in consort with a vigorous injection of federal economic stimuli and oversight.[32]

The NCWC's statement on social reconstruction was far from unanimously approved by the bishops. William Cardinal O'Connell, the imperious Archbishop of Boston, who had opposed the formation of the NCWC and seemed in many respects constitutionally immune to episcopal collegiality, claimed that the text reeked of socialism. Along with the rise in class consciousness precipitated by the Second Industrial Revolution—as evinced by Eugene Debs's persistence in (if not conquest of) the national polls—came the inclination to radically restructure the American economic system, and organized socialism appealed to members of the laboring class across the board of denominational affiliation. From the outset, it seems, Church leadership was anxious over the prospects of spiritual endogamy that might result from nonsectarian fraternal groups, such as the Knights of Labor, which had narrowly escaped papal condemnation through the intervention of James Cardinal Gibbons in 1887.[33] The most radical forerunner of John Ryan was New York City's Lower East Side parish priest, Edward McGlynn—a philosophical disciple of the "lapsed Episcopalian" Henry George, whose 1879 *Progress and Poverty* made an international splash by advocating a communal "single tax" and analogized the privatization of land to the slave trade.[34] McGlynn was beloved among the New York Irish, who were primed for tenants' rights agitation by the popular lecture circuit of their "Old Country" Land League compatriots, Charles Stewart Parnell and Michael Davitt. John Cardinal McCloskey, then archbishop of New York, intervened to prevent McGlynn's suppression by Rome, but his successor, Michael Corrigan, was substantially less sympathetic and openly clashed with the diocesan priest over his public support of George's 1886 mayoral bid.

But for all of the concerns, among William O'Connell and other institutional ultramontanes, that the 1919 NCWC's declaration hinted at insurrectionism, the US bishops' self-organization and formal engagement with the "Social Question" represented a shift in their own priorities, as well as a tactical awareness of the material concerns that consumed the laity and a healthy paranoia regarding the practical threats of Protestant and Marxist proselytization. Catholics moved in droves among the laboring class, and the tension between American and Roman allegiances simultaneously compelled the Catholic leadership to engage the topic of economic justice while causing them some angst about the repercussions of entering into the political realm in such a public manner. In spite of Leo XIII's encyclical and the proletarian agitation of local clergy such as McGlynn, the Church leadership had different priorities, such as debates over philosophical and institutional Americanism, sexual morality, managing the integration of diverse immigrant ethnicities, and building cultural infrastructure.[35] However, regardless of individual bishops' personal sentiments on the industrial economy, labor, capital, and the right to collective bargaining, the ground-level reality was that Catholics were affected by structural inequalities in the workplace, and they were unionizing, with or without official sanction. Prior to the rise of the AFL, the Knights of Labor was the most influential union in the country. Founded in 1879 as a secret society and led by the lay Catholic Terence Powderly, the Knights ran afoul of the archbishop of Québec, Elzéar-Alexandre Taschereau, and were formally condemned in 1886.[36] After some confusion, it was determined that the ban did not actually apply to the organization's American permutation, and Baltimore's James Gibbons interceded on their behalf, arguing for union rights as a theoretical ideal that should be supported on ethical grounds, but also tactfully warning of the anti-Catholic backlash that a papal condemnation might inspire.

That the American hierarchy would come out publicly on the side of organized labor was not as self-intuitive as it might appear retrospectively. The whole concept of a proletarian Catholic "Church of the Poor" was not something primordial but rather developed as a reflection of—and concerted response to—practical demographic realities and evangelical concerns. Outside of frontier nations like the United States and Protestant-dominated regions like the United Kingdom, the Church's symbiosis—and complicity—with power, wealth, and government authority had been a matter of course. The experience of a largely immigrant Church, as has been documented by successive generations of American Catholic historians, was an unusual—if not unique—predicament and fostered a particular form of institutional orientation.[37] As much as John Courtney Murray, SJ, and John F. Kennedy begged to differ, the separation of Church and State was not a traditionally Catholic ideal, and the early American leadership had to acclimate itself with the reality of disestablishment, voluntary lay participation, and their own financial instability.[38] The psychological trauma of Italian insurrection in the 1840s—which forced Pius IX's evacuation of Rome and was credited with converting the once progressive pope to reactionary antimodernism—exacerbated latent suspicions of revolutionary rhetoric and political instability, even if "stability" meant the maintenance of a socially immobilized status quo. Social hierarchy was not morally suspect, and American Catholics held no unified perspective on the immorality of what are now consensed to be labor exploitation and child abuse. Furthermore, powerbrokers among the higher-end, lace-curtain Catholic gentry assimilated quite nicely into their newfound social strata, dominated by the American entrepreneurial spirit.[39] However, the changing face of American Catholicism, most conspicuously represented by the hordes of Famine Irish flooding northeastern ports, precipitated a more inflexible, aggressive, urban Catholic subculture, personified by New York's own intransigent archbishop, "Dagger John" Hughes, who had armed guards stand watch over local churches following the Philadelphia anti-Catholic riots of 1844 and proclaimed that "if a single Catholic church were burned in New York, the city would become a second Moscow."[40] "The Social Question" became an increasingly urgent matter for the US bishops and blurred the theoretically rigid distinction between ecclesiastical and secular affairs that was formally breached by the *Bishops' Program of Social Reconstruction*.

In a 1986 essay for the *U.S. Catholic Historian*, R. Emmett Curran, SJ, went out on a limb with his observation that "the American bishops as a body have not been renowned for prophetic activity."[41] Although he proceeds to argue that its contemporary articulation is self-consciously doing just that, his point was made. Even in 1919, following the publication of the *Bishops' Program*, the American hierarchy did not rush headlong into social reconstruction, in spite of the Ryan statement's steadfast rhetoric. The postbellum influx of immigrants had tripled the nation's Catholic population by 1890 and labor self-empowerment pressed the issue, forcing the American hierarchy to rethink the church's historical anxiety regarding unions.[42] As with the Knights of Labor, many of the fraternal orders originated as, shared common aesthetics with, or actually persisted as secret societies, which touched on some sensitivities cultivated in anticlerical Europe earlier in the century by Giuseppe Mazzini and the revolutionary syndicate Young Italy. Some groups were dubbed suspicious on account of their connections—actual or perceived—to Irish revolutionary groups, such as the excommunicated Fenian Brotherhood. The Molly Maguires—made moderately famous by an uninnovatively named 1970 Sean Connery film (*The Molly Maguires*)—protected rural coal-mining pogues in eastern Pennsylvania's anthracite region through their own eccentric blend of industrial sabotage, murder, and tactical cross-dressing.[43] As in Ireland under the watch of the thoroughly Roman cardinal Paul Cullen, radicalism was eschewed by the hierarchy in favor of a more conciliatory engagement with the secular authorities.[44] The association of the Knights with the Chicago Haymarket Square Riot on May 4, 1886, marked the beginning of the end and was subsequently employed as prosecutorial ammunition by the Vatican, which pitted the Americanist leaders John Ireland, James Gibbons, John Keane, and Denis O'Connell against ultramontanes Bernard McQuaid and Michael Corrigan.[45] The Americanists narrowly won the day and laid the foundation for more systematic advocacy on behalf of the working poor—although their argument was based on a sober assessment of the Knights' probability of imminent collapse and the bad publicity a condemnation might generate. Similarly, although Edward McGlynn was, in fact, formally excommunicated for insubordination the very next year—again Corrigan was at the heart of it—he was rehabilitated on Christmas Eve, 1892. Both episodes have been credited with having an impact on the social posture of *Rerum Novarum*, although it would be some decades before the encyclical's principles were thoroughly digested by the US bishops.[46]

Muscular Catholicism

That institutional Catholicism began to assert itself more prominently in American socio-economic criticism was symptomatic of a renewed sense of collective social access and cultural stability. Although they were still far from having fully assimilated into the homogenized civil religion of the US melting pot depicted in Will Herberg's *Protestant, Catholic, Jew*—testified to by Al Smith's ill-fated presidential campaign in 1928—American Catholics had grown considerably more acceptable to the mainstream populace by the time the *Bishops' Program* went public.[47] A decade later, widespread support for Spain's Francisco Franco coupled with some enduring sympathy for the Italian Mussolini—which might be plausibly written off, to some extent, as self-interested opportunism rather than pure ideology—revived questions about Catholicism's supranational allegiance and compatibility with democratic principles.[48] Concerns raised by Roman Catholicism's seeming affinity for fascist dictators preyed upon the Church's own ambiguity regarding individualism and inspired much of the prodigious output of the pejoratively dubbed "New Theology"—a misnomer for the preconciliar *ressourcement* turn to classic theological authorities. Nevertheless, the Catholic intelligentsia sprang at the opportunity created by the WWI crisis of Protestant liberalism, courageously armed with, as it were, Thomism. While by 1955, Catholic University of America's venerable historian John Tracy Ellis would bemoan American Catholicism's underwhelming contribution to American intellectual life, blaming their "self-imposed ghetto mentality" and "lack of industry and the habits of work," his Thomist predecessors of the 1920s and '30s would have unanimously concurred that the Church claimed ownership over "the oldest, wisest, and most sublime tradition of learning that the world has ever known" and was well-primed to use it.[49]

In the 1879 encyclical *Aeterni Patris*, Leo XIII cemented Thomas Aquinas's position as the Church's pre-eminent philosophical authority. This institutionalized and shaped the Neo-Scholastic revival, making Thomism the de facto standard of Catholic orthodoxy. For all of aesthetic medievalism's appeal to bourgeois Anglo-Protestants, its official sanction—coupled with the Vatican's official opprobrium against Modernism—reinforced Catholicism's reputation as intellectually retrograde. Although Patrick Carey stipulates that "Al Smith lost the campaign not only because of his Catholicism, but also because of his urban identification, his stand against Prohibition, Republican prosperity, and Herbert Hoover's popularity," these very distasteful red flags—he was "wet" and gritty—were all stereotypically Catholic features.[50] Even by 1940, when University of Chicago faculty members attempted to procure a visiting scholar's post for Jacques Maritain—the once-suicidal French convert turned neo-Thomist democrat—the philosophy department's chair, Charner M. Perry, declined to take up the cause on the grounds of Maritain's reputation as a Catholic apologist.[51] However, lingering anti-Catholic prejudices notwithstanding, Halsey characterizes the early twentieth century as "a period of arrival."[52] As with *Rerum Novarum*, Vatican authorization did not translate into an immediate renovation of US infrastructure—by 1895, Catholic University still had but a single philosophy professor and meager scholarly resources.[53] That all changed, gradually at first, and by 1925 Saint Louis University hatched the first self-professed Neo-Scholastic journal, *The Modern Schoolman*—soon followed by *Thought* (Fordham University), *The New Scholasticism* (which morphed into the *American Catholic Philosophical Quarterly*), and the *Thomist*.[54] American neo-Thomism was syncretic, providing a holistic approach to modern concerns while appealing to Catholicism's veneration for tradition. It was sufficiently antimodern and rejected materialist individualism, along with the liberal Protestant fallacy of inevitable upward progress and human self-sufficiency. In its later incarnations—popularized by the television guru Fulton Sheen, as well as Maritain and John Courtney Murray—neo-Thomism was reconstituted as the ultimate American reserve ammunition in the Cold War struggle against global Communism.[55]

Scholasticism was not the only aspect of Roman Catholic tradition that was conscripted in the interests of Red Scare nationalism. Socialist power loomed over international politics but also threatened to devour American democracy from within. Labor was particularly susceptible to Marxist propaganda, having been ravaged by unchecked laissez-faire capitalism. While Catholicism gathered its resources on intellectual and organizational fronts, a liturgical revival movement tended to the interior needs of the community. Virgil Michel, OSB, of St. John's Abbey in Collegeville, Minnesota, led the charge, founding *Orate Fratres* (now *Worship*) as a journal dedicated to liturgical reform in 1926, along with the Liturgical Press. The doctrine of the Mystical Body of Christ—which would be formally promulgated by Pius XII in 1943—provided a handy metaphor for an orthodox Catholic middle road between individualism and collectivism.[56] The "body" model of Church was considerably more participatory than previous Catholic ecclesiology, while maintaining a formalized hierarchy locating the papacy firmly at the "head." Insofar as Andrew Greeley's assertion that "Catholics live in an enchanted world" could aspire to be more than mere poetic license, that world within *the* world had to be maintained through a consistent spiritual infrastructure.[57] The cultural self-confidence among American Catholics fostered a proliferation of the adjective "Catholic" as a descriptor for shared analogical formation across disciplines—the *Catholic* novel, *Catholic* sociology, etc.[58]

The lay retreat movement emerged in the United States as part of the comprehensive support network that American Catholics developed to attend to contemporary needs, material and spiritual. James T. Fisher has noted that, while the retreat phenomenon bore some strong resemblance to the more traditional parish mission—with itinerant priests migrating from town to town on a revival circuit—it was "by nature more elitist," on account of the practical logistics involved.[59] As with many of the Catholic lay associations of the era, the retreat movement was formed through a combination of organic lay initiative and institutional oversight. The reforming priest Terence J. Shealy, SJ, is largely credited for overseeing the national consolidation of retreats, which he viewed as instrumental in reinforcing the foundations of the institutional Church, at this precarious stage in the maturation of American Catholicism.[60] Analogous to the ideology of Social Gospel reformers such as Walter Rauschenbusch, Shealy's vision of retreats attempted to strike a balance between individual salvation, spiritual perfection, and social reconstruction. A militant antimodernist, Pope Pius XI—elevated on February 6, 1922—gave his imprimatur in the encyclical *Mens nostra*, which outlined a vision of the lay retreat providing spiritual nourishment for politicized parochial organs such as Catholic Action, the "participation of the laity in the apostolate of the hierarchy."[61] Throughout the 1930s, Pius XI's model became increasingly normative, essentially segregating the spiritual and political realms—with retreats cornering the market on interior rigorism, which was then shaped through participants' subsequent participation in Church-sanctioned avenues of progressive engagement.[62] As Joseph Chinnici, OFM, notes in reference to Shealy's generation of spiritual reform, "the retreat, like the nineteenth-century mission, was designed to create a stronger and more organized institutional church."[63]

The format of the Catholic retreat was aimed at fostering individual religious experience rather than muscle-memory ritual practice—although they certainly were not devoid of ritual. Their predecessor, the parish mission, had more mass appeal and relied heavily on a platoon of charismatic, trained professionals furnished by the Paulists, Jesuits, and Redemptorists.[64] On the opposite end of the spectrum from the brick-and-mortar clergy who bottom-lined American Catholic infrastructure—and the network of schools, hospitals, lay societies, and guilds—these itinerant conference preachers focused on (re)converting souls and drumming up spiritual fervor. Particularly in rural areas, circuit priests had administered the sacraments to a vulnerable and spiritually isolated laity.[65] During the colonial period, nomadic clergy attempted to minister to at-risk Catholics in danger of endogamy, succumbing to Protestant proselytism, or lapsing due to lack of support.[66] Evangelical Catholicism provided skilled ministry to perform outreach to laity who did not have regular access to priests, but also to give healthy congregations an injection of spiritual adrenaline and some much-needed support to overworked diocesan clergy. It protected susceptible Catholics from caving and aided in boundary maintenance, but it also improved the quality of already habitual churchgoers by inspiring moral vigilance, devotional piety, and sacramental observance. Whether it was a matter of aiding women religious' ministering to remote frontier Catholics, lending a colingual ear for ethnic immigrant parishioners, preempting modernist or socialist threats, or indoctrinating blue-collar workers into the gospel of democratic process, collective bargaining, and ultramontanism, missionary priests served a critical function in the preservation and fortification of American Catholic vitality.[67]

The Iron City Trinity

> Unionization is a perfectly normal, Christian thing. That it ever has been regarded otherwise is proof of the twisted viewpoint that has prevailed in our modern civilization. Why should not the worker organize? Why should he be compelled to go through his working life like a grain of sand and not like the social organism he is? Why does anyone want to keep the workers apart, disorganized? Why other than through the desire to keep them weak and easy to exploit?
>
> —Charles Owen Rice to the Textile Workers Organizing Committee in Utica, New York, 1938

Although Port of New York longshoremen—along with Marlon Brando—might demur, Pittsburgh Steel made the Iron City *the* premier hub of organized labor in early twentieth-century America.[68] As in New York, the proletarian workforce became a battleground in the domestic standoff between the Roman Catholic Church and international Communism. The financial collapse that devolved into the Great Depression gutted American jobs, with unemployment peaking at close to twenty-five percent by 1933.[69] Although Catholics had already made inroads into mainstream assimilation in the United States, they were still a conspicuous minority—albeit a sizeable one—somewhat on the fringes of American society. The post–World War I era was not the worst time to be an American "Papist," and Catholic philosophers were anxious to advertise the Universal Church's intellectual resources in a climate dominated by disenchanted Christian Realists. However, while the "myth of progress" opened up avenues for asserting a measure of Catholic exceptionalism, the practical concerns of the Depression fostered a groundswell of social engagement that inspired a reapplication of traditional thought to the harsh realities that surged below the surface of industrial capitalism.

One name that looms singularly large in the history of Pittsburgh Catholic labor activism is Charles Owen Rice. Born to a pair of Brooklyn-Irish immigrants in 1908, just two and a half years before John Hugo, Rice entered St. Vincent's (as would Hugo)—after a childhood spent in Ireland and undergraduate studies at Duquesne—and was ordained in 1934. The year before, he had met Dorothy Day during a visit to New York and was inspired by her socially engaged, practical theology—

albeit in a relatively nascent state, given the fact that she had only converted in 1927.[70] Subsequently, Rice cofounded the St. Joseph House of Hospitality with Carl Hensler—another local priest—became executive director of the Pittsburgh Catholic Worker School, wrote regularly on social matters in Pittsburgh's *Catholic*, and was a ubiquitous presence on local radio. Simultaneously the Rice-Hensler duo also organized the Catholic Radical Alliance (CRA), which mobilized local Irish and Poles to support the families of laborers on strike. In 1937, the CRA publicly defended the Congress of Industrial Organizations (CIO) against Republican charges of Communist atheism.[71] This won them the eternal allegiance of Pittsburgh's working class—at least until the Civil Rights Movement, which saw Rice temporarily alienated from his base—but it also instigated a confrontation between them and another venerable labor priest, James Cox, who had briefly run for president on the Jobless Party ticket in 1932. Although Cox had terminated his candidacy in support of Franklin Delano Roosevelt, he eventually soured on the New Deal, which he determined to be overly collectivist.[72]

Cox, similarly Duquesne- and St. Vincent's-educated, was the pastor of Old St. Patrick's Church, located in Pittsburgh's Strip District, an industrial hub that was variously home to U. S. Steel, Westinghouse Electric, and the H. J. Heinz Company, among other less prolific tenants. Old St. Pat's was the oldest parish in the city but boasted a miniscule eighteen families in regular Mass attendance. During the Depression, Cox founded an enormous soup kitchen that served two million meals between 1930 and 1934. He also facilitated a relationship between St. Patrick's Relief Fund and Acme Coal and Coke Company, which funneled 2,120 tons of coal to the local poor.[73] Additionally, the industrious priest became the unofficial mayor of his very own "Shantytown," which was constructed on church land primarily using recycled broken-down wooden crates. Perhaps his most dramatic endeavor, however, was organizing between twelve and twenty-five thousand militant pedestrians—dubbed "Cox's Army"—which he led to Washington, DC, in protest of rampant unemployment and government neglect. As reported in *Time* magazine in 1932, the long, frigid march, at its time the largest protest of its kind in American history, drew inspiration—along with its nickname—from the Social Gospeler Jacob Coxey's 1894 "Army of the Commonweal in Christ":

> In 1894, when poor people walked, one Jacob Sechler Coxey—now the respectable Republican Mayor of Massillon, Ohio—marched a ragged army of 100 men from his hometown to Washington to get the Government to do something about hard times. Last month when Congress opened, 1,600 Red "hunger marchers" arrived at the Capital in trucks, tried to muscle their way into the Senate chamber and, failing, traipsed off yelling the "International." Last week another, far larger "army" invaded Washington. No handful of disgruntled partisans were they, but more than 10,000 orderly men who differed from the silent crowds that watched them pass only in that they were wet, hungry and out of work.[74]

Then-president Herbert Hoover was unsurprisingly disturbed and irritated by the massive turnout descending on the nation's capital. To make matters worse, at every stop, it seemed Cox and his army were greeted with open arms by locals and treated to warm hospitality all along the route. Republicans suspected that the march was being backed by an unlikely coalition of Communist, Vatican, and Al Smith–voting supporters, and although these conspiracy theories proved groundless it was true that Andrew Mellon had been surreptitiously supplying the caravan with free gasoline along the route.[75] Cox's Army demanded that deeper government resources be appropriated for domestic relief work, and President Hoover begrudgingly agreed to meet with a delegation of thirteen to discuss a program for economic recovery. However, in the pre-FDR era, Hoover's platitudes failed to satisfy and left a vacuum, prompting Cox's presidential bid. Bishop Hugh Boyle, a friend to Charles Owen Rice and, as it were, John Hugo, supported Cox's candidacy as a skillful means of promoting Catholic social teaching.[76] Cox's establishment of "Blue Shirt battalions" seemed eerily reminiscent of the German National Socialists and fostered unsubstantiated rumors that he was a fascist. However, by the winter of 1934, Cox had stepped somewhat out of the limelight and found himself working as a full-time operator for Roosevelt, pacifying Catholic Democrats who resented the Episcopalian for defeating Al Smith in the primaries—an outcome that they blamed largely on nepotism and southern bigotry.[77]

As the *Time* piece indicates, Cox's march on Washington, while being enormously successful, was not particularly innovative from a tactical level. The Communist Hunger March a year earlier, though not an overwhelming success in terms of numbers, nevertheless pushed Cox to be more aggressive, demanding, and openly confrontational (albeit peaceful). Kenneth Heineman has noted that US labor historians have conventionally condemned proletarian clerics for their anti-Red paranoia that undermined the good works of civic-minded Communist activists. Pittsburgh was not all that different from the rest of the nation, and Catholics competed with various forms of organized socialism for membership, while often being conflated or mistaken for one another in the minds of capital holders and stability-minded conservatives:

> For the sake of history, let it be noted that there was a perduring streak of Catholic opposition to the New Deal, to Liberalism, to the Roosevelts, to Trade Unionism, especially the CIO brand, and to those of us who supported all of the above. There were very few rich Catholics, but we had a bourgeoisie, which could be vehement. Even some workers, then as now, had the bourgeois mentality. Father Charles E. Coughlin was unbelievably influential with the laity, even workers, some of the clergy and hierarchy. Through his radio program and his magazine, he promoted isolationism, anti-Liberalism, and anti-Semitism. After he was silenced, those seeds lay dormant during WWII, but when the war was over, blossomed again. Isolationists re-emerged as cold warriors, and Senator Joseph McCarthy burst on the scene, calling us all Communists.[78]

As perhaps the premier industrial hub in the United States, Pittsburgh evolved into a vortex of anti-Communist activity during World War I, supporting a substantial web of government agencies and infrastructure.[79] A cornucopia of urban working-class immigrants imported their collectivist ethic of DIY political muscle, which overflowed into rural industrial agitation.[80] Because they drew from a similar base—disenfranchised victims of laissez-faire capitalism and labor exploitation—and were similarly international, progressive Catholics and Communists were both painted as patently unpatriotic and dangerous to the American way of life by corporate propagandists and reactionary politicians. Similarly, both were accused of making straw men out of one another—amplifying their "dangers to the nation" in the interest of their own American identity and patriotic legitimacy.[81] The Canadian-born Detroit priest Charles Coughlin had become a radio sensation with tens of millions of listeners tuning into his weekly talk show, which received so much fan mail that it was assigned its own postal code. An initial supporter of FDR, Coughlin eventually turned on the New Deal, crafting a panicked anti-Semitic theory that denounced the US president for being a Manchurian of foreign Jewish puppet masters. A younger, less racist Coughlin had nominally supported organized labor but balked at the concept of striking as a bridge too far. By 1936, he was publicly excoriating the CIO, alleging they harbored Communist sympathizers.[82] Himself an immigrant—albeit a proximate one—Coughlin's manic appeal spoke to the legitimizing force of mainstream anti-Communist sensationalism, although Ken Heineman is careful not to overstate the tactically opportunist character of the American Catholic-Communist confrontation.[83]

While it has been alleged that race relations in Depression-era Pittsburgh were not as clannish as their urban East Coast counterparts, the CIO—which emerged out of the American Federation of Labor (AFL) in 1935 to support specifically mechanized-labor concerns—was almost exclusively white. More specifically, it was dominated by Jews and Catholics, who entered into organized labor at high rates and subsequently became allied with Democratic interests through the tightknit political machine dubbed the "Iron City Trinity," composed of the Church, the party, and the steel workers' union.[84] Charles Owen Rice, James Cox, and other prominent labor priests were cut from blue-collar cloth—as was their bishop, Hugh Boyle. They were grassroots activists, not mercenarial imports such as populated the ranks of their Communist nemeses, who were depicted by Catholic leaders as opportunist outsiders with little compassion for, or interest in, the practical needs of local families. While both Catholics and Communists were portrayed as questionably loyal Americans, the diocesan-level Church in Pittsburgh was successful in identifying itself with marginalized workers on a visceral, emotive level. While the Shantytown mayor Cox made international headlines, Rice was *the* Iron City labor icon. He was a ubiquitous presence at CIO events and served as their unofficial chaplain:[85]

> What we need is not less CIO and less progressive legislation. We need more of both. I beg the workers to be loyal to their leaders and refuse to be shaken by hardship, calumnies, or campaigns of any kind. Labor is on the march. On the march to a goal that will bring justice and happiness to all classes of people. Labor's right is everyone's fight. It is a fight for decency, justice, and a Christian social order.[86]

Rice was also an expert anti-Communist who used his spare time to compose tactical activist manuals, such as the ominously named *How to Decontrol Your Union of Communists*.[87] Heineman argues that personalist Catholic labor activists such as Rice, while occasionally manic in their anti-Communism, were, by and large, sincere and not simply pandering to assimilationist opportunities—although the recalibration of mainstream US insider-outsider boundaries to include Catholics at the expense of Communists may have been a welcomed side effect. Although prominent activist-priests allied themselves with big government, others found the traditional Catholic concept of subsidiarity to be a more attractive guiding principle.[88] Rice was also closely affiliated with the Association of Catholic Trade Unionists (ACTU)—cofounded by New York Catholic Worker John Cort in 1937—whose avowed mission was to promote Catholic social teaching among laborers.[89] Although it was founded by and for the Catholic laity, the ACTU was heavily clerical and afforded Rice an added layer of institutional authority, which he parlayed to his advantage in the campaign to eradicate Communism from Pittsburgh labor.[90]

In the activist ferment that swirled around Pittsburgh in the mid-1930s—which produced epic labor priests like Cox and Rice—John Hugo's interest in economic injustice tracked him into the discipline of sociology fit with prevailing trends then afoot. It was an electric atmosphere, and it is no wonder that a young seminarian with a flair for the dramatic would be attracted to the Social Question; it would have been more astonishing if he was not. The very same year as Hugo's priestly ordination, 1936, Paul Hanly Furfey—CUA's "supernatural sociologist"—published his dynamic text *Fire on the Earth*, outlining a theological imperative behind radical politics.[91] Furfey, "a goader, fire-breather and renegade," became a favorite of Peter Maurin, who added *Fire on the Earth* to the reading list of his perpetually hypothetical book club.[92] Similarly, Hugo was not at all unique among Pittsburghers in his attraction to the Catholic Worker's incarnational spirituality and embedded form of ministry—although this would come a bit later in life. With Rice at the helm, Pittsburgh would become a stronghold of Catholic Worker activity—and the site of at least one dramatic community schism. However, although it is inconceivable that Hugo might never have intersected with the Catholic Worker down the road if things had panned out just a bit differently, it was his unanticipated and slightly random encounter with the Lacouture retreat that detached him somewhat from scholastic aspirations and simultaneously laid the groundwork for a future, deeply fruitful, relationship with Dorothy Day. Much like the retreat itself, Hugo's contemplative vocation inadvertently—he would say providentially—found a dramatic social application through his ability to facilitate deep spiritual conversion. Hugo's synthesis was in large part a recontextualization of the austere, scrupulous, disengaged interiority of Lacouturite theology into a medium that could form a radical social analysis of structural sin and activist noncompliance with the machines of death. The vibrant lifeworld of Pittsburgh Catholic labor gave him the mettle to transpose Lacouture's Sermon on the Mount critique of government economic and military policies, as well as of mass corporations whose profits seemed to require the dependency and destitution of multitudes; it also conditioned Hugo's laser-like focus on complicity within the halls of Catholic power, which he believed to be particularly susceptible to the allure of secular paganism.

5 John Hugo and the Retreat's Southward Migration

> Let us take the case of a priest, who is fond of smoking, enjoys a good meal, likes to go to the ball-game, listen to the radio, etc. . . . Now, it is a false application of Catholic principles to say that this priest, in the indulgence of these pleasures is committing any sin or preparing the way for a fall from grace. He enjoys these pleasures, it is true, but his ultimate purpose is to recreate himself in body and in soul, so that he can perform his priestly duties with greater zest and efficacy. It is a false asceticism that would reprove a priest of this type.
>
> —Francis J. Connell, "Comments on 'Applied Christianity' by Fr. Hugo"

By the winter of 1949, the debate over Lacouturisme had become firmly rooted in US soil and had developed a distinct, somewhat more frenzied, tone. The figurehead of the American movement was Pittsburgh diocesan priest John Hugo, who had first stumbled upon the Lacouture retreat eleven years prior. Hugo translated the retreat into American idioms and almost single-handedly reconstituted what had been a primarily clerical, socially withdrawn, insular francophone movement within Québécois Catholicism into a powerful stimulant for Lacouturite spiritual regeneration in the United States. Unlike Lacouture's original permutation of the retreat, Hugo's tapped into the laity directly—anticipating the Second Vatican Council's articulation of "holiness for all." Under Hugo's stewardship, the retreat gained a more public, populist slant and also became more organized in its confrontational posture than it ever was in Québec. Hugo was a natural scrapper and was galvanized further by his beloved teacher's suppression, which he—in good Lacouturite form—interpreted in semi-apocalyptic, highly cinematic terms.

From his first taste of "*the* retreat," Hugo's career might be read as a lifelong homage to his spiritual father. By his own account, he experienced a profound interior transformation during his first retreat with Lacouture in September 1938—during the Canadien's brief revival circuit along the US Atlantic coastline—that mimicked Lacouture's own interior revelations in Alaska.[1] As with Lacouture, following this seminal event, Hugo seems never to have wavered from his extreme new course of maximalist, countercultural Catholicism—although the cultural backdrop that served as their foil of paganism differed markedly. While his mentor relied on subterfuge and a certain level of disingenuous manipulation to promote his rigorist program, Hugo was, from the start, fully transparent about his position, as well as his visceral antagonism to the theological status quo. While Lacouture relied on anonymously leaked correspondences to serve as his mouthpiece during the suppression, Hugo published in both popular and academic journals and spoke publicly with a fiery rhetoric that transgressed the boundaries of civility. Hugo's retreat inspired a form of "public Catholicism" that marked an evolutionary mutation in the American model.[2] Historically, the Church's "immigrant" strain had predominated and was eventually replaced by an assimilationist New Dealing Catholicism that was thoroughly and intentionally American—if persistently off-modern. Hugo's posture was formed out of the bedrock of Lacouturite revivalism but bore an unmistakably social orientation that Lacouture never possessed—and which, indeed, caused him some degree of concern. But nonetheless, it did so in a manner that was profoundly nonconformist and in some respects patently un-American.

The tale of John Hugo's interior development so closely resembles Lacouture's that observers might hypothesize that the latter's influence may have retroactively colored his memory—although the fact remains that Lacouture's own story in many ways simply recast the typical Pauline-Augustinian conversion narrative that has been template for the conventional Christian imagination for approaching two thousand years. Hugo habitually referred to himself as "Irish Catholic," although his Celtic bloodline was a slightly more complex composite of Irish, Welsh, and French. His mother, née Mary Caulfield, being an Irish thoroughbred, exercised a stereotypically autocratic, albeit relatively benign, influence on her children. The Hugo family was solidly middle-class, situated in the Pittsburgh suburb of McKeesport, and nourished by the combined incomes of

Mary and Lawrence, who worked as a steel company secretary and combined real estate and insurance agent, respectively—only to see their finances decimated during the 1929 economic collapse.[3] Nonetheless, their close proximity to St. Vincent's Archabbey in nearby Latrobe guaranteed the Hugo children a thoroughly Catholic education.[4] John (b. 1911) was the oldest of four—a miniscule number in comparison to Lacouture's twenty-one—who all went on to higher education and, eventually, teaching at both the high school and university levels. Mary Hugo set a high standard of religious observance that permeated the household, while Lawrence fostered a climate of academic excellence. After a series of consultations with his father during middle school, a young John Hugo divined that he was predestined to matriculate at Carnegie Tech University in order to pursue his blossoming interest in engineering.[5] However, these plans were derailed by his entry into St. Vincent's Prep in 1924. Over the next decade in Latrobe, at the prep, college, and diocesan seminary—and although he never formally entered into the Benedictine life—he was profoundly formed by its contemplative influence:

> Why did I become a priest? . . . If I may use a figure, it would be a magnet, subtle, at first almost unfelt, but growing in force until it became all but overpowering. So perhaps it is simpler and truer just to compare it to falling in love. And genuine love, of whatever kind, exacts a high price.[6]

Hugo was ordained into a life of active ministry but was unknowingly primed to receive Lacouture's retreat spirituality of interior withdrawal and moral perfectionism. Although Hugo's assimilation into religious life was not as unflinching as Lacouture's—he notes his strong inclination toward women as a major impediment to accepting his ascetic calling—it was also met with substantially less sensational resistance from his parents. In fact, Hugo credits his father's counsel on the stoic life with helping him resist sexual temptation during his adolescence. If Lacouture's autobiographical narrative played up his almost sui generis deocentric focus from childhood, Hugo's seems to pay special attention to establish conventional masculine bona fides. As the gravitational pull of clerical life drew him closer, Hugo showed little of the radical supernaturalism that would color his later enthusiasm.

John Hugo Gets Religion

> And so, we have scarcely begun to enjoy this world when we must begin to give up its pleasures; we have no sooner started to live than we must learn to die: just as the happiness of the caterpillar, grubbing about the earth for food, is interrupted by the law of growth which turns him into the dead-looking chrysalis. . . . And yet as the chrysalis is but an intermediate stage, from which the graceful butterfly will soon emerge, so the mortification of this life is also but an intermediate stage from which we too shall emerge "new creatures" capable of entering upon and enjoying the glory of heaven.
>
> —John J. Hugo, *Why Must I Suffer? Or, How to Become a Butterfly*

According to John Hugo's self-report, his young adulthood was characterized by diligent but unambitious study and a wholesome social interest inspired by the Catholic social teachings of Pope Pius XI, whose encyclical *Quadragesimo Anno* commemorated the fortieth anniversary of Leo XIII's landmark *Rerum Novarum*.[7] This compelled him to pursue an academic program in the social sciences that eventually landed him a position at Seton Hill College, some ten miles west in Greensburg, Pennsylvania—run by the Sisters of Charity—following his ordination to the diaconate. Although he would later come to resent his seminary education for what he perceived to be an overreliance on casuistry and permissive spiritual laxity, this only seems to have bubbled to the surface retrospectively following his encounter with Onésime Lacouture. This occurred following his second year at Seton Hill, just in time for his first assignment teaching undergraduate Scripture. By the time he had returned for the fall semester, his whole vision of academic life and theological education had shifted decidedly: he grew disillusioned with academic theology, which—in his mind—simply reproduced spiritually sterile philosophical formulas and segregated the mystical Doctors of the Church like Teresa of Avila, John of the Cross, and Francis de Sales to marginal posts as material for unencouraged extracurricular study.[8] Given the Lacouture retreat's heavy reliance on Scripture, Hugo was fired up and eagerly launched himself into his class with a newfound zeal, using it as an opportunity to clarify his own thoughts as well as evangelize fertile young minds. Unfortunately, Fr. James A. Reeves, Seton Hill's president—who had possessed exclusive rights to the course up until then and had assigned it to Hugo in the first place as a vote of confidence—did not share his protégé's radical interpretation of Scripture. Hugo's less than objective account of the incident described it with characteristic cheek:

> The sudden appearance on the campus of the doctrine of holiness for all was too much for a regime committed to "common sense religion." There was sudden turmoil on the campus, further agitated as news of the "Lacouture Affair" filtered through. Catholics are generally tolerant of their priests as long as they do not "get religion." The people, comfortable in our affluent society, fear getting caught up in any excessive religious enthusiasm.[9]

Before the year was out, Hugo had been removed from his post and replaced by an older, more conventionally user-friendly priest. Without substantial variation, this pattern would be repeated—albeit punctuated by extended lulls—for the next forty years.

As Hugo described his first encounter with Lacouture, the Jesuit "*fertilized* my mind, until then rendered barren by a spirit of rationalism and inhibiting minimalism such as has in fact long dominated practically all Catholic spirituality."[10] This all might never have come to pass, had Hugo not enrolled in summer classes at the University of Chicago, skipping his annual diocesan retreat in 1938. As restitution, Hugo traveled to St. Mary's Seminary in Baltimore to make a retreat with Lacouture, who was then touring the eastern seaboard.[11] Throughout his life, Hugo was more or less tight-lipped about his own religious experiences and certainly never alluded to anything approaching his Jesuit mentor's mystical encounters. But even if Hugo never even had a direct experience of God, he did encounter Onésime Lacouture, whose impact was practically sacramental. Lacouture radicalized Hugo, transfiguring him from a conventional, socially minded liberal into a Catholic barnstormer. Lacouture introduced Hugo to a new way of reading Scripture, as well as to the litany of Catholic contemplatives—most particularly John of the Cross. The scrupulous attention to minor attachments did not come naturally, but it became clear to Hugo that they were the real battlefield for Christian holiness:

> That first time I was struggling with relatively superficial things like smoking, eating, dietary habits. Eat, drink, and make good cheer—that's perpetually the slogan of the pagan, you know. Drinking, recreation, various attachments that are innocent enough—this was our fight.[12]

Hugo also appears to have absorbed Lacouture's messianic interpretation of their prophetic role in Church renewal, sowing the seeds of authentic, vibrant Christianity in a Church under siege from without as well as within by the forces of modernism, secularism, and moral laxity. Similarly, he assimilated Lacouture's extremist tendency to view opposition in cosmic terms and perceived a supernatural conspiracy lying below the surface of anti-Lacouture agitation. As he grew in stature—even within the Lacouturite microcosm—Hugo painted himself into a venerable lineage of subversive reformers and spiritual heroes tracing its origins directly back to Israel's prophets and Christ.

To Hugo, Onésime Lacouture was the personification of the Gospel. Although he had not dreamed of academic triumph in the grandiose, epic terms that colored his Québécois predecessor's pre-conversion fantasies, Hugo seems to have bought Lacouture's maximalist doctrine wholesale and adopted the Jesuit's trademark laconic anti-intellectualism. From that very first retreat, Hugo's devotion to his Jesuit mentor was characterized by a pronounced and unflagging reverence that verged on fanaticism. Although there is no indication that Hugo had previously found his chosen lifestyle unfulfilling or bland, Lacouture opened his eyes to a new realm of existence that disenchanted Hugo with the conventional, accommodationist Christianity that had defined his formation thus far. His prior vocation now appeared bland by comparison. Lacouture seemed to inhabit a thoroughly supernatural stratum that electrified the impressionable young seminarian: "Possibly there have been, and are holier men among the clergy; but I have never heard of any teacher of spirituality in America to compare with him in excellence of doctrine, clarity and vigour of presentation, and extent of influence. Certainly it is the Holy Spirit who converts souls; but it is His design to convert them through human instruments, through the preaching of His apostles."[13] While Hugo was unashamed of his zeal for Lacouturism, he was tactfully insistent that retreat participants had not been sucked into a personality cult, drawing a sharp distinction between their guide and the doctrine that was taught in the retreats. Following Lacouture's own testimonies—and conventional wisdom—Hugo went to great lengths to emphasize the Canadien preacher's theological orthodoxy, traditional pedigree, and lack of innovation. Although quite young, Hugo already knew enough to realize that charges of doctrinal novelty were toxic to theological credibility—particularly one as iconoclastic, controversial, and divisive as Lacouture had been in Québec, and was increasingly becoming south of the border. Similarly, it could not have escaped Hugo from early on that his own reputation was integrally intertwined with that of his newfound abba. That being said, the claim of antiquity was heartfelt and earnest—Hugo was being indoctrinated into a self-consciously primitivist spirituality that defined itself in terms of return to a primordial, pure, martyr's Christianity.

Applied Christianity *and Lacouturite Apologetics*

As a Lacouture devotee, Hugo was predictably scandalized by his mentor's undignified mishandling and the triumph of the dark conspiracy to extinguish his revival of the faith. Toward the end of his life, Hugo exhibited a measure of grim resignation that the "return to the Gospel" had been so thwarted by those very Church leaders whose vocation was to care for ecclesiastical welfare.[14] As part of his program to evangelize mainline American Catholicism, and simultaneously defend his master from slander south of the border, Hugo composed a detailed apology entitled *Applied Christianity*. Insofar as criticism in the United States was as-yet unarticulated publicly, *Applied Christianity* was something of a preemptive strike. Privately published in 1944, the text is essentially a consolidation of retreat notes that Hugo compiled during Lacouture's conferences, with some additional stabs at imagined inquisitors lurking in the shadows. His stated purpose for composing *Applied Christianity* was to fortify the content of retreats he had given himself, in response to the requests of former participants.[15] Additionally, and more optimistically, Hugo hoped to publicize the Lacouturite doctrine that had animated his own spiritual life, and which he believed held the potential to resuscitate American Catholic theology and clerical formation. For the uninitiated who did not have the good fortune to find the retreat on their own, *Applied Christianity* was to be a piece of bait and an invitation to conversion. The text contained an implicit indictment of seminary theology, which Hugo—like Lacouture—condemned for being overly rationalistic and spiritually sterile in its reliance on Thomism. More to the point, Hugo bristled at the Neo-Scholastic presentation of Saint Thomas, not the Angelic Doctor himself, who he admired deeply. In fact, Hugo contended that "there is really no such thing as Thomistic philosophy."[16] *Applied Christianity* outlined vintage Lacouture themes: the doctrine of samples, the Folly of the Cross, the relationship between nature and grace, our supernatural destiny, and the "supreme dominion of God."[17]

Applied Christianity was a manifesto of maximalist Christian spirituality. It operated under the basic assumption that we are all, indeed, called to the summit of perfection by our creation as *imago Dei*. In fact, Hugo might have avoided some of the biting criticisms that surfaced if he had restricted his target audience to seasoned professional contemplatives—as had John of the Cross—rather than writing for popular consumption.[18] However, that would have run contrary to his egalitarian anthropology. Benjamin Peters's very detailed work on Hugo has shown that, in a manner similar Henri de Lubac, he rejected the proposition that there is an appropriately designated "natural" end to human life but rather that a supernatural orientation is inscribed in our very DNA, which therefore lays a claim on all Christians without exception or variance.[19] Hugo emphasized our interior disposition as the locus of the spiritual combat and the defining platform for Christian ethical conduct:

> When can we be sure that our lives are actually *dominated* by the love of God? When our actions are *motivated* by this love. The motive of an action fixes its end and thereby reveals, as it also determines, the animating principle of the action. . . . Hence we can say that an action is made supernatural by a supernatural motive, being performed for the love of God. . . . If, on the other hand, our motive is merely natural and selfish, grace no longer impels the action, but is kept locked up in the soul; the practical impulsion and motive for the action comes from a selfishness, from concupiscence, from the love of creatures.[20]

Hugo argued that it is only in our motives that we are truly free.[21] The embodied nature of the human condition dictates that we live in a state of almost perpetual compulsion, both in terms of biological necessity and socio-psychological obligation. Our motivation alone is where we exercise liberty—we may be motivated by practical expediency, personal ambition, fear, or pleasure. Or, we may "supernaturalize" all our activity by being existentially oriented toward God, doing all things in God's name. For Hugo, this marks the sanctification that humans have been summoned to by Christ's mandate—or what he interpreted as a mandate—"Be ye perfect" (Matt. 5:48). Although Hugo does not go so far as to state explicitly that there are no actions that are, in themselves, intrinsically wrong, always and everywhere, his extreme focus on motives did leave him open to skeptical inquiry.[22] Additionally, Hugo's monocular focus on spiritual perfection appeared to relegate anything less to the margins.

Applied Christianity parrots Lacouture's attack on the modern pagan mentality and its emphasis on theory at the expense of practicality—the distinction between *in se* and *in nobis*, evoking Dorothy Day's beloved Dostoevsky quote: "love in action is a harsh and dreadful thing compared with love in dreams."[23] Thus Hugo could stipulate that "it is . . . false and artificial to speak of actions *in themselves*. This is accurate for philosophers, who deal with things *in the abstract*; but it is dangerous for us who must decide the merits of our actions *in the concrete*. For in the concrete, every action takes us either closer to God, or further away from Him."[24] Similarly, while Hugo could affirm that the natural and supernatural operate in tandem, our embodied experience is characterized by conflict—and this formed the basis for the Lacouturite emphasis on ascetic discipline. Displaying a studious fixation on the Lacouture affair, Hugo attempted to preempt anticipated criticisms regarding perceptions of excessive austerity: "There is nothing wrong with austerity in itself. The Saints were austere; and the Man Who said: 'Deny thyself and take up thy cross daily' was certainly teaching an austere doctrine; and He lived an austere life."[25] Hugo vigorously defended his doctrine of mortification, arguing that it did not constitute a condemnation of creation or natural forms of happiness; it was a functional practice rooted in the love of God and conformity to God's will, which is also the source of our ever-greater happiness. In the supernatural cost/benefit analysis, self-mortification is simply the practice of denying temporary, ephemeral pleasures that conventionally pass as happiness for what is innately superior. In Hugo's logic, asceticism is actually a proactive "yes" rather than a "no"—an openness to God that involves, on a secondary level, a denial of base pleasures. However, his proposition does evince a fundamentalist adherence to Matthew 22:37's injunction against idolatry in exclusivist terms and an occasionally unanalogical tendency toward created phenomena—despite his adherence to the doctrine of samples. Hugo's alternation between formal affirmation of creation and rejection of "the world" was dialectical and the question of theological orthodoxy a matter of emphasis and balance. According to Hugo, ascetic practices are the outward expression of self-renunciation, which emerges as a response to the supernatural, itself an imitation of Christ: "This is why Christian joy is a fruit of the Holy Ghost: it proceeds from supernatural charity, the love of God, and is introduced into our hearts by the Holy Ghost with grace; moreover, it increases as the activity of the Holy Ghost more and more predominates in the soul, which is at the expense of merely natural affections."[26]

Hugo's permutation of retreat theology differed from Lacouture's in two distinct but interrelated ways. Hugo's primary antagonists were not religious superiors or bishops but nationally renowned scholars. And as such, his persecution of the retreat did not come in the form of pastoral advice, surreptitious politicking, or binding edicts but as written works in the pages of influential academic journals. By 1941, Hugo had already grown weary of the theatrics involving professional critics who seemed to make it their personal mission to smear his good name:

> Concerning the charges of heresy (which come thick and fast), I do not intend to answer them. Seminarians do not have the authority to set down anathemas, neither do seminary professors. I have a hard time keeping my patience with these self-appointed inquisitors who shout heresy as soon as they see an idea unfamiliar to them. . . . My bishop has given me faculties to teach and he knows what I teach. And bishops are the sole custodians of faith and morals. I am answerable to only him.[27]

Whether he actually meant it at the time or was just taking the moral high road, Hugo's fortitude did not endure. Additionally, Hugo's cycle of the controversy was more indiscrete and venomous than Lacouture's. There was minimal behind-closed-doors dialoguing. However—as was the case in Québec—the record leads one to suspect that the "victim" in question drew some measure of satisfaction from the whole ordeal. The tone of *Applied Christianity* was not exactly conciliatory, and Hugo does seem to have instigated—or at least exacerbated—some of the conflict, which he no doubt considered justifiable retribution for sins perpetrated against his mentor and mission critical to combat the mounting—if then-anonymous—pagan opposition. Throughout the ordeal, Hugo's skill at taking refuge underneath the wing of sympathetic bishops like Hugh Boyle leads one to puzzle whether his professed adoration of the role of the magisterium was genuine or opportunistically tactical—or both. Hugo repeatedly flaunted *Applied Christianity*'s *nihil obstat* from former Dunwoodie rector Msgr. Arthur J. Scanlon, and imprimatur from the Archbishop of New York, Francis J. Spellman—the doctrinaire, hawkish future cardinal nicknamed "the American Pope."[28]

The Best Defense

For all the lip service he paid to the virtue of humility and voluntary suffering, Hugo was not above mounting a vigorous, polemical self-defense, often laden with vitriolic ad hominem attacks that were fairly clearly intended to maim. In fact, he seemed to think of it as his prophetic duty. Not only did John Hugo not abstain from answering the charges of heresy—and *Applied Christianity* was itself at least partially an apologia for Onésime Lacouture—but he actually wrote two additional volumes on the subject, chronicling the controversy and meticulously addressing the critiques on an almost line-by-line basis.[29] This is not to say that his critics did not goad him, even if their intentions were fairly benign, initially. The first broadside to address John Hugo by name was printed in the July 1945 edition of the venerable *American Ecclesiastical Review* (*AER*)—the oldest American Catholic theological journal (now defunct)—and composed by the Catholic University's own Francis Connell, CSsR, a Redemptorist priest and frequent contributor to the *AER*. The essay was, in fact, an abridged version of a more detailed critique of *Applied Christianity* that Connell had circulated privately among colleagues. Connell began his review with what seems like an attempt at empathy (if a patronizing empathy) before taking a turn toward the alarmist and accusatory:

> Any writer who attempts to inspire his readers with the spirit of self-denial and conformity to the divine will deserves commendation for his good intention. But this does not necessarily include approbation of the particular type of virtue he wishes to inculcate or of the doctrines on which he bases his arguments. The Church has frequently condemned books evidently intended to foster Christian sanctity, but reprehensible either because they presented an incorrect norm of virtue

> or because the methods they suggested or the ascetical ideas they upheld were not in conformity with Catholic teaching.[30]

Connell's review emphasized that he was not calling for a formal ecclesiastical censure but alleged that *Applied Christianity* "contains statements which, if taken in their literal sense, bear a close resemblance to propositions condemned by the Church."[31] For instance, Connell inquired into Hugo's depiction of "supernatural actions" as necessarily demanding pure charity, which seemed to imply that sinners (i.e., most humans) might never perform such acts. The looming concern that Connell raised was what Hugo thinks of imperfect Christians and whether humanity's fallen nature is capable of performing meritorious action, unaided by an injection of grace.[32] Although Connell never mentions Jansenism explicitly, he favorably compares Hugo to both Michel de Bay (a.k.a. "Baius," 1513–1589) and Pasquier Quesnel (1634–1719), an influential forerunner of Jansenius and Jansenist archtheologian, respectively. Within the span of four pages, Connell's essay mentions Baius, Quesnel, Manichaeism, and Catharism—at the very least a passive-aggressive indictment of heresy, regardless of preceding commendations for Hugo's good intentions.

While the retreat's uncompromising demand for Christian perfection invited allegations of Pelagianism, conversely, its dim assessment of modern culture and natural human desire accounted for its Jansenist reputation—the most oft-cited and most challenging for the movement to shake.[33] Jansenism—as described by its leading seventeenth-century apologist, Antoine Arnauld—was more spectral than actual; the term itself laden with pejorative overtones of radical Augustinianism. For the most part, almost no one actually employed the term "Jansenist" as a self-identifier. Rather, the word was more commonly wielded as a derogatory mallet.[34] It has been suggested that the phenomenon might be more accurately renamed in deference to Jansenius's classmate and occasional benefactor, Jean Duvergier de Hauranne—better known as the Abbé de Saint-Cyran, who was arguably more influential in the movement's history.[35] Jansenism has commonly been defined in terms of doctrines explicitly anathematized in the 1653 papal bull *Cum occasione*, promulgated by Innocent X,[36] and Clement XI's anti-Quesnelian document *Unigenitus* in 1713. However, in practice it was substantially more obscure and fluid. In his concise treatment of the topic, Jonathan Wright concedes:

John Hugo at Maryfarm (Easton, PA), early 1940s (Department of Special Collections and University Archives, Marquette University Libraries)

> Jansenism, like most isms, was a convenient, homogenizing fiction, but like most convenient fictions it was a shadow, a reflection, of a real, unruly squabble: a fault line running through the Roman Catholic Church. . . . At root it was a Catholic attempt to reclaim Augustine, and this did not strike some people as an especially disreputable cause.[37]

While the term itself was coined by Jesuit provocateurs, and eventually became associated with a specific set of theological propositions that attacked nominally "laxist" tendencies prevalent in contemporary Christianity, the term "Jansenist" has historically been employed as a more general designation to indicate a dour, pessimistic Christian rigorism—stereotyped as mystically sterile "remote God" theology, although not exclusively.[38] It has been used to name multiple characteristics of Catholic anti-modernism: suspicion regarding the free use of reason, "progress," human nature's purportedly inherent virtue, and engagement with secular culture—although just as often it is used (more colloquially) as an object of blame for Catholic cultural guilt (particularly of the Irish variety) and sexual prudishness. If early Jansenism was characterized by anti-Jesuitism, then the Lacouture movement—particularly in its first redaction—really might have qualified, the not-so-subtle irony being that the "heresiarch" of this Jansenist outbreak was himself a member of the Society of Jesus.

The narrative history of the Lacouturite movement mimics its Jansenist analogue in form, with primary characters filling particular, if sometimes overlapping, roles: its roster of luminous personalities (Jansenius, Saint-Cyran, Quesnel: Lacouture, Hugo, Dorothy Day), primary sites (the Abbey of Port-Royal: the retreat), staunch apologists (Antoine Arnauld, Blaise Pascal: Louis Farina, Anselme Longpré), and antagonistic villains (the Society, Armand Jean du Plessis [Cardinal Richelieu]: universities, the *American Ecclesiastical Review*, various local hierarchy). If Lacouture himself provided the bedrock inspiration, Hugo was the movement's most successful publicist and imbued it with his own ultra-supernaturalist vision of Christian heroism. In his explanation of the term "ultra-supernaturalism," Ronald Knox writes:

> For that is the real character of the enthusiast, he expects more evident results from the grace of God than we others. He sees what effects religion can have, does sometimes have, in transforming a man's whole life and outlook; these exceptional cases (so we are content to think them) are for him the average standard of religious achievement. He will have no "almost-Christians," no weaker brethren who plod and stumble, who (if the truth must be told) would like to have one foot in either world, whose ambition is to qualify, not to excel. He has before his eyes a picture of the early Church, visibly penetrated with the supernatural influences; and nothing less will serve him for a model.[39]

The ultra-supernaturalist is inherently evangelical, Knox suggests, for it is the work of the "experimentalist," who has herself undergone a profound conversion (in the sense that William James describes—a new worldview) and invites others to do likewise.[40] The narrative of Lacouturite history could be read as a sequence of conversions, like a falling row of dominos—beginning with Lacouture's own foundational experience and subsequent proselytizing efforts. As the movement's popularity grew—first among the Québécois professed, later among both American clergy and laity, which consequently drew increasingly public scrutiny—it also adopted a substantially more combative tone. John Hugo may be credited with composing Lacouturism's most sophisticated, aggressive, and polarizing polemics—which increasingly isolated it from the fold of conventional American Catholicism.

Indeed, that Lacouturites retaliated in the first place seems somewhat counterintuitive, especially given their stated doctrine of suffering, which reached its apex in John Hugo—who went so far as to state, quite frankly, that *all* manner of affliction was a net positive for the soul's development (including natural disasters and genocide) and that suffering should actually be pursued by the Christian; he wrote an entire pamphlet on this, colorfully titled *Why Must I Suffer? Or, How to Become a Butterfly.* On paper, Hugo exuded a zeal for martyrdom reminiscent of Ignatius of Antioch, but unlike him, when push came to shove, he went to great lengths to court the sympathies of his persecutors and showed a particular concern with popular opinion—seemingly contradicting his emphasis on cultivating *apatheia* and alleged affinity for suffering and what Dorothy Day would glibly call her "poverty of reputation."[41] This logical disconnect was justified on the grounds that Hugo felt compelled to defend his position precisely because of the heresy charge, which had the capacity to infect others and thus had to be clarified, "in all Christian charity," so as to avoid scandal—precisely the logic that inspired the anti-Lacouturite polemics in the first place.

American Inquisition

Six months following the publication of Connell's review, Joseph Clifford Fenton—an imposing CUA theology professor and student of the great French Thomist, Réginald Marie Garrigou-Lagrange, OP—entered into the fray. His article "Nature and the Supernatural Life," printed in the *AER* (which Fenton edited) took a more tactful approach, even if it opted for a slightly more saccharine form of defamation.[42] Evidently, the condition of the dispute had escalated to such a level in the United States that a reticent Fenton felt compelled to address the conflict systematically: "Nature and the Supernatural Life" gives an overview of the controversy, including a relatively favorable appraisal of Anselme Longpré's synopsis of Lacouturite spirituality in *La folie de la croix*—or at least a respectful assessment of its lucid presentation, if not its theological acumen.[43] In the United States, Hugo had been the most dominant proponent of the doctrine, and thus, Fenton reasoned, it was imperative that his work be scrutinized comprehensively. Similarly, the fallout from *Applied Christianity* and Connell's review—including Hugo's subsequent circulation of retreat notes as something of a retort—had reached a critical mass that required clarification to bring it to conclusion:

> It would be tragic if a seminarian were to take the doctrine of *Applied Christianity* seriously and strive to interpret the truths of fundamental dogmatic theology in the light of the passages we have quoted. He would be led to imagine that the only reason which does not contradict faith is merely a non-existent abstraction.[44]

Although he was exceptionally polite about it and, like Connell, laid the praise rather thick on the front end when it came to Hugo's intentions and genuine piety, the letter had some serious bite to it. Throughout, Fenton's article had a tone that might be alternately interpreted as either pastoral or patronizing, meticulously enumerating Hugo's linguistic imprecisions and fretting over the menace of the hypothetical proliferation of Lacouturite doctrine.[45]

Fenton defended "natural" forms of love, which he believed Hugo's doctrine obliterated. He found error in Hugo's apparently impermeable divisions between our natural and supernatural capacities, which, in his reading, actually degraded the latter, and "definitely leaves the impression that the supernatural order is above all something which merely fills in the gap which original sin produced in the natural order of human activity."[46] The love of God above all things is inscribed in the natural law, and Fenton evaluated Hugo's "good pagan" as a straw man, virtually indistinguishable from any common animal. Rather, the two great commandments and the Decalogue itself belong to the natural order, as does our knowledge of God as He is known through creation, even in the case of mystical "mediated immediacy": "At the same time we must remember that any love for creatures to the exclusion of God, or any preference of a creature of God, must be classed as something evil, even judged by purely natural standards."[47] Fenton vigorously rejected Hugo's charges of moral laxity and the proposition that his camp of critics are advocating some modified form of permissive Catholicism. Rather, he witnessed some "definitely pernicious" and spiritually debilitating errors in *Applied Christianity*, a "strange sort of book" that risked corrupting the vulnerable reader not armed with graduate degrees in theology.[48] By the end of his essay, Fenton had clearly lost his patience, or perhaps just his poise, curtly dismissing Hugo as a "Lutheran" (which presumably carried more sting then than it might now), although he did not repeat Connell's earlier Jansenist charge—a development Hugo interpreted as something of a moral victory for the cause.

Temperamentally similar to Lacouture, Hugo was potentially even more susceptible to theatrical immoderation and the petty gibe than his mentor. At the very least, he was quite a bit more extroverted and seems to have somewhat relished the public nature of the controversy as it grew more heated. No doubt, like Fenton, he perceived the issues at stake to be critically important to the modern Church and welcomed the publicity as both an opportunity and a challenge. Although they were prodigious scholars in their own right, Fenton and Connell are known to history primarily as the two leaders of the pre-conciliar opposition to John Courtney Murray and beacons of the conservative establishment against the insidious advance of secularism:

> Fenton and Connell fought doggedly for well over a decade against what they perceived as a rising tide of Catholic indifferentism that threatened the very core of distinctive Catholic identity in the United States. . . . To these advocates of the strenuous spiritual life, the Catholic's relationship to American society was ineluctably adversarial; any change in the church's position would indicate capitulation, a failure of nerve, or dogmatic treason.[49]

Given their reputations as critics of American secularism and bogeymen of Catholic progress, there is some irony at work in their role in the Hugo controversy. Fenton and Connell positioned themselves as guardians of orthodoxy from extremes on both ends of the spectrum: contemporary relativism and moral laxity, along with Hugo's alleged excesses. If John Courtney Murray could have been judged too liberal in his openness to "the world," the autonomy of the individual conscience, and human nature, Hugo and his ilk represented an opposite problem—a troublingly Calvinist-sounding degradation of human nature and affect.[50] As Fenton noted: if all Hugo was saying was that the underlying motivation for all loves should be the love of God, then there is nothing inconsonant with fundamental Christian teaching; however, "The Last Supernaturalists" feared that Hugo's exclusivist supernaturalism banished "natural affections" altogether, something that seemed not only irreconcilable with orthodox Catholic thought but logically impossible, considering our creaturely composition.

Presumably to no one's great surprise, John Hugo withheld the benefit of the doubt from Fenton's article—as he had with Connell's initial treatment of *Applied Christianity*. Nevertheless, like Fenton and Connell themselves, Hugo attempted to claim the moral high ground, in response to those who may have thought that the whole situation had become rather undignified. He gave an account for his persistence in the controversy: the mandate of defending oneself—particularly as a priest—against charges of heresy, the growing influence of Lacouturism and *Applied Christianity*, and the mandate to defend truth regardless of the scandal it might cause to popular sensibilities: "To sacrifice truth for the sake of charity would be ultimately to sacrifice charity itself."[51] This did not, however, preclude him from glibly slagging Fenton and Connell as "the cardboard soldiers" on the very same page and much, much worse elsewhere. Thematically, Hugo's tone mirrored that of both Fenton and Connell, alleging that the critics had misunderstood, acted in bad faith by alleging that he had said things that he had not said, and projected theological missteps where none existed. Firmly persuaded of his intellectual pedigree and moral righteousness, Hugo repeated the Lacouturite rejection of innovation charges and alleged that it was actually his critics' laxity—that is, lack of a comprehensive supernatural doctrine—that underlay their theological errors.[52]

The Paranoid Style and Anti-intellectualism among the "Lacoutermites"

Given their explicitly radical program, it would have seemed somewhat disingenuous for Lacouturites to act surprised that their brand of fire-and-brimstone revivalism was not greeted with open arms by sentinels of mainline Catholicism. Every volley of critical attacks reconfirmed their lofty self-identity as a remnant of authentic Christianity, sojourning in a Church dominated by worldliness and base materialism. The sheer volume of material he produced, and its rather meticulous attention to detail, indicates that Hugo, in one way or the other, did in fact relish his role as theological outlaw. However, although the punishment doled out lacked gory fireworks, the Lacouturites' depiction of antagonism as a "white martyrdom" was more than paranoia.[53] Lacouture's and Hugo's depictions of their critics were infused with hyperbole, but although they were not drawn and quartered, they actually *were* persecuted in some fashion and prevented from carrying on the singular work that defined their supernatural vocations. Souls were at stake, and while at times they both seemed as much concerned with ad hominem attacks on their opponents as they were with the substance of the controversy, this should not obscure the fact that their passion was deep-seated and authentic.

In the mid-1960s, Richard Hofstadter investigated the social psychology behind anti-intellectualism along with the recurrent phenomenon of "the paranoid style" in American politics. Hofstadter witnessed profound similarities between his generally secular subjects and Christian millenarianism (although the distinction is not as clean as he seems to hope, especially in his treatment of anti-Catholicism):

> The distinguishing thing about the paranoid style is not that its exponents see conspiracies or plots here and there in history, but that they regards a "vast" or "gigantic" conspiracy *as the motive force* in historical events. History *is* a conspiracy, set in motion by demonic forces of almost transcendent power, and what is felt to be needed to defeat it is not the usual methods of political give-and-take, but an all-out crusade. The paranoid spokesman sees the fate of this conspiracy in apocalyptic terms—he traffics in the birth and death of whole worlds, whole political orders, whole systems of human values. He is always manning the barricades of civilization. He constantly lives at a turning point: it is now or never in organizing resistance to conspiracy.[54]

For Hofstadter, the secular paranoid—much like Knox's enthusiast—is constitutionally immoderate. The matters he is engaged in are absolutely critical, not just to himself but on a universal scale. From this perspective, the subject of unjust persecution is not simply oneself but a larger, transcendent ideal.[55] The visceral indignation aroused in Lacouture, along with Hugo and his colleagues, certainly matched characteristics of Hofstadter's paranoia—particularly evident, for instance, in the movement's repeated allegations that antagonists were clandestine satanic operatives. While Hofstadter himself recognized that, as a turn of phrase, the term "paranoid style" is inherently prejudicial, he attempted to show that it was, in fact, a pervasive and altogether common social phenomenon.[56] Oftentimes—as evident in the Lacouture debate—there are inclinations toward paranoia on both sides, and opposing factions feed off each other's reactionary aggression. Lacouturite devotees increasingly viewed their authentically spiritual community as under attack from Church authorities. Conversely, as the toxic controversy between Hugo and his enemies went public, Lacouturism was increasingly depicted as a threat to Church stability.

Much of the rhetoric employed by both Lacouture and Hugo was symptomatic of the anti-intellectualism that Hofstadter isolated as another enduring, and complementary, trend of the American character, along with the paranoia. Originating in profound interior conversion experiences during his regency in Alaska, Lacouture's spirituality was infused with a deep suspicion of what he considered to be the sterile legalism of academic theology. His revelations led him to shun formal education from that period onward and develop an increasingly adversarial assessment of the relationship between the speculative intellect and the affect as authoritative conduits of spiritual truth. This tone was absorbed by Hugo from the very outset. The fact that the most vocal—and prestigious—critics of the Lacouture movement wielded hefty academic credentials further cemented the community's suspicion of genteel intellectualism:

> Intellectuals, it may be held, are pretentious, conceited, effeminate, and snobbish; and very likely immoral, dangerous, and subversive. . . . Even at the level of elementary education, a schooling that puts too much stress on the acquisition of mere knowledge, as opposed to the vigorous development of physical and emotional life, is heartless in its mode of conduct and threatens to produce social decadence.[57]

Hofstadter's caricature closely models depictions of Lacouture adversaries by Hugo and his contemporaries. As an essentially grassroots revival movement, Lacouturism was hypersensitive to what it viewed as a manualist sophistry represented by nemeses such as the Catholic University of America's Francis Connell, whose systematic dissection of Hugo's text *Applied Christianity* effectively catalyzed the conflict between the two factions in the United States; although the first cause can be traced to *Applied Christianity* itself (or even Onésime Lacouture), once Connell's piece broke, the die was pretty well cast. It was, in a sense, a symptom of the division that itself further amplified the conflict exponentially. However, this is not to say that Lacouture disciples—even Hugo, certainly not Dorothy Day—were intellectual Luddites, categorically averse to scholarship or reticent to employ its support when opportune. Nevertheless, the basic tenor of the movement was constitutionally lowbrow and proudly embodied some of what John Tracy Ellis regarded as the "deplorable" misfortune of the American Catholic intellectual legacy.[58]

Although Fenton's and Connell's *American Ecclesiastical Review* articles were the most technical of the volleys directed at Hugo's theology, they were neither the first nor the last. In "Nature and the Supernatural Life," Fenton noted that the initial intervention against American Lacouturism was by Pascal Parente in a 1943 *AER* issue, before *Applied Christianity* had even hit the press. Parente's essay appears to have been prompted by the circulation of preliminary edits of *Applied Christianity*. Although Parente's text did not mention Hugo by name, the volatile Yinzer read between the lines and was understandably wounded by the imputed charges of heterodoxy: "This would be *exaggerated supernaturalism* leading to all the follies of false mysticism. Instead of eliminating what is naturally good in the 'natural,' we must elevate it to the supernatural and sanctify it, otherwise life itself will become an impossibility and a crime, and we are right back among the old heresies of the Manichaeans and Albigensians."[59] Parente, who had written on the topic of ascetic theology, also leveled allegations of Lutheranism, Gnosticism, and Jansenism. Perhaps the most damaging blow was Parente's coining of the phrase "exaggerated supernaturalism," a term that would be adopted by future Hugo critics.

In January 1947, the English spiritual theologian Gerald Vann, OP, lobbed his two cents from across the Atlantic, in the Benedictine liturgical reform journal *Orate Fratres* (now *Worship*), hosted by St. John's Abbey in Collegeville, Minnesota.[60] While his essay carried none of the detailed line-by-line analysis of Fenton's and Connell's earlier works, it struck a tone that was increasingly snide and inflammatory. Vann repeated previously enumerated concerns regarding Hugo's treatment of grace and nature, which he read as unforgivably Manichean: "Fr. Hugo's picture of life as a Christian should lead it, is a picture of two entirely separate, and inimical, regions: one filled with natural things which are essentially deeds of darkness, the other filled with the supernatural which, somehow or another, has no contact with nature."[61] *Applied Christianity*, which Vann characterizes as "a muddle," failed in its attempt to reconcile the apparent Christian paradox: to love "two apparently contradictory things," God and the world.[62] The Dominican interpreted Hugo as completely disavowing the natural world, contradicting God's own assessment of creation as "good," which he somewhat simplistically and condescendingly proposed as a uniquely "Protestant" trait opposed to orthodox Catholicism's supposed constitutional "optimism."[63] This essay might be viewed as marking the end of professional, at least nominally dignified, debate and the beginning of Hugo-era polemical mudslinging. While Vann's critique was more impressionistic than Parente's, Connell's, or Fenton's articles and focused more on what it deemed to be heterodox tendencies rather than particular quotations or theological propositions (although it is not completely devoid of this), Hugo predictably dismissed it as "preposterous" and suffused with the "spirit of naturalism" that he saw proliferating throughout "pagan" Christianity.[64] Vann's "attack," like essentially all the others throughout the years, seems to have little effect on Hugo other than to embolden his spirit of retrenchment and exacerbate the more prickly side of his character.[65]

Up in Smoke: Brother Nathaniel's Brainstorm and the Devolution of Theological Debate

> The Catholic religion, he reflected—a religion of sacrifice; a religion of the Cross and the Crucified. No one who smokes can live it fully; no one who smokes can teach it fully; rejecting in practice, as he does many times each day—in fact, with every puff—the basic principle of Christian asceticism: self-denial. Little wonder Christianity today is a hollow shell!
>
> —Anonymous, *Brother Nathaniel Has a Brainstorm: A Story*

As an enthusiastic student of Saint Paul, Hugo relentlessly preached the gospel of interior conversion. He argued that the external ascetic practices—while in and of themselves not essential—were only valuable insofar as they facilitated a radical transformation of the heart.

However, Lacouturites were skeptical of those who claimed asceticism was unnecessary for those firmly rooted in Christian charity. Nonetheless, throughout the controversy both supporters and critics alike often got hung up on the form, rather than substance, of Lacouturite teachings.[66] In 1948, "The Fourth Attack," as John Hugo named it (although, all told, it was technically the fifth), was directed less explicitly at him but rather "against a particular application of the *Applied Christianity*'s teaching on detachment, which had appeared in a pamphlet, *Brother Nathaniel's Brainstorm*."[67] Four years earlier, Hugo and Fr. Louis Farina—his right-hand man in all missionary endeavors—published the anonymously authored short story, although there was much speculation that the two of them had authored the text themselves. Certainly, it had the character of cheek that permeated their more tart polemics. The story sardonically narrated the tale of a dim but sincere and charitable friar who is drafted by his superior to compose an annual donor's appeal for his (unspecified) religious order. Brother Nathaniel inadvertently causes great scandal by innocently focusing on the order's cigarette consumption in his annual appeal, asking for $500,000 to cover tobacco-related expenses. Although the text itself was a mix of slightly bland tongue-in-cheek humor and ethical finger-wagging, *Nathaniel's Brainstorm* was fundamentally an indictment of clerical avarice and—more broadly—secularized, pagan Christianity. The subsequent alarm that the text precipitated had pundits on both sides of the issue seemingly missing the point in their defense or condemnation of nicotine. The author's underlying message was classic Lacouture spirituality, prompted by the basic proposition that so long as we maintain any worldly attachments, our love for God is deficient—not, in itself, a unique Christian proposition on the theoretical level.[68] If *Applied Christianity* was an attempt to codify the theological content of the Lacouture retreat into respectable academic prose, *Brother Nathaniel Has a Brainstorm* represented a tack in quite a different direction.

In the irony-laden bit of spiritual pulp fiction—twenty-five cents a copy—Brother Nathaniel himself is represented as earnest and naïve. In fact, as a rhetorical device, Brother Nathaniel is an unwitting instrument of authorial malice. In the story, Brother Nathaniel's "smoking fund" appeal predictably infuriated would-be donors and caused no shortage of trouble for the order's Father Superior, who was then faced with the dilemma—as administrators sometimes are—of having to do damage control. He also provided the satirical author an opportunity for theological reflection on the topic of ascetic spirituality and "Hugonut" proselytism—not to mention the revival of the time-honored Lacouturite doctrine of nicotine abstinence—an icon of pagan self-indulgence with no discernible benefits outside the simple pleasures of smoking itself.[69] Flustered, the Father Superior sought the council of a Carmelite Prior, and their dialogue constitutes the bulk of the text's explicit theological reflection. Regardless of the story's intent, it was received by skeptics as negatively as it was welcomed by Lacouture aficionados. In the August 1948 issue of the *Homiletic and Pastoral Review*, Joseph P. Donovan, CM—the Vincentian rector of St. Louis's Kenrick Seminary—penned a retort in the form of an article entitled "A Bit of Puritanical Catholicity."[70] The title of the essay says it all; throughout Donovan did not mince his words: he thought that the focus on cigarettes was ludicrous, as if the simple act of smoking itself was indicative of spiritual laxity and that its cessation magically transform sinners into saints:

> The poor man forgot that if non-smoking makes saints, the Methodists, especially the preachers, would provide saints in troops. . . . As in the case of Savonarola, the attempted reforms of the superior came to nothing. . . . If the priests and brothers were not as fervent as they well might have been, it wasn't because they smoked, but because they were wanting in the desired intensity of Religious observance, and neither smoking nor non-smoking constitutes that.[71]

The apparent laughableness of Methodist sanctity aside, Donovan contended that the anonymous author—who he clearly believed was Hugo—had missed the boat with his fixation on smoking: it is not smoking that is the problem but a deeper, more existential, aridity, of which compulsive smoking is an indicator. Without a more proactive approach, Donovan's concern was that, while a prohibition on smoking might save some cash and a few priests might live longer, their overall spiritual quality would not have improved one iota. Rather, this dormant tepidity would manifest in some other peculiar fashion.

Two months later—perhaps sensing the regrettable dearth of Christian charity on both sides of the debate—the industrious Leo Trese joined in, using his regular column in *Emmanuel Magazine* as a platform for injecting a bit of calm circumspection.[72] Perhaps taking a cue from the satire of *Brother Nathaniel's Brainstorm*, Trese similarly eschewed direct op-ed communication in favor of some creative license. His essay took the form of a rambling dissociative dialogue between himself and his conscience, occasioned by the pangs of nocturnal nicotine craving. Trese played Switzerland, apparently sympathetic to both camps simultaneously, with his conscience standing in for Hugo:

> *Self:* Now don't tell me, my friend, that you don't know that interior mortification is more important than exterior. . . . If I were mortified interiorly, I shouldn't have had to argue with myself for fifteen minutes before going to the phone and volunteering to drive her. There are a few examples of what I mean more important mortifications. I could quit smoking, and still be mighty selfish, and thoughtless, and cantankerous. Abstinence from nicotine wouldn't profit me half as much as another thirty minutes a day spent in prayer. If I loved God enough. . . .
>
> *Conscience:* Yes, I can see what you're getting at. If you loved God enough, mortification would come easy. Heroic self-denial is the result of goodness, rather than the cause. If you can advance in the love of God, your self-attachments will shed themselves like the peeling of an onion, layer by layer until there's nothing left.[73]

Certainly, Trese's musings were more pastoral, gentle, and legible than were any of the previous publications during the Hugo controversy. Trese's role as diplomatic peacemaker empowered him to neutrally play both sides, somewhat: he lauded Hugo's piety and religious fervor, while chiding him for an elitist sense of superiority that bordered on spiritual snobbery. Similarly, Trese wondered out loud if it was really the Christian thing to do, to double down on the right to smoke cigarettes as a matter of principle. Certainly the controversy was, itself, morphing into an unbecoming row among otherwise distinguished members of the American Church.

If Leo Trese's intention was to nip things in the bud and inject a bit of sober civility into the increasingly snide and polemical—and decreasingly substantive—theological skirmish, his musings did not have the desired effect. In February 1949, Louis Farina injected himself into the exhausting feud and published a curt retort to Donovan in the *Homiletic and Pastoral Review*, "Is Detachment Puritanical?"[74] As Hugo had been—and would continue to be in perpetuity—a fervent defender of his mentor Onésime Lacouture, so would Farina be of Hugo, although their relationship was substantially more collegial. Early in the essay, Farina actually quotes the "sticks and stones" nursery rhyme, and dismisses Trese's critical heterodoxy allegations as the frail ravings of a pagan—apparently unaware that employing ad hominem remarks against his opponent might come across as a tad hypocritical and sour his indictment of Donovan for the very same practice. Name-calling aside, the meat of the essay was a defense of ascetic practices of self-mortification:

> St. John the Baptist is praised by the Scriptures because he drank no wine. Was *he* a Jansenist? . . .
>
> All the ancient Fathers who renounced the world and lived heroically austere and mortified lives in the desert, were they Jansenists? All the holy monks and hermits of the Church's history, all the holy priests and bishops who renounced the pleasures of the world . . . were they Jansenists? And apart from the worldly pleasures and comforts they abandoned was not the marriage they also renounced at least as great a good among god's creatures as the tobacco whose use the critic so vigorously defends? Why are they, then, not Jansenists? Why is it virtuous to give up home, marriage, riches, pleasures—but Jansenistic to give up cigarettes? . . . By the critic's standard, the Church Triumphant is filled with Jansenists![75]

Farina conscripts a litany of austere saints and blesseds to establish a well-worn precedent, including Peter of Alcántara—the pioneer of sixteenth-century Spanish *recogimiento* and a spiritual consultant of Teresa of Avila, who modeled a new development of interiority that bore similarities to Lacouturism—although the fact that Alcántara was, in fact, investigated on account of perceived severity indicates that under different spatial-temporal conditions he very likely might also have been accused of Jansenism, had he not predated Cornelius Jansen by some eighty-five years.[76] And while there has certainly been no shortage of theological disputes over the intervening fifteen hundred years raised by the perceived antisocial asceticism of the desert *abbas* and *ammas*, Farina's point was made: the Christian tradition has a long history of supporting, even romanticizing, dramatic forms of self-mortification that conventional society—even conventional Christians—perceived as prohibitively extreme. Farina repeated Hugo's defense against the charges of missing the forest for the trees with the cigarette debacle. It was not cigarettes in particular that they were arguing to be "inherently evil": "It is an attack on the *attachment* to smoking; or, rather, it is an attack on the attachment to any creature-pleasure. It is an attack on the *mentality* that permits or even fosters habitual self-indulgence."[77] If indulging one's attachments—smoking, drinking, compulsive behavior of any sort—is an expression of a deeper infidelity to God, Farina encouraged self-mortification as an athletic means of spiritual restoration but not itself constitutive of holiness. Although he does not dispute the redemptive potential of the single act of martyrdom, increasing in personal holiness is a gradual interior process that may serve a pastoral function, as one's interior grace overflows. In response to counsels of temperance, Farina retorted that love of God is the one thing that demands *im*moderation and to which the term "excess" does not actually apply: compromise was the language of the devil.[78]

In Saecula Saeculorum

> Father Trese, again rejecting the idea that he wrongly attributes to me, tells his conscience, "I thought we were talking about sin, rather than sanctity. If you put it on the basis of sanctity, maybe we could get together!" For it is precisely because this attachment is an impediment to sanctity, and not because I consider it sinful, that I believe it should be given up.
>
> —John J. Hugo, letter to the editor, *Emmanuel*

In a later issue of *Emmanuel*, Hugo seemed to have missed the conciliatory objective of Trese's essay, penning a sarcastic letter to the editor, stiffening at what he interpreted as Trese's suggestion that exterior mortification were but trifles. With Farina's entry into the conflict, the opposition appears to have desisted somewhat, or simply moved on with their lives, realizing that the substance of the debate had long-since stagnated and grown rather tiresome. This marked the end of published attacks on Hugo or *Applied Christianity*, although this restraint was not matched by Hugo. Apparently unable to let the matter go, Hugo continued to ruminate, further dramatizing the episode and amalgamating it into the cosmic conspiracy that once brought Onésime Lacouture down. In the 1950s, he reissued *Nature and the Supernatural* as a 250-page history of the controversy sparked by *Applied Christianity*, for the obvious purpose of setting the record straight and getting in a last word. Furthermore, he consistently prodded Dorothy Day—who had become an avid participant in, and apologist for, the retreat—to publish her own meditations on the "Encounter with Silence" (as it was later called) theology. A year after his death in an automobile accident on October 1, 1985, Hugo's two-volume magnum opus, *Your Ways Are Not My Ways*, was published. The first section is a familiar defense of Lacouture coupled with one more expanded account of the retreat—much of which is essentially an amalgamation of *Nature and the Supernatural* and Anselme Longpré's *Un mouvement spirituel au Québec*, while the second volume is yet another attempt to reformulate Lacouturite theology. Just like Lacouture himself, Hugo went to the grave relentlessly defending "the strong meat of the Gospel" long after his nemeses had apparently moved on and the retreat's popular appeal subsided (although not vanished).

The rhetoric in *Your Ways Are Not My Ways* is considerably more aggressive than even his previous publications, and Hugo has never been accused of excessive tact. He spit venom at Lacouture's enemies and compiled a list of unjustly persecuted spiritual allies: John of the Cross, Teresa of Avila, Joan of Arc, Galileo, even Martin Luther—misunderstood theological mavericks, all of them, who were blacklisted by contemporary pagan powerbrokers and spiritually weak cowards who would not aid those under attack for fear of self-preservation.[79] The self-vindicated Hugo likened his opponents to the Inquisition and the Pharisaic Christ-killers, alleging diabolical motives and even outright demon possession. Evidently, the heterodox accusations still stung four decades later, and Hugo appears to have assimilated Lacouture's supernatural perspective and more paranoid hermeneutics. Even as late as the 1980s, Hugo was still mounting an impassioned defense against the litany of long-since-passed allegations of Jansenism, Manichaeism, moral rigorism, and the like—years after most people had stopped paying attention and most of the major players in the case had passed on.

Although John Hugo was forced into parish work, engaged in antiwar agitation (sharing some of Day's own unpopular pacifism, albeit with some remainder), and apparently thrived as a minister to recovering substance abusers and the incarcerated felons, his encounter with Onésime Lacouture as a young priest categorically rearranged the trajectory of his career. Like Lacouture, his early orientation toward scholarship—albeit of a dif-

John Hugo portrait (Department of Special Collections and University Archives, Marquette University Libraries)

ferent sort—was transformed into a vigorous anti-intellectualism that was only cemented by the decidedly negative response that his theology received within more polished, genteel circles. While counting Thomism and numerous Church Doctors in its arsenal, Hugo's revivalism had a visceral grittiness to it that was distinctly American and reminiscent of a stereotypically Protestant fundamentalist swagger. Hugo was considerably more at ease in the twentieth century than was his teacher—we sense none of Lacouture's anxiety at the accelerated pace of modern society. He considered himself a man of his times, when a certain amount of political engagement, particularly on the subject of militarism, was a moral imperative, which perplexed his mentor somewhat.[80] This should not be taken to mean, however, that he was any less zealous in his condemnation of contemporary trappings. Hugo's primitivism equaled Lacouture's in substance but differed in tone: he was more secure in his place in modern urban-industrial culture and was therefore more empowered to openly resist its allure. Thus Hugo, the once-budding sociologist, made his name not in the Pittsburgh tradition of labor activism and progressive social Catholicism, nor as a community leader, but as a provincial zealot and revivalist thaumaturge, temperamentally ill-suited to the pride-swallowing world of scholarly peer review. Although it could be reasonably argued that he was unfairly targeted by sensationalist rhetoric, Hugo's scorched earth approach to theological dispute cemented his marginal position relative to respectable Catholicism and established his immutable reputation as an uncompromising, dyed-in-the-wool enthusiast.

6 Dorothy Day, Anti-triumphalism, and a Personalist Approach to Voluntary Poverty

> This is a story of a spiritual adventure which began with reading the works of St. Teresa of Avila twenty years ago during an idle beautiful summer, which led me on new paths, laid me open and receptive to strange adventures of the spirit. . . . She was a journalist too in a way, and reported an attempt to take up and use spiritual weapons during the turbulent times.
>
> This story is about an attempt to discover and use spiritual weapons, in a day of atomic war and preparation for war.
>
> —Dorothy Day, *All Is Grace*

Within the ranks of the Lacouturite disciples, Dorothy Day stands out as its most historically conspicuous—which is to say, the most famous. During her lifetime and following her death in 1980, the retreat gained publicity and credibility directly from her close affiliation. Day first learned of the Lacouture retreat in the late 1930s (through her friend, publisher Maisie Ward) and was subsequently introduced to its doctrinal substance by a Josephite priest named Pacifique Roy, who had himself become an avid student of Lacouture and great admirer of John Hugo.[1] The effect on Day was as profound as it was instantaneous, unraveling her previous disenchantment with the stark, hollow veneer of Catholic contemplative life—based on a particularly unpleasant experience at the Convent of Mary Reparatrix in Manhattan's Midtown (just north of Madison Square Park).[2] Although based in Baltimore, Roy was Québécois in both origin and temperament—stereotypically rugged and passionate. While some of the Workers viewed him as overly severe, Day was drawn to his aura of sanctity:

> What he talked to us about was not the social order, but love and holiness without which man cannot see God. He spoke with such absorption

> that all who came, stayed to listen. . . . For me it was like falling in love again. I began to understand many things.[3]

Roy was unapologetically perfectionist and mandated personal interior conversion, augmented by a stark juxtaposition of the life of Christ contrasted against "the world."[4] To Day's eyes, he modeled the ecstatic love of God that seemed to naturally overflow into love of neighbors. His social program was the devout life of prayer, and his desire to work for others an expression of piety rather than a political agenda. In Roy, Dorothy Day witnessed a comprehensive interior life that was cultivated by Onésime Lacouture's program of contemplation. She was hooked. Roy frequently made the trip north to give conferences at the New York Worker houses, if even just for a day. But in addition to preaching Lacouture's more general maximalist doctrine, Roy promoted John Hugo's retreat program as its most authentic iteration and urged the Catholic Workers—Dorothy Day in particular—to seek him out.[5] Eventually, Roy's mental faculties failed, and he was forced to retire to Montréal, suffering from a form of dementia that was heartbreakingly similar to the later unraveling of Peter Maurin.[6] In both incidents, Day interpreted their suffering as instructive examples of ascetic purification and ascribed Christic properties to their, albeit at this stage purely passive, mortification.

In serving as a gateway to John Hugo, Pacifique Roy played a critical animating role in Dorothy Day's formation: he introduced her to Lacouturite theology and enticed her to go deeper, wherein she discovered a vigorous spirituality that resonated with her own interior predisposition. However, it was not until the summer of 1941 that she experienced "*the* retreat" formally, which she made under Hugo's care.[7] As it was for him, Day's first experience of the retreat proved foundational. She would later rave about her first exposure to the retreat in an unfinished manuscript, which she tentatively titled *All Is Grace*:

> I made this retreat, as the saying is, many times. The first time brought with it a shock of recognition that this was what I was looking for in the way of an explanation of the mystery of the Christian Life, the plan of God for us all. Though still I saw through a glass darkly, I saw things as a whole for the first time with a delight, a joy, an excitement, which is hard to describe. This is what I expected when I became a Catholic. This is what all my reading had led me to expect in the way of teach-

> ing and guidance in the spiritual life. I came away with what I can only consider to be an increased knowledge of the supernatural life, the feeling that I had grown in faith, hope and charity, that I had been fed the strong meat of the gospel and was now prepared to run the race, to journey onward with that food which would sustain me for forty days in any wilderness. I felt prepared for deserts and underground tunnels, for the dark night of the senses and of the soul. And I knew too that this strong light would dim with the ensuing months and that the next year I would again have to make the retreat, to adjust my vision to the blazing truth which was set before us, to get things into perspective once again.[8]

Most important, the retreat provided spiritual nourishment for Day's uncompromising, heroic approach to Christianity by introducing her to "the mind of Christ."[9] She wrote about her experiences on retreat as serving a rejuvenating function that both preempted her from falling into personal despair and recommitted her to the supernatural life as a lived protest against Christian mediocrity. As she testified: "For too long, too little has been expected of us."[10] Hugo's own activist posture bolstered Day's vision of the Catholic Worker's apostolate as a non-utilitarian form of Christian witness, existentially founded on what she called "precarity"—a liminal extension of a dedication to voluntary poverty that took inspiration from the Beatitudes and the Folly of the Cross.[11]

Dorothy Day and the Downward Path to Salvation

A Brooklyn native (b. November 8, 1897), Dorothy May Day was raised—in Oakland and later Chicago—in a household largely devoid of religion, although the Day children were all baptized Episcopalians. John Day, the *pater familias*, spent most of Dorothy's childhood at the horse track as a racing journalist and was, by her own estimation, a rather distant figure—largely aloof during her childhood and disapproving of her later radicalism. In her youth and adolescence, Day displayed an early empathetic tendency, galvanized by the devastating San Francisco earthquake of 1906 and later encounters with factory labor conditions—first in the pages of Upton Sinclair's *The Jungle* and later walking the streets of Chicago's West Side industrial wasteland.[12] In both of these instances, she experienced a spontaneous and enduring identification with the suffering of others, accompanied by a recognition of humanity's innate cooperative impulse lying beneath an apparently harsh exterior of American rugged individualism. And although the Day household did briefly plunge into dire financial straits immediately upon arrival (before John Sr. secured steady employment), Dorothy Day's experience of urban poverty in Chicago was somewhat voyeuristic, simply by virtue of the fact that the poverty she witnessed was not her own. Nevertheless, slight glimmers of her developing incarnational aesthetic were emitted, marked by the ability to extract beauty from the depths of apparent destitution.[13] Although at the time she lacked the conceptual tools to articulate her experience of divinity amid—even fused with—the bleak suffering of humanity's underclass, Day marked this period as the beginning of her radical education.

After the conclusion of her second year at the University of Illinois–Urbana, Day opted to leave college and move back east to her native New York. Her parents had preceded her, when John Day won a position at the *New York Telegraph*. Dorothy Day herself began to look for employment as a reporter, with no immediate success, before finally convincing the managing editor of the Socialist paper the *Call* to give her a shot, in the form of an experimental piece that called for Day to chronicle her attempts to subsist for a month on five dollars a day—a forerunner of Barbara Ehrenreich's 2001 undercover investigation *Nickel and Dimed*, and retrospectively, an exercise that some might plausibly find offensive, even with the purest of intentions.[14] Life at the *Call* launched her headfirst into the heart of downtown radicalism, and she soon found herself engulfed in nightly debates between anarchists (largely in the form of IWW Wobblies) and all manner of socialists.[15]

Day, already a member of the Socialist Party, soon joined the Wobblies, was beaten by the riot police who evidently failed to recognize her journalist credentials, and interviewed Leon Trotsky—just before his return to Russia on the front end of the revolution in 1917. She also befriended a fellow employee at the *Call* named Mike Gold, who, later in life, edited the Communist *Daily Worker* zine—whose name Day would blatantly riff on—and composed the enduring memoir of urban blight, *Jews Without Money*.[16] This marked the first of a succession of incredibly intimate—although sexually ambiguous—relationships that Day would foster over the next years with charismatic, sometimes emotionally disturbed, or disturb*ing*, men who comingled in New York's salty downtown artistic and radical scenes. Perhaps most notable among these was the playwright Eugene O'Neill, who, along with Day herself, was part of a motley crew of regulars who drank away the night at a tavern named the Golden Swan on the corner of West Fourth Street and Sixth Avenue—now a city park of the same name—which earned the uninviting nickname "The Hell Hole."[17] Owned by the former boxer Tom Wallace, it boasted a diverse clientele—predominately a patchwork of writers, thespians, and bona fide mobsters.[18] Much to her dismay, fellow traveler Malcolm Cowley later immortalized Day's participation in the Hell Hole's climate of debauchery in his account of the time, noting that, "the gangsters admired Dorothy Day because she could drink them under the table."[19] It was here that a thoroughly lubricated O'Neill would stumble through garbled recitations of Francis Thompson's poem "The Hound of Heaven," which impressed upon Day a then-amorphous sense of grace that she would absorb into her conceptual framework of "the downward path" to salvation.[20]After a night of heavy drinking, Day would often trudge by Catholics on their way to early morning Mass, sometimes even stopping into St. Joseph's on Sixth Avenue herself.[21] Although Day's family was only nominally religious, Dorothy had been nursing a growing affinity for Christianity for years by reading the Bible and Thomas à Kempis's *Imitation of Christ*. Even though her radical disposition revolted against hierarchy and she disapproved of the consolidation of wealth among Church leaders at the expense of the bulk of its membership, the Church's gravitational pull proved irresistible: "It seems to me a long time that I led this wavering life, in my ignorance not knowing that we are of body, mind and soul, and that all our faculties can be brought into harmony. I felt strongly that the life of nature warred against the life of grace."[22] Dorothy Day would retrospectively interpret her wavering period in distinctly Pauline terms as a—albeit largely subconscious and inarticulate—struggle between natural inclination toward sin and God's persistent, gracious, draw toward the supernatural. Looking back years later, she would attribute an Augustinian sense of cognitive dissonance to this period, depicting herself as an almost textbook example of William James's "divided self."[23] In time, Day would grow weary of her bohemianism, with its romantic rhetoric that coopted others' suffering and smacked of self-indulgent escapism—an impulse that she witnessed with a critical eye among younger Catholic Workers, although she was herself accused of persistently harboring a similar inclination.[24] By

1918, the war was in full swing and Day's enthusiasm for her affected radicalism had waned, partially on account of the *Masses* (the respectable leftist journal where she worked) being terminated, partially resulting from a succession of personal tragedies, partially as a response to the psychological vertigo brought on by a war that disillusioned many progressives during that era. Although the severance from her old bohemian social circle was not—and never would be—a clean break, Day increasingly immersed herself directly in the lives of the afflicted, what she would later translate into Roman Catholic parlance as the "Works of Mercy."

By 1918, Day and her younger sister Della had taken positions as nurse apprentices at Brooklyn's Kings County Hospital, where she would get a crash course in service work, "changing bed pans, giving sponge baths and alcohol rubs, taking temperatures, administering injections and enemas, changing dressings, keeping charts, and dispensing medication."[25] Early on, an irate ninety-four-year-old grandmother hurled a used chamber pot at her, causing Day to break into tears—an understandable reaction but uncharacteristically delicate given her later robust reputation for virtually limitless patience with difficult clientele.[26] Kings County provided her with the opportunity to drench herself in human suffering, rather than simply writing about it, but in a proactive way that honed her skills while reaffirming her commitment to engaged radicalism. Kings County also set the stage for Day's soon-to-be all-consuming romance with a journalist named Lionel Moise, who arrived at the hospital after having been drugged and robbed outside a waterfront bar. It was, by all accounts, a lopsided partnership, and Day doted on Moise while he maintained a stoic self-possession that simultaneously confounded and lured her even deeper into psychological dependence. What is more, if Day's "autobiographical novel" *The Eleventh Virgin* can be read as truly autobiographical, Moise was also responsible for an unexpected and unwanted pregnancy that Day eventually terminated at his recommendation, just before he uprooted to Venezuela, leaving Day to fend for herself.[27] Since her death, the specter of Day's abortion has been raised in relation to her cause for canonization, but she remained tight-lipped on the subject for the rest of her days. After Moise left to Venezuela, Day met an older man named Berkeley Tobey, whom she married at some slightly vague point in the early 1920s.[28] Upon learning of Moise's return to the United States, Day relocated back to Chicago, took a job with the Communist Party's *Liberator*, and resumed what she would later call her "disorderly life" with Moise.[29]

During this time, Dorothy Day was swept up in a Palmer Raid on an IWW house and arrested on trumped-up charges of prostitution.[30] It was not her first time in jail; she had been arrested once in Washington, DC, in the spring of 1917 as part of a suffragist picket in front of the White House. She and her group were initially sentenced to thirty days of jail time but were granted a presidential pardon by Woodrow Wilson, following a week-long hunger strike. This time around, as opposed to feeling empowered through collective jail solidarity, Day was processed as a sex worker and tossed into general population, while a neighboring inmate suffered through the effects of early narcotic withdrawal.[31] In Day's uniquely reflective analogical imagination, this chilling encounter proved instructive of the human condition. Of the myriad ways she could have responded, Day portrays the experience as providing a teachable moment by eliciting a profound awareness of the tragic character of our disordered life that a more doctrinaire iteration of herself would attribute to Original Sin. Or at least that is how she depicts events in her memoir, composed for public consumption decades after the fact. She chose to interpret the experience as allowing her to more deeply identify with the underclass. In her natural impulse toward self-preservation, Day recognized that her own relative privilege precluded her from fully submerging herself in this life: "I could get away, paying no penalty, because of my friends, my background, my education, my privilege."[32] This insight mimicked a recurring feature of Day's meditations on the gulf between her more or less voluntary, ascetic acceptance of suffering as a choice and that of the truly destitute. Although her care for Lionel Moise eventually dissipated—that is, he "left town with another woman"—she credited him with reviving her love for Dostoevsky, high praise coming from Dorothy Day, given the Russian author's pivotal influence on her development.[33] Furthermore, it was her tenure in Chicago that planted the seeds of her vision of Roman Catholicism as the Church of the Poor, seeds that would germinate deep in her spirit upon her return to New York and eventually contribute mightily to her conversion. But that was still in the semi-distant future. Perhaps colored by the experience in jail, and the eventual dissolution of her second relationship with Moise, Day's memories of this period of her life were bleak. However, she left Chicago in the fall of 1923 on an emotional upswing, as word came that *The Eleventh Virgin* would be published by Albert and Charles Boni. Within six months, Day had relocated once more, this time to New Orleans with her sister Della and a woman named Mary whom she had befriended in Chicago. *The Eleventh Virgin* came out in print and was eventually optioned as a film—though never progressed any further—but Day almost instantaneously soured on the book, a sentiment that would only be amplified down the road, when as mother superior of the Catholic Worker, she conscripted collaborators for a search-and-destroy mission, seeking all publicly held copies of the text. In a 1924 letter to Llewellyn Jones—then literary editor of the *Chicago Evening Post*—Day remarked with the disaffected wisdom that comes with age (albeit still a relatively young twenty-seven years): "My book, now that it is in cold print, doesn't please me, but I console myself by remembering that I wrote it when I was twenty-two."[34] Her correspondence during the period indicates that she made a conscious effort to curb her prodigious drinking habits. Although she enjoyed her time in New Orleans and found steady work at the *New Orleans Item*, she soon migrated back to New York, using her share of *The Eleventh Virgin*'s film money ($2,500) to purchase a beachfront shack on Staten Island.[35]

In her tin-roofed hideaway, Dorothy Day had her fill of solitude and sparse scenery, near-perfect conditions for a recovering bohemian writer. Shortly, Day began a relationship with with a friend of Malcolm Cowley's, William Batterham, better known to posterity by his middle name, Forster. Once more, Day gravitated to an emotionally aloof, countercultural stoic, whom historians seem to resent for the heartbreak that he caused Day—although, typically, they treat him as more of a stock character, playing a necessary yet morally revolting role in her pre-conversion narrative, the love of her life who stood in the way of her total surrender to God. For her part, Day's dramatic profile of Batterham captures some of the allure that she felt at the time, with a characteristic romantic color that contrasted with her avowed tendency toward stark realism: "The man I loved, with whom I entered into a common-law marriage, was an anarchist, an Englishman by descent, and a biologist."[36] As Robert Ellsberg has noted, Batterham in reality was rather less epic than illustrated in Day's published recollection:

> Actually, he was from North Carolina. His "anarchism" was chiefly expressed in opposition to the institution of marriage. And though he was fascinated by natural history and anything to do with fishing, it was a stretch to call him a biologist; he worked in a factory making gauges and later owned a store in Manhattan.[37]

Dorothy Day in her Staten Island, NY cottage, ca. 1925 (Department of Special Collections and University Archives, Marquette University Libraries)

Day historians' protective impulses seem to embolden depictions of Batterham—or "Battingham" as William Miller mistakenly calls him—as something of a prototype: the emotionally volatile, cold narcissist, who took advantage of a vulnerable and pure Day (her years of drinking mobsters "under the table" notwithstanding) only to desert her in her time of greatest need—a kind of recapitulation of Lionel Moise, but armed with a rowboat and anarchism.[38] He is the final obstacle to her conversion—even after Day had settled her own radical's cognitive dissonance at the prospect of voluntarily joining just about the most hierarchical religious institution on the market. In Day's own accounts, Batterham fills a role in the narrative of her own personal development; she treats him more like a supporting character in a novel than the love of her life—or rather, she only tells her side of the story, which is understandable. Batterham tempts her to choose the created over the Creator but also presents the opportunity for Day's surrender to God and an end to her "wavering."[39]

Day aficionados' sympathies with her agonizing choice between her love of Batterham and her increasingly clear, and ultimately greater, love for God—a choice that she was forced into by Batterham's intransigent atheism—has tended to cloud his more redeeming characteristics and his positive influence on Day—which she herself did enumerate, his subsequent "pig-headedness" notwithstanding.[40] Batterham provided Day with a keen insight into the beauty of the natural world—one that had been obscured by her immersion in urban poverty but emerged during her more rural existence on Staten Island. Batterham's misanthropic streak was matched by a deep and abiding passion for solitude and wildlife.[41] In her memoir, Day represents Batterham as the prototypical "natural man," who introduces her to the wonders of nature but balks at her increasingly analogical, Augustinian redirection toward the supernatural—which he wants absolutely nothing to do with.[42] While Day used nature as a prism to refract the glory of the divine, Batterham insistently halted at any intellectual or spiritual extrapolation from steadfast materialism. Although he had introduced her to nature, he increasingly resented Day's impulse to evolve beyond a purely biological worldview.

Strange as it may seem, as she looked back on their time together, Dorothy Day also credited Batterham with her first awareness of the interconnected web of humanity, which she would later conceptualize as the Mystical Body of Christ. Although someone apparently so disenchanted with the human race as Batterham might appear a rather unlikely candidate for this type of influence, Day traces the origins of her socially transcendent sensibility to the infamous Sacco and Vanzetti trial and its devastating impact on her "common-law husband"—as she liked to identify him. Nicola Sacco and Bartolomeo Vanzetti were arrested on highly questionable murder and attempted burglary charges in 1920 Braintree, Massachusetts—just outside of Boston. Antiauthoritarian cynics concluded that the pair of loosely affiliated Italian immigrants had been targeted on account of their ties with militant Galleanist anarchism.[43] Although the evidence was circumstantial at best, and the defense produced a bevy of alibi witnesses, the pair was convicted and sentenced to death by electric chair. They were executed, along with an ex-con named Celestino Madeiros who had himself copped to the Braintree killings without effect, while being convicted on a separate murder charge. In *The Long Loneliness*, Day recalled that day, August 15, 1927: "All the nation mourned. All the nation, I mean, that is made up of the poor, the worker, the trade unionist—those who felt most keenly the sense of solidarity—that very sense of solidarity which made me gradually understand the doctrine of the Mystical Body of Christ whereby we are the members of one another."[44] Although both Sacco and Vanzetti had long-since disavowed organized religion, and actually refused multiple opportunities to consult with a priest on their execution day, their dignity throughout the ordeal, and, in particular, Vanzetti's eloquent and compassionate reflection on their misfortune—coupled with a profound sense of solidarity with those who suffer injustice—earned them widespread admiration and sympathy from such disparate supporters as George Bernard Shaw, H. G. Wells, Walter Lippmann, and Albert Einstein.[45] Protests, many of them violent, erupted around the world, and over ten thousand mourners paid their respects in person over the two days the bodies lay in state. Popular depictions of Sacco and Vanzetti represented the anarchists in expiatory messianic terms, falsely convicted and suffering unto death for the sins of a morally bankrupt, decadent society. The outpouring of communal support and messianic interpretations of the two blue-collar radicals resonated deeply with Dorothy Day; but even decades later, she would exhibit a profound sense of exasperation at the lack of support for justice among Christians across denominational lines, even as she found her soul hurtling toward the Church.[46] For his part, Forster Batterham sunk into a deep depression, the episode confirming for him all that he thought was wretched in humanity. Unlike Day, he saw no redemptive silver lining, only the horror of injustice and cruelty.

Dorothy Day's growing sense of the supernatural, even in the very midst of gross injustice, was augmented, perhaps, by a pivotal, life-changing occasion that had pushed her even closer to the edge. A year and a half before Sacco and Vanzetti were sentenced to death, Day gave birth to a daughter named Tamar Teresa, on March 4, 1926.[47] Day was absolutely thrilled; following her abortion, she persistently had harbored a suspicion that the procedure had left her sterile.[48] News of her pregnancy precipitated an ecstatic overflow of gratitude at her place within the cosmos and the relationship with Batterham. In the fall of 1925, Day had traveled south to Florida to visit her mother with Della, and her letters to Batterham during this period exhibit a profound sense of belonging, coupled with her deep love for him—which seemed to intensify all the more because of their shared role in bringing on new life.[49] However, Batterham did not share this enthusiasm at the prospect of progeny.[50] Batterham's dim outlook on procreation was rooted in a bleak interpretation of human nature and contemporary society, paired with his intense and uncompromising desire to be unfettered from obligations that might impinge on his freedom. He interpreted parenthood as a huge responsibility that would take up his time, money, and ability to come and go as he pleased. In a sense, he was, of course, correct; but he failed to recognize any of the draws that might make parenthood appealing—his unrelentingly dark assessment of humanity precluded any such optimism.

While Batterham's almost predictable tepidity at the idea of parenthood cast a pall of anxiety over Day's otherwise unflappable enthusiasm, not even he could dampen her spirits for long. Day experienced an uncontrollable urge to pray, as if her own participation in creation drew her ever closer to her Creator. Without any formal direction, she fumbled her way through the rosary, making use of a souvenir set of prayer beads that she had picked up during her stay in New Orleans. Even with Batterham's periodic doom-and-gloom reminders, Day seems to have willfully persisted in her optimism, her clear sense of place evolving and growing in clarity. The months of relative convalescence and waiting occasioned a period of introspection and clarification of her sense of self.[51] Jim Forest—a one-time *Catholic Worker* managing editor, founding member of the Catholic Peace

Fellowship, and Day's friend and biographer—has speculated that part of Batterham's distaste for the whole business of parenthood stemmed from a suspicion that the introduction of a third party—albeit in the form of an infant—could mark the beginning of the end of their bond, or at least his exclusive claim on Day's affections—competition, as it were.[52] He was absolutely right. The birth of Tamar Teresa marked a decisive shift in Day's priorities and served as a catalyst for her imminent conversion to Roman Catholicism, which, in truth, had been in the works for some time, however slowly developing. Insofar as her rustic lifestyle with Batterham on Staten Island—although she had not completely renounced the world of leftist intellectual socialites—marked a shift toward a more halcyon way, Day's new status as a mother—now responsible for the spiritual, as well as material, needs of her newborn—marked a tipping point that brought the fervent countercultural radical firmly to the doorstep of, of all things, the Roman Catholic Church.

The Dynamite of the Church: Early Years at the Catholic Worker

> People who try to live their everyday lives according to an ideal are likely to make fools of themselves, which some critics think is just what the Catholic Workers have been doing for nearly twenty years. Others, more charitable, hold that there are two differences between their folly and plain foolishness. One is that theirs is premeditated; they are, so to speak, fools on principle. . . . The other difference is that, unlike plain fools, the Catholic Workers, in spite of the most appalling miscalculations, cross-purposes, lack of planning and general confusion, have accomplished a lot even by worldly standards.
>
> —Dwight MacDonald, "The Foolish Things of the World—I"

What blossomed into an unswerving intention to commend her daughter's soul to the care of the Church gave Day the nudge she needed to enter the Church herself. After years of feeling a growing inclination toward the supernatural, warring with herself over the discrepancy between the "Church of the Poor" that she saw on display among immigrants and the urban working class contrasted with the consolidated opulence of Catholic power, and anxiety regarding what joining the Church would do to her credibility as a radical, Day finally gave in.[53] The decision was neither instantaneous nor unflinching, although her later rendition of the events might lead one to believe otherwise. Day's murky account of the timeline in *The Long Loneliness*, coupled with William Miller's misdating of Tamar's birth year—1926 instead of 1927—has resulted in a commonly accepted conversion narrative that is *too* seamless, too clean.[54] Tamar was baptized in July of 1927, and Day was received into the Catholic Church—*re*baptized, actually—on December 29, more than a year and a half after her daughter's birth, for reasons that remain opaque.[55] The widely accepted notion that her conversion—and the impending dissolution of her relationship with Batterham—was inevitable following the birth of her child obscures the fact that she wanted reconciliation, as demonstrated by her barrage of uncharacteristically unguarded love letters, which persisted through at least 1932.[56] Even though Day's conversion was not as clear as traditionally represented, and she appears to have persisted in her "wavering" for some time, her final decision was as much a response of self-surrender and renunciation of her former life as it was an entrance into a new, supernatural communion.

If Batterham had worried that the arrival of their daughter would drive a wedge between him and Day, he interpreted her conversion to Roman Catholicism as an adulterous betrayal—at least as crystallized in Day's memory. It is notable that her later reflection on the conversion experience and the irreparable rift that it caused between her and Batterham are framed in distinctly Lacouturite terms. She struggled between loving Batterham and her superseding love of God, which in the end were mutually exclusive.[57] In the retreats that she would turn to with fervor—still years off, at this point—she was steeped in the "*nada, nada, nada*" ascetic theology of John of the Cross and the virtually oppositional relationship between natural and supernatural affections that permeated John Hugo's teaching. Hugo, as Lacouture, often employed the analogy between Christian self-mortification and romantic love, and Day's own conversion to Catholicism—which truly marked the end of her partnership with Forster Batterham—provided her with an explicit template for proactively choosing between what is "good" and what is infinitely greater, and ultimately the fountain of all goodness.[58] She had been reading William James—whom she credits for introducing her to Teresa of Avila and the Catholic mystical tradition—and came to understand her own spiritual dilemma as a struggle between oppositional impulses, and a quest for internal unification.[59] However, the apparent contradiction of voluntary self-mortification was not completely lost on Day, whose "talent for self-dramatization" prompted her to simultaneously marvel and puzzle at her own change of affairs.[60]

The Making of a Catholic Anarchist: Peter Maurin Indoctrinates Dorothy Day

In the intervening half decade, Day struggled with the dissolution of her partnership with Forster Batterham—although she was edified to see that he was a much more engaged father to Tamar than his doom-and-gloom rhetoric had led her to expect—and relocated several times in search of meaningful work: first a modest move to Manhattan, then to Hollywood, then Mexico. Mexico City provided Day with a refuge from the emotional ties of her lingering attraction to Batterham and steeped her in a thoroughly Catholic atmosphere. Day was able to eke out a living writing articles for *Commonweal* and *America* but was forced to leave the country prematurely, when Tamar came down with malaria. By the summer of 1931, Day had returned to New York and moved into an apartment in what is now Alphabet City with Tamar, Day's younger brother John, and his wife Tessa. By that time, the United States was thoroughly embedded in the Great Depression and provided Day with ample material for introspective reflection, but no easy avenues for proactive engagement. She grew frustrated with her inability to integrate her religious and political orientations, coupled with her own sense of personal disengagement from social movements of the era. Although she had formally joined the Church, she still had no real community and felt crippled by loneliness and indecision.[61] That would all permanently change on December 9, 1932, when—seemingly out of the blue—fate deposited a weathered, idiosyncratic, fifty-five-year-old homeless French chatterbox named Peter Maurin on her doorstep.[62]

While she may not have realized it at the time, Day's unexpected introduction to Maurin would basically set the tone for the next two decades of her life. Whatever structure or direction she had lacked since converting to Catholicism she now had in spades, at least vicariously. Among all his peculiarities, Maurin came with a prepackaged socio-spiritual agenda and never lacked for confidence—although in his case it might be more charitably described as a sense of vocation. His "indoctrination" of Day into his program began instantly, and he chose their first meeting as an opportunity to introduce her to his "Easy Essays"—Maurin's preferred medium of public theology—brief, pithy, semi-poetic, grammatically toxic tongue twisters about politics, holiness, and anarchism.[63] Maurin has been portrayed somewhat dismissively as a "mystical self-described philosopher" and his quirks, lack of "social intelligence," problematic gender politics,[64] burdensome self-confidence, and general foreignness spawned a gamut-running variety of responses.[65] His enigmatic personality has spawned a cottage industry of scholarship, with the seemingly collective, if unstated, objective of trying to figure out exactly what made him so peculiar.[66] To Day, however, he was a contemporary prophet, draped in a ratty dress suit—"the kind of old clothes that have so lost their shape and finish that it's impossible to tell if they are clean or not."[67] He was compulsively vernacular and inaugurated the Catholic Worker tradition of avoiding formality and restricting direct addresses to the forename, under the presupposition that the salutation "Mrs." or "Mr." was code for "outsider."[68]

Perhaps more than anything else, Peter Maurin was a man with a vision of revolution. He was indelicate, sometimes tactless, in his delivery, but was just the militant blend of medieval romanticism, incarnational social vision, and anarchist politics that Dorothy Day needed to resuscitate her flagging sense of vocation. In Maurin's mind, her purpose in life was obvious—to work with him on starting a holistic spiritual and social revolution. Maurin came from earthy peasant stock, and—unlike Day—was an avowed back-to-the-land, agrarian anarcho-primitivist, promoting what he called a "green revolution." His philosophy was steeped in the French personalism of Mounier and Berdyaev—whose critique of "bourgeois culture" deeply affected Day's social vision.[69] He rebelled against intellectually elaborate moral casuistry and vehemently subscribed to a form of biblical literalism and a brand of realized eschatology that took the hardline interpretations of the Sermon on the Mount as a baseline for Christian ethics. Maurin's social program had an immediacy that required personal sacrifice and rejected the conventional reliance on state intervention—predicated upon a radical appreciation of the doctrine of the Mystical Body:

> We are our brother's keeper, and all men are our brothers whether they be Catholic or not. But of course the tie that binds Catholics is closer, the tie of grace. We partake of the same food, Christ. We put off the old man and put on Christ. The same blood flows through our veins, Christ's. We are the same flesh, Christ's.[70]

Put simply, Peter Maurin dreamed of creating "a society where it will be easier for men to be good."[71] For Dorothy Day, he would provide instant community, the antidote to what she would call "the long loneliness"—a persistent source of darkness for Day, even following her entrance into the Church. Paul Elie notes the peculiarity of the fact that, for years following her conversion, Day really did not know any Catholics—at least not any that she considered real friends by any stretch of the imagination.[72] Peter Maurin served as a spiritual mentor and validated her new identity by, as it were, taking it for granted. Until this point, Day had struggled with the apparent paradox of her religious impulse coupled with her radical socio-political tastes—a tension that could never be fully resolved. And while Day worried that the apparently mutually exclusive aspects of her personality might prove irreconcilable, Maurin never seems to have acknowledged any contradiction in the first place, possibly because he shared them, and—in a way very much like Onésime Lacouture—Maurin seems to have been nothing if not reconciled to himself.

While his bizarre mannerisms and occasionally exasperating personality derived more from lapses in self-awareness than anything approaching malice, Dorothy Day seems to have viewed him in almost biblical terms as the Folly of the Cross incarnate—or a prophetic inversion of the conventionally accepted order.[73] Through her lens, Maurin was a prophetic iconoclast in the tradition of Isaiah and Francis of Assisi—and thus could not really be expected to, well, blend. In his case, the form matched the substance—and his vocation was clearly, in the oft-paraphrased tradition of Finley Peter Dunne and Mary Harris "Mother" Jones, "to comfort the afflicted, and afflict the comfortable."[74] His Easy Essays were a concise brand of evangelization that capitalized on his broken immigrant English and theatrical flair.[75] Possibly more than anything, however, Maurin enjoyed making pronouncements to Day—and whoever else happened to be within earshot: "Man proposes and woman disposes," he loved to say.[76] He was an unrepentant dreamer and left the nuts and bolts of implementation to Day, along with an increasingly unwieldy conglomerate of ragtag disenfranchised skid row outpatients and college honor roll candidates that eventually composed the Catholic Worker, which became Day's adopted family for the next fifty years.

Peter Maurin—a former Lasallian Christian Brother and lowbagging handyperson—sought out an avenue for proselytizing his synthesis of "cult, culture, and cultivation," which drew moral fiber from the Church Magisterium's modern turn toward the Social Question. He had memorized passages from *Rerum Novarum* and *Quadragesimo Anno* and eventually composed his own syllabus for a program of theological formation in his brand of Catholic personalism. Although he did not share Day's affinity for frontline protest, Maurin set the ethical bar rather high and taught Day to model herself on the lives of the saints.[77] He was a tireless advocate of study but showed an aversion to abstraction in favor of practical theology. Day, being a journalist, was in many ways his perfect sidekick: she was moderately connected, had an eye for literary style, a keen desire for purpose that was both political and spiritual, and she listened. Maurin's vision of an impending anticapitalist, communitarian "Green Revolution" required some form of platform, some means of communicating his ideas to the world that was more efficient than his soapbox in Union Square. And thus was born the *Catholic Worker*, a radical paper selling—then as now—for a penny a copy. The paper hit the newsstands on May Day, 1933:

> For those who are sitting on park benches in the warm spring sunlight.
>
> For those who are huddling in shelters trying to escape the rain.
>
> For those who are walking the streets in the all but futile search for work.
>
> For those who think that there is no hope for the future, no recognition of their plight—this paper is addressed.[78]

"The Bread of the Strong"

> How can we love our husbands, our wives, our children? All the other loves I have I must use as samples of love of God. . . . They are the totems, instruments of love.—all the world and everything in it must be used as [a] means of loving God. We must love the world intensely but not for *itself*. We are human beings, but *baptized* human beings. We must use things as we need them.
>
> —Dorothy Day, *All Is Grace* retreat notes

Over the next several months, the *Catholic Worker*'s readership multiplied exponentially (not necessarily a remarkable feat, given their modest baseline)—at least partially owing to parish subscriptions, which spoke to the paper's relatively unanticipated mass appeal. By May of 1936, the *Worker*'s monthly print run clocked in at 110,000.[79] One of the earliest issues that contributors took on—following Maurin's lead—was the issue of urban poverty, which many of them had experienced firsthand and which they saw in their midst in increasingly amplified numbers as the United States struggled through the Great Depression. Maurin fortified his position with references to Catholic Social Teaching, the *Rule* of Saint Benedict, and the example of Saint Basil the Great's Cappadocian "city of hospitality," which all manifested sentiments mirroring his own. Structured primarily as an internally focused critique of the Church, by practicing, committed Catholics, the *Worker*'s position stressed the need for a more radical approach to addressing homelessness and financial destitution on an immediate, local level, rather than instinctively relying on the New Deal. Organically, the *Catholic Worker*'s office—that would be Day's apartment on the Lower East Side—evolved into a "house of hospitality," which became another signature feature of Dorothy Day's ministry. Inevitably, their work and socio-political orientation brought the paper's staff into routine contact with the "housing-deficient," and when Day's brother John moved out to Dobbs Ferry—up the Hudson, just north of Yonkers—Maurin and several others moved in and turned it into an impromptu flophouse. The journal's success soon enabled them to begin renting apartments specifically to provide homes for those in need, and free meals followed soon behind. The *Worker*'s infrastructure and capacity seemed to increase in direct proportion to the deepening financial crisis that was rapidly expanding their unfortunate client base.

Although Maurin's rigorous—rigorist—indoctrination formed the bedrock of Dorothy Day's spiritual development, she found profound nourishment from her auspicious encounter with Lacouturite theology. Although she felt called to live and work in the city, Day's divergent disposition toward solitude thirsted for a deeper contemplative life. Her relationship with Hugo—her confessor for a time—and other Lacouturite clergy was highly symbiotic: the priests found fertile soil for their radical doctrine of Christian maximalism, which they had hoped to promote directly among the laity.[80] "*The* retreat" provided Day with interior nourishment: she routinely employed biblical culinary metaphors to describe the retreat—meat, bread, water. The anti-modernist and anti-intellectual strands within Hugo's thought blended nicely with Day's own theological temperament, molded as it had been by Peter Maurin—an avowed medievalist "reactionary."[81] It spoke to her developing moral perfectionism and seemed to provide a practical method for cultivating holiness. Day's notes from a 1943 retreat held at St. Anthony's Orphanage in Oakmont, Pennsylvania—an enterprise overseen by Louis Farina—chronicles her studied attention to traditionally Lacouturite concepts, such as the use of creatures, ordered affections, and the pagan mentality, using the analogy of an infant running around with a pair of scissors: it is not the scissors that make it dangerous but the combination of the subject and object.[82] In a similar way, only the spiritually perfect may enjoy all creation while remaining detached. Although the notes are somewhat stilted, they show Day in the process of digesting Lacouture's teachings on the relative opposition between natural and supernatural motives. This passage highlights a few of the principles in Lacouturite theology that were focal points of controversy—in both its Canadian and American permutations: an unforgiving deocentric focus; the tragic misappropriation of creation's inherent "goodness;" the distinction between evaluating phenomena *in se* and *in nobis*; the critical function of supernatural motives; and the imperative for ascetic discipline along the spiritual path. Diminutive, self-degrading comments aside, Day's ruminations might have made useful fodder for more belligerent Lacouturite apologists.

Retreat at Maryfarm, 1941; in the back row, Pacifique Roy is flanked by Peter Maurin and Dorothy Day (Department of Special Collections and University Archives, Marquette University Libraries)

Hugo's rendition of the spiritual combat appealed to Day's visceral attraction to "self-abnegation" and ego transcendence.[83] The retreat was austere: no idle conversation for ten days (more or less), no listening to the radio, no smoking. They ate groundhog—Day's recollections of life "in retreat" are smattered with references to eating locally harvested groundhog, which seemed to fascinate as well as repel. The overabundance of downtime coupled with enforced silence recalibrated Day's rhythms and served a rejuvenating function that revitalized her for reentry into the chaotic world of Catholic Worker ministry—a sentiment that was emphatically supported by Hugo and found itself something of a minority opinion among the more garrulous Catholic Worker community.[84] However, all the external appearances of serenity notwithstanding, there was dynamic interior work being done below the surface. Hugo's conferences unflinchingly and somewhat relentlessly attacked the status quo of Christian mediocrity not in abstractions, but practically, in our motives, whereby we—even subconsciously—opt for proximate and temporal "goods," to the relative marginalization of the supernatural. An ascetic heart was cultivated, and Day's retreat notes evince a heightened sensitivity to Hugo's redemptive theology of suffering:

> The sins of my entire past life from earliest childhood come often to my mind to fill me with a sense of iniquity. . . . Yes, compunction is good, and the desire for penance instinctive in every human heart. . . . One

> *desires* to share in the sufferings of Christ. One desires to share in the hardships of the beloved, hunger, thirst, vigils, and this means self-imposed mortifications, self-imposed dying to self. . . . But it is *love* that gives these desires and love is a glowing, happy thing, a radiant, warming fire. . . . This blindness of love, this folly of love,—this seeing Christ in others, everywhere and not seeing the ugly, the obvious the dirty, the sinful—this means we do not see the faults of others,—only our own. We see only Christ in them. We have eyes only for our beloved, ears for His voice.[85]

Day carried her notes around with her when she returned to "the world" as a reminder of the principles she had digested during the retreats—as a means of prolonging their effect. And while the retreats reinvigorated her fervor, they also provided a new framework within which to view her multi-pronged vocation as a radical political activist, writer, non-profit innkeeper, and manager of the decidedly unmanageable. She viewed the content of the retreats as seamlessly compatible with Peter Maurin's theology—as Day testified during her funeral oration for Onésime Lacouture, she considered the tandem influence of Lacouture and Maurin to have been unmatched in her formation. While Maurin seemed to Day to be an almost sui generis incarnation of Lacouturite principles, the retreat—for all its occasionally boorish rhetoric—presented a decidedly practical education in ascetic theology that gave her hearty food for thought.

Although she delighted in the freedom that came with the retreats—that is, the freedom to contemplate, pray, and indulge her instinctive moral scrupulosity—she did, nevertheless, continue to endure bouts of loneliness, boredom, and self-doubt. In the heart of the city, swarmed by a seemingly endless barrage of demands, the austere silence of the retreat held great appeal. And while this was more than simply a figment of Day's exhausted but obstinately romantic imagination, the reality of the retreat's routine could be somewhat more tedious.[86] Day prayed for the gift of perseverance, in terms of resisting the noonday devil of listlessness during both the retreat and in her ministries at the Catholic Worker. While she fantasized about a monastic vocation in her correspondence with her pen pal, the celebrity Trappist monk–author Thomas Merton—who, in turn, habitually daydreamed about life as a radical activist, among many other things and, indeed, eventually became a Benedictine oblate attached to St. Procopius Abbey in the Chicago suburbs—this did not insulate her from the conventional trappings of solitude. While her enthusiasm for the retreat seems to have wavered little over the decades of her active participation, her expectations could only have been tempered, or rather deepened, by experience.

The expectation of mystical fireworks and spiritual heroism—perhaps embodied most clearly in the newly minted monastic Thomas Merton's memoir, *The Seven Storey Mountain*—were part and parcel of the retreat's practical obstacles. As a safeguard, the program followed tradition by attempting to counsel against attachments to what John of the Cross termed "consolations," lest the contemplative develop attachments to interior objects (as subtle as self-awareness or even hope) and unwittingly convert them into idols. In *The Dark Night*, his guide for fellow Discalced Carmelites, John went to great lengths to explain how the positive reinforcement given to the spiritual novice as encouragement is eventually withheld as the soul progresses along the way to perfection, in order that they may not become a hindrance to its deocentric focus. During his conferences, Hugo applied his supernatural perspective to the practice of contemplation, emphasizing the dangers of obsessing over the fruits of prayer, which—similar to more profane phenomena such as wealth, power, and prestige—distract the soul from its proper supernatural orientation; the main point being that loving the feeling that one gets during prayer is not the same as loving God. In her notes from a 1942 retreat at Oakmont led by Hugo and Farina, Day reflected on the obstacles and attachments that prey upon the contemplative: "People love consolations. That is why there are so few saints. . . . The more you pray, the worse things get."[87] The Lacouture retreat was not meant to be easy—it was "the bread of the strong," as Day said.[88] And while much was asked of retreatants, much was also promised in return—an expansion of their exclusive love for God that would paradoxically empower them to love their neighbors all the more, without reservation. The self-abnegation and abandonment preached during the retreat resonated clearly with Dorothy Day's strong affection for Thérèse of Lisieux—the infirm Carmelite who aspired to missionary heroics but was restricted to the cloister, developing a fervent spirituality that transfigured seemingly minor acts (such as enduring annoying sister nuns with charitable equanimity) with cosmic significance.[89]

A World of Pain: The Retreat's Doctrine of Suffering

> Whenever I make this retreat it seems as though I were transplanted back through the centuries to the time when the Church was in its pristine fervor and the sole absorbtion [*sic*] of those who had received the great treasure of the Faith was to imitate Christ just as closely as they possibly could in every phase of their lives. . . . After all, God knew about the "industrial revolution, the "atomic age," and all the "ages," and growing complications of the world until the end of time, and yet, His command to "be perfect" is for everyone, in all walks of life and in every century till the end of the world.
>
> —Emma Grenier, letter to Dorothy Day, 24 August 1952

In order for the profound conversion that the retreat aimed at to stick, a certain degree of suffering was expected—even embraced—along the way. However, undergirding this programmatic consideration was a more comprehensive belief about the phenomena, in its myriad forms. The Lacouturite philosophy of suffering both attracted and repelled; indeed, on occasion it was alleged to be almost masochistic: retreat aficionados were depicted as self-flagellating dupes, their leaders pathological fanatics. If the process of ongoing conversion to the supernatural *mentalité* includes—even demands—pain, would it not be logical to welcome obstacles as they arise? And if so, would this truly constitute suffering? Although Hugo's intransigent belligerence throughout the Lacouture controversy might indicate some personal inertia on the subject, in his preaching and written work he touted the virtue of righteous suffering. The venom he spewed at his opponents throughout the ordeal leads one to suspect that he found the controversy more offensive than his circumspect, willing-martyr-for-the-cause disclaimers might lead one to assume. Nevertheless, while he allegorized his own persecution—along with that of Onésime Lacouture—to Christ's Passion, during his retreats Hugo treated suffering as a precondition of holiness that merits eternal life:

> And so, we have to face the fact that to work for this kingdom is going to mean, not a picnic; it's going to mean . . . confronting darkness and suffering, and labor. And if we're unwilling for the labor or the suffering, then forget about the kingdom. . . . We suffer and die for the Kingdom of God.[90]

The doctrine of suffering that Hugo espoused throughout the retreats was augmented by more complex theological works, such as *Applied Christianity*, but also by short, pithy little pamphlets that were distributed with colorful titles such as *Pruning* (a Hugo metaphor for the ascetic life) and the aforementioned *How to Become a Butterfly*.[91] Hugo's ethic of suffering had two primary components: suffering as an ascetic practice that detaches the soul from temporal matters, freeing it to order itself properly toward the supernatural, and suffering as imitation of Christ. In the former, Hugo discusses the redemptive value of all forms of suffering, both voluntary and involuntary, because they foster a sense of dissatisfaction with ephemeral forms of happiness, redirecting the soul toward God: "It is precisely by sufferings that our attachments for the pleasures and the good things of the world are severed."[92] And while Hugo wove his more severe rhetoric into a defensibly orthodox framework of Christian renunciation, his deep-seated conviction regarding the "relative opposition" between the natural and supernatural—*in nobis*—precipitated some turns of phrase that were apt to instigate conflict: "We have no sooner started to live than we must learn to die. . . . Our life here on earth, with its arduous duties, with its self-denial and unending trials, is itself a kind of death, a mortification or dying . . . ."[93] Although Hugo proceeded to identify the developmental function of self-mortification in shaping the soul for the beatific vision and a kenotic overflow of charity toward all creatures, his assessment of conventional life understandably struck skeptics as rather severe.[94]

This, Then, Is Perfect Joy: Catholic Workers and Self-mortification on Retreat

> A retreat is an oasis in the desert of this life, in the midst of the aridities of our daily life. It is a spiritual training, of the spirit, as training for the body is undertaken. We do not feel our spiritual growth, but exercises persevered in give facility and grace. We often do not feel the action of the sun, but sitting before the Eucharist, in the presence of Jesus in the Eucharist warms and gives health to the spirit as the sun gives health to the body.
>
> —Dorothy Day, *All Is Grace*

For her part, Dorothy Day seems to have found the Lacouturite doctrine of suffering profoundly exhilarating, which perhaps did precious little to reassure concerned friends who worried about her tendency toward self-recrimination and moral scrupulosity. Although the living conditions were sparse—even for someone acclimated to Catholic Worker city life, Day envisioned the interior and exterior trials of the retreat as sandpaper for the soul, which would condition her to spiritual detachment.[95] Hugo's ascetic language began working its way into Day's lexicon and colored her interpretation of trials as spiritual refinement. As they aged, both Peter Maurin and Pacifique Roy's minds slowly blunted, and they experienced diminished mental capacities; Day interpreted their disorienting vertigo as passive purification, of God stripping away the last vestiges of attachments—to their very own selves. During the last years of his life, the pathologically talkative Peter Maurin grew quiet, his thought process confused. Outsiders often took his silence as an indication of deafness or cognitive deficiency and infantilized him in a manner that Day found excruciating.[96] By the time Maurin died, Day was steeped in the Lacouturite ideology of mortification and the dynamic, cooperative relationship between the ascetic and God in bringing the soul to perfection. In Day's regular "On Pilgrimage" column in the *Catholic Worker*, she began to speak of "pruning" and counseled the acceptance of—even enthusiasm for—suffering; the catch twenty-two being the fact that those who have the capacity to take solace in the redemptive value of their suffering are then, properly speaking, experiencing a diminished form of it, as with John of the Cross's "dark night." Hugo's ascetic theology synced closely with Day's reading of Thérèse of Lisieux's "Little Way" and seems to have fortified her resolve during periods of pointed unpopularity, particularly regarding her resolute absolute pacifism, which set her at odds with more moderate pacifists like Thomas Merton and even John Hugo—who had published a personalist indictment of military conscription in the November 1944 edition of the *Catholic Worker*—to say nothing of more hawkish establishment powerbrokers like New York's Cardinal Spellman.[97]

Although Dorothy Day marshaled great strength and vitality from the anti-triumphalist rigorism that saturated Hugo's teaching, her attempts to promulgate it within the ranks of the Catholic Worker were not unopposed. From the beginning, some within the community protested, apparently not concurring with Day's opinion of the social application of contemplative withdrawal. To some, the quiet stillness of retreat life seemed altogether too comfortable:

> I did not think of retreats for a long time again. We were living a retreat, some of us said smugly. Others said scornfully that with all our talk of voluntary poverty, with shelters like our houses of hospitality and with farming communes, we were indeed fleeing to the fields, retreating from the world, living in ivory towers. I wanted to start a farming commune called Tower of Ivory, one of the titles of the Blessed Virgin in the litany dedicated to her.[98]

Compared to the urban poverty that surrounded and saturated the Catholic Worker through and through, the perceived tranquility of the retreat seemed self-indulgent and unproductive. Somewhat ironically, this was also the root of Thomas Merton's mercurial "vocation issues"—at least when he wasn't yearning for the greater solitude of the Carthusians or Camaldolese—which he confided to Day throughout their lively correspondence (mirroring her own wearied fantasies about eremitic life).[99] This critique mimicked more typical popular antagonism toward the apparent unproductivity of monasticism—the extreme withdrawal from sociopolitical participation. Although the Catholic Worker sometimes prided itself on its determined *im*practicality, closed retreats seemed excessively disengaged for the social concerns that composed the heart of the Worker's apostolate. Now while the Lacouturite retreat's *fuga mundi* actually fostered an ethic of radical social engagement, ten days of quiet prayer in the countryside seemed decadent to some—indicating, perhaps, a lack of sympathy or appreciation for the spiritual combat that was waged amid the quiet stillness.

Among those who did participate, the Lacouture retreat met with mixed reviews. Although Day's deep reverence for it was echoed by many, others found it too Spartan, pessimistic, spiritually melodramatic, and rather dull. In his memoir, *Wings of Dawn*, Stanley Vishnewski notes that many were impressed with Roy and Hugo's pluck—to preach detachment at a time when the mainstream clergy seemed, like the laity, to be increasingly drawn to material comfort and social respectability.[100] However, Vishnewski's enthusiasm for the retreat was rather muted; he bristled at the puritanical overtones of Hugo's ascetic teaching and worried over the internal fractures it precipitated within the Worker community. Yet again, nicotine distinguished itself as a key point of conflict:

> It seemed to me, that the most controversial part of the retreat revolved around the question of smoking vs. non-smoking. Theological

Maryfarm, Easton PA (Department of Special Collections and University Archives, Marquette University Libraries)

> and abstract questions made little appeal to the average Catholic but cigarettes were a concrete fact and could be touched and smoked. The retreat masters stressed, perhaps unduly, that it was impossible to live a good Christian life and to smoke at the same time. If one wanted to love God, he had to give up his attachment to cigarette smoking.
>
> As a consequence, those who had made the retreat and gave up smoking began to act as spiritual policemen in an effort to persuade their friends to stop smoking. It was possible for a worldly person to collect cartons and packets of cigarettes at the end of every retreat. I sometimes suspected that a few of the most vociferous anti-smokers were secret smokers who used the retreat as a pretext to collect free cigarettes.
>
> The reformed smokers would point an accusing finger at anyone smoking and would taunt them by saying that it was impossible for them to be doing it for the love of God and that they just had to be on the road to hell. The smokers would counter by blowing smoke rings into the air and telling the retreatants to go to hell. It was hell either way.[101]

Vishnewski acknowledged the benefits of the retreat on receptive souls and took some slightly smug satisfaction in the anxiety it appeared to provoke among the more worldly clergy, to see themselves spiritually outdone by the laity. However, the perpetual Lent that was preached during the retreat seemed more appropriate to the Trappists, and the conviction that observant Christians ought to restrict themselves to "no joy except that of the Cross" was bound to inspire bitterness, dissension, and among some outright envy toward the unbaptized who had not yet fallen subject to the heroic demands of Christian morality.[102] Additionally, many who left the retreat feeling quite invigorated about the "strong meat of the Gospel," and running the extra mile, soon backslid upon reentry into normal society without the comprehensive support structure of retreat discipline and suffered deep existential wounds as a result. Additionally, Vishnewski thought the food was altogether ghastly and soon realized the unfortunate truth that a silent retreat is no place to stoke the flames of romance—and the constant, forced refrain of "Rejoice!" grated on him like nails on a chalkboard.[103]

Hugo and Day were both well aware of some of the pitfalls of the retreat—of the social pressures that might arise and the potential for excess. Although—as with the depiction of himself and Onésime Lacouture as the persecuted Christ—Hugo's anti-triumphalist dismissal of the retreat's unpopularity sometimes seemed like a coping mechanism, it never quite caught on as much as he had hoped:

> Miller: Were there others there that found in the retreat the same truth that Dorothy Did? Were there any of the other Workers that you recall?
>
> Hugo: I think so. It would be hard for me to give names right now because I've met so many over the years. . . . So I really don't know. But we never achieved the results we wanted, I'll say that. Of course, a great consolation is that Jesus Christ himself didn't. He only had twelve followers after his Galilean journey. So we weren't looking for great success, humanly speaking.[104]

In the heady stratosphere of ascetic theology, extremism and affected spiritual materialism might well derail actual progress in the contemplative life and cause divisions within the community. Father Paul Judge described it as "T.N.T. and then some," which risked overwhelming the unprepared.[105] As competitive penance arose among retreatants, outdoing one another in ascetic gymnastics, Hugo worried that this tendency actually contradicted the process of *metanoia* that self-mortification was intended to foster—and occasionally found himself in the rather unfamiliar position of counseling moderation.[106] Both within the retreat and without, the Catholic Worker seemed to attract individuals who tragically undermined themselves by growing attached to their own reputation for detachment. However, this is perhaps not shocking, considering that the corpus of Christian ascetic literature is rife with warnings against the trappings of spiritual pride, indicating the phenomenon's relative predictability. In Montréal and Milwaukee, communities formed that adopted practices commonly associated with cult activity in the popular imagination—uniform dress codes, parroting catchphrases, rigorous self-policing, and social insularity; the Pittsburgh "Spirituals" excommunicated their fellow Workers before descending into drunken disorder; part of the Catholic Worker farm in Easton ("Maryfarm"), Pennsylvania, was commandeered by a manipulative, questionably sane, schismatic sect that caused Day and others an endless series of headaches and actually led the Catholic Worker to vacate the premises and sign away its property to the squatters. While the theatrics added perhaps a bit too much color to Catholic Worker life, they also provided fodder for Day's introspective journalism, including a cheeky unpublished essay aptly titled "Oh the Bitter Scorn that Religion Calls Up," that had a bit of fun at the expense of some of the more colorful characters she had stumbled across over the years—such as "Hugh," who publicized his piety by habitually approaching the Blessed Sacrament on his knees, which was certainly cinematic, if a bit disruptive to fellow worshipers in terms of Communion gridlock.[107]

While the regulars at the Lacouturite retreats generally cherished the environment for its remarkable austerity, this sentiment was certainly not shared by all, and some found it, actually, rather too pleasant—not on principle but in practice. Rather than smirking at the contemplative life itself as one of relative ease and unproductivity, some critics subscribed to the values of periodic withdrawal but wanted more austerity, less structure, more isolation. But the retreat was controlled and coordinated—in a sense lacking a certain amount of precarity. After all, although retreatants had to maintain a virtually complete state of silence, and ate food that Stanley Vishnewski thought more appropriate for horses, they did not want for much.[108] Skeptics within the community were not necessarily wrong—retreat participants had their needs cared for, albeit in a relatively modest fashion. But they had meals, even if they consisted of groundhog and oatmeal (which some sardonically referred to as "cruel gruel").[109] The experience of relative deprivation juxtaposed against the even greater destitution faced by some was a consistent source of scrupulous guilt for Dorothy Day, both within the retreat itself and back at home in the "world" of the Catholic Worker on the Lower East Side. What passed for austerity among most—seemingly masochistic to some—was all rather plush to others, who might well have puzzled over the rhetoric of self-mortification within a community that subsisted on a predictable three squares a day. The rough conditions were meant to precipitate a sense of detachment that was conducive to the spiritual combat, but this was predicated on the expectation that the conditions would, in fact, be experienced as a hardship, which would prime participants for extended bouts of interior prayer. Otherwise the whole thing might have seemed somewhat anticlimactic. Ten days of intensive contemplation proved a challenge for even the pious but could make for a positively insufferable trial for those who found themselves spiritually arid.

Dorothy Day promoted the retreat energetically among the Catholic Worker community and publicly through her articles in the paper. She touted the profound rejuvenating and formative effects it had on her personally, as well as its contribution to creating a dense maelstrom of prayer that radiated throughout the Mystical Body—based on her "power plant" conception of contemplative activity as reverberating throughout the Church.[110] This functional vision of prayer was evident in her comforting letters to an ever-restless Thomas Merton, which teased out Day's vision of its social function, of bonding humanity to itself as well as to God. She took this somewhat more literally in 1943 and—with Hugo's encouragement—withdrew herself from active ministry and retired to Long Island as a time of extended retreat (although she only lasted six months out of the intended year).[111] Additionally, she saw it as a more intimate occasion for building community within the Worker family, collecting members from different geographic regions and resuscitating their collective enthusiasm, which was put to task so often in the day-to-day. Father Harvey Egan once remarked to Day that the retreat had been, "in spite of the apparent coolness of so many faithful workers, the salvation of the CW. In the retreat lies our only hope for ourselves, for the apostolate."[112] Inevitably, not everyone appreciated these opportunities for supernatural community building, and some viewed the retreat more as a venue for Day to flex her authoritarianism. In the summer of 1939, as debate about US intervention in the growing conflict in Europe simmered, Day put out a call for as many members of the Catholic Worker family who had the means to travel to convene at the Easton farm. Even though the Worker had persistently organized against militarism for the past half-decade, debates about conscientious military invention in the face of impending global war stretched the community thin. Workers gathered for a retreat presided over by Joachim Benson, a priest of the Missionary Servants of the Most Holy Trinity, and Day emerged spiritually recharged and comforted that fractures had been mended—if only temporarily.[113] But for all their transformative power, retreats could not predictably guarantee participants would all emerge as pacifist conscientious objectors.

Epilogue: To Afflict the Comfortable and Comfort the Afflicted

Catholic Worker Pacifism as a Form-of-Life

> I was thinking this morning about our neighbor's attitudes toward us, their respect for the ideas of the paper. I do not think however that they have respect for us personally for trying to live these ideals. They respect our "success" . . . . They respect us because "important" people come to see us. But if we should be suppressed, and could not pay our bills, they would be just as contemptuous, or rather much more contemptuous than they are to the poor around us. They would despise us for our failure.
>
> We have yet to learn what voluntary poverty really means.
>
> —Dorothy Day, *The Duty of Delight: The Diaries of Dorothy Day*

On August 10, 1940, Dorothy Day penned a circular letter from the Worker's root hub in Lower Manhattan to its constellation of affiliated communities, as the United States teetered on the brink of entry into World War II. Subsequently dubbed "Dorothy's Encyclical," the letter was a rare occasion for Day to directly assert her charismatic authority, in contrast to the Worker's conventional decentralized mode of operation.[1] From its inception in 1933, the *Catholic Worker* hit the streets with a distinctive amalgamation of radical politics and maximalist Christian spirituality, maintaining a dogged opposition to all forms of militarism as an evangelical sign of contradiction against the prevailing "just war" traditions that dominated Catholic moral theology and international policy. Indeed, pacifism would not even be sanctioned as a legitimate conscientious option for Catholics until the publication of *Gaudium et Spes* (the Pastoral Constitution on the Church in the Modern World) in 1965, during the Second Vatican Council.[2] At issue in Day's address was the question of dissent within the Worker on fundamental questions—triggered by the revelation that certain communities that challenged Day's platform of pacifist nonintervention had suppressed the circulation of the New York paper. And although it was framed as an open letter, the note was rather baldly directed at the Chicago houses and perhaps even more surgically at John Cogley—a local organizer who had been most vocal about his dissent.

Within just over a month Franklin Delano Roosevelt would reinstate the military draft, and the Catholic Worker offshoot Association of Catholic Conscientious Objectors (ACCO) would form a small (135 at its apex) nucleus of opposition to military conscription.[3] In her letter, Day suggested that those houses that were fundamentally unable to affirm to the Worker's position disavow themselves from the network:

> Our workers have taken it upon themselves to try to follow the counsels of perfection. . . . Many can only go part of the way, what with family obligations, health considerations, even a different point of view. If they wish to work with us, we are glad and thankful to have them, but they cannot be said to be representing the Catholic Worker position. . . . Perhaps it would be better in these cases for the House to disassociate themselves from the Catholic Worker movement.[4]

While Day seemed at pains to not condemn more moderate positions, less charitable readers interpreted the letter as a thinly veiled purge by an autocratic leader whose anarchist sensibilities extended only insofar as she was the "Grand Anarch" (a somewhat tongue-in-cheek epithet coined by longtime Worker and close friend, Tom Cornell).[5] Even within the Catholic Worker's horizontal framework, the military question was an ideological borderline—Day's absolute pacifism being, by definition, inflexible. The proximate cause of the "excommunication" (the suppression of the paper) was overshadowed by this more substantial underlying issue, and Day used her bully pulpit as an opportunity for a monologic clarification of thought regarding the Catholic Worker's collective conscience.

At about the same time, and at Day's prompting, Catholic Workers from across the United States descended on Maryfarm for another pan–Catholic Worker retreat, this time led by CUA's "supernatural sociologist" and unofficial Worker systematician, Paul Hanley Furfey.[6] As she had the year before, Day emerged from the retreat deeply consoled and rejuvenated.[7] John Cogley had a very different experience and concluded that his conscientious military interventionism was anathema within the Catholic

Worker umbrella—which he would later describe as "dictatorially" pacifist.[8] Imagining that Day's intransigent position not only diverged from his own but flirted with heresy, he subsequently left the Catholic Worker and enlisted in the army—albeit with some difficulty, because of a well-meaning but nepotistic exemption previously garnered for him by the influential cleric Reynold Henry Hillenbrand.[9] The Chicago Worker houses disbanded for a time and were eventually followed by others, including two in Pittsburgh under the stewardship of Charles Owen Rice.[10]

In June of 1940—the month the German *Wehrmacht* invaded Paris—Dorothy Day had composed an editorial in the *Catholic Worker* titled "Our Stand," which asserted the "orthodox" Catholic Worker position against coercion and militarism:

> Many of our readers ask, "What is the stand of the CATHOLIC WORKER in regard to the present war?" . . . We repeat, that as in the Ethiopian war, the Spanish war, the Japanese and Chinese war, the Russian-Finnish war—so in the present war we stand unalterably opposed to war as a means of saving "Christianity," "civilization," "democracy." We do not believe that they can be saved by these means.[11]

In this op-ed, which first put her on the FBI's radar (although as late as 1943, J. Edgar Hoover speculated that she was a Russian secret agent), Day invoked the Beatitudes—which she considered the Catholic Worker's manifesto—as a framing matrix to bolster her inverted vision of the Folly of the Cross as heroic spiritual path.[12] Thus the question of militarism was not something accidental but rather more integral to her understanding of the Catholic Worker's calling. Day's praxis of conscientious impracticality incorporated pacifism as both an approach to particular historically embedded events and an interior disposition encompassing the entirety of her being-in-relationship to others—what the Italian philosopher Giorgio Agamben has called a "form-of-life": "a life that is linked so closely to its form that it proves to be inseparable from it."[13]

Day's refusal to objectify or instrumentalize—in her mind, dehumanize—others in order to achieve practical ends was essential to her absolute pacifism, and the sharp criticism she drew synced tightly with her vision of prophetic Christianity and the Worker's aforementioned poverty of reputation, which rendered it to a certain extent unintelligible, even to progressive Catholics. This was amplified during the summer of 1940,

Dorothy Day on retreat at Maryfarm in the 1950s (Photo credit: Margaret Dagenais, Department of Special Collections and University Archives, Marquette University Libraries)

following the publication of the *Catholic Worker*'s controversial "Peace Edition," and Day's journals from that period bulge with meditations on spiritual poverty and penitential repetitions of "This then is perfect joy," harvested from Saint Francis's dialogues with Brother Leo in *The Little Flowers*.[14] The incongruity with the ways of the world encapsulated in the recklessly impractical Folly of the Cross theology that Day had at least partially imbibed from Lacouturism formed much of the basis for accusations of Catholic Worker romanticism and hyper-sentimentality, which rendered the Worker functionally ill-equipped to do the "real work" of addressing meta-level structural oppression. Day piqued at the dismissive-sounding term "sentimentality" and indignantly defied those who dismissed the Worker as sappy to "mortify" themselves by trying their hand at life on the breadline, quoting a favorite line from Dostoevsky's *The Brothers Karamazov* that became something of a Catholic Worker motto: "Love in practice is a harsh and dreadful thing compared to love in dreams."[15] Perhaps the term "sentimentality" particularly riled Day since she herself employed the term pejoratively. One example was her treatment of a Catholic Worker episode in which a rabid faction defected from the mainstream Pittsburgh community, dubbing themselves the "Spirituals" (as opposed to the more measured "Br. Eliases")—which melodramatically recalled an early Franciscan rift following the thirteenth-century death of the *Poverello*. They claimed a more authentically Franciscan voluntary poverty than their Catholic Worker contemporaries but soon imploded through a mixture of cultivated alcoholism and logistical incompetence.[16] Dorothy Day dialectically oscillated between an analogical incarnationalism and a more Sanjuanist asceticism—on the basis of which it has been suggested that she harbored a masochistic expiatory-suffering-as-vocation "victim soul" mentality, along with the allegations of Jansenist proclivities that came with her relationship to Hugo.[17] The Catholic Worker's field of forces was a conglomerate of charisms that contrasted sharply with the hegemonic shadows of both Church and State, intermingled with the mundane, self-abnegating grind of tending to human suffering—the effects of the tectonic forces of social sin.

The pacifist form-of-life that Day defended in the face of World War II corresponded to her evangelical poverty as both a form of witness and technique for forming Christian conscience. It was an impoverished lifestyle, destitute of recourse (Reinhold Niebuhr's argument about the coercive power of nonviolence notwithstanding)—a nonparticipation in the conventional mechanisms of hard power.[18] The same disregard for self cultivated through Catholic Worker pacifism also informed the community's praxis of voluntary poverty and the Works of Mercy. Thomas Merton once noted that for Dorothy Day, poverty was "more than a sociological problem: it is also a religious mystery"—a "strange and elusive thing," symptomatic of human suffering, while potentially also a remedy; paradoxically both a sacrament and scandal.[19] In 1948 Day penned an incendiary editorial, "We Are Un-American: We Are Catholics," in which she protested the proposition of universal military training, fusing militarism with free-market capitalism, which both liquidate marginalized swaths of humanity in favor of preserving and extending the privileges of a relatively small few:

> The policy of the United States is anti-Catholic because it is atheistic. God does not enter into it for in place of Him there is EXPEDIENCY. It has become expedient that we murder, it has become expedient that we ignore the precepts of Jesus Christ laid down in the Sermon on the Mount and applicable to ALL MEN, not just to a chosen few who are to be perfect.
>
> . . .
>
> We are against war because it is contrary to the spirit of Jesus Christ, and the only important thing is that we abide in His spirit. It is more important than being American, more important than being respectable, more important than obedience to the State.[20]

This editorial highlights the point at which Day's class analysis collided with the Christian pacifist tradition. In a globalized economy, capitalism is inexorably tied to militarism—it forms the basis, means, and ends of so much military conflict. And if capitalism is violence, then pacifism and voluntary poverty are intertwined, both standing in stark contrast to the norms by which we are socialized into respectable mainstream US culture.[21] In this context, the asceticism of Lacouturite theology was part of a process of self-deconstruction without remainder that, for Day, was bound up in the generation of a radically pacifist subjectivity.

In the lead-up to the 1940 retreat at Easton that would confirm his alienation from Catholic Worker orthodoxy, Dorothy Day typed out a brief letter to John Cogley, in which she seemed reconciled to their differences on the military question and nudged him to attend, signing off: "You are bone of our bone, and flesh of our flesh, not bone of contention."[22] The question of Cogley's excommunication seemed to have had less to do with particular transgressions than the form-of-life that he cultivated, reflecting a distinct—in this case particularly grave—gap in Christian ways of being. If Day saw the Catholic Worker's vocation as intrinsically pacifist—albeit previously informally, as suited its communitarian anti-structure—she considered Cogley's realist lens incompatible. This divergence presented an opportunity for erecting a semi-porous boundary that foregrounded integral Catholic Worker principles—although this intervention was laden with some considerable ambiguity regarding whose conscience was authoritative in the process of community spiritual formation.

The Strong Meat of the Gospel: The Formation of a Comprehensive Maximalist Christianity

> Those were beautiful days. It was as though we were listening to the gospel for the first time. We saw all things new. There was a freshness about everything as though we were in love, as indeed we were. After a day of recollection . . . we went back to New York or Philadelphia refreshed, and "went for forty days and forty nights," like the prophets, on that food. It was good bread. Indeed, it was strong meat.
>
> —Dorothy Day, *The Long Loneliness*

Although she once depicted herself as an exemplar of "the wavering life," Dorothy Day's narrative exhibits a fairly linear trajectory when examined as a whole—although her depictions may have been retroactively shaded by memory and the influence of the Augustinian archetype.[23] I was once asked if I thought Dorothy Day could have become "Dorothy Day" had she not serendipitously encountered the Lacouture retreat—a question that I still feel incapable of answering in any intelligible way. It feels like an impossible question. If the whole gestalt of our lifeworld is predicated upon the web of causes and conditions that have preceded us at any moment, then isolating any but the most trivial influences as ancillary seems like the unravelling of the space-time continuum. However, the considerable perseverance in the heroic Christian maximalism that became the hallmark of Catholic Worker personalism owes a great debt to the influence of Lacouturisme (largely under the stewardship of John Hugo), along with Peter Maurin and a myriad of other critical interventions in her spiritual development. Certainly, she considered it critical. Day made the retreat regularly for some thirty-five years and promoted it vigorously both in person and publicly in the pages of the *Catholic Worker.* She made it "virtually mandatory" within the New York Worker community and devoted substantial resources toward establishing a permanent retreat house on one of their farms, albeit without enduring success.[24] The ascetic detachment—from both external and interior objects and, finally, one's self—at the core of Lacouturite theology was constitutive of the evangelical poverty that was vital to Dorothy Day's form-of-life.

Day's relative celebrity brought increased interest in the retreat, both sympathetic and critical. However, unlike her clerical counterparts, Day managed to avoid anything approaching official censure—possibly because she was a layperson, possibly because she was a woman. Indeed, Day appears to have mimed Teresa of Avila by downplaying her theological credentials as a means of sidestepping ecclesiastical scrutiny—although one may detect a muted sarcasm buried beneath her intellectual self-deprecation.[25] The Lacouture retreat afforded her an opportunity to digest the rigorous ethic of self-renunciation that she espoused in her writing and the Catholic Worker's variation on the Works of Mercy. In Day's mind, the Catholic Worker was distinguished—perhaps above all else—by its interior prayer life, and the retreat was its heartbeat. Although this formed a point of conflict within the larger community, Day's own subjectivity was critically shaped by Lacouture, Roy, Hugo, Farina, and a small battalion of other spiritual directors who espoused the extreme self-abnegation embedded in the Christian vocation to be a sign of contradiction. Through them, she absorbed the perfectionist mandate to do all things in God's name, purify supernatural motives, oppose the impulse to fashion idols out of temporal phenomena; to quietly and patiently (if not always cheerfully) endure bouts of suffering, and pattern oneself on an exigent reading of the Sermon on the Mount—which Day called a "manifesto" for all Catholics, but in an exceptional way for the Catholic Worker.[26]

In the development of Lacouturisme, Hugo contributed both an activist sensibility and a high estimation of lay spiritual potential. Inspired by

Pius XI's vision of prayer's evangelical dimensions, Hugo morphed the Lacouture retreat into a spiritual wellspring for revolutionary social action.[27] Personal holiness continued to be a central focus of the retreat, but Hugo combined this with an exacting political sensibility. It was even further politicized through his merger with Dorothy Day, who spoke of the Catholic Worker's apostolate in non-utilitarian terms as a form of witness.[28] This commitment to impracticality, as expression of the Folly of the Cross, became a signature characteristic of Catholic Worker activism. In both Québec and the United States, the self-consciously countercultural, deocentric focus of Lacouturite theology aggressively called on Catholics to reject secular propriety and assimilation. The retreat's iconoclastic enthusiasm drew the ire of powerful mainstream critics, and the movement threatened to implode under the weight of the vitriolic—and often unbecoming—conflict. However, its formative role in Day's spiritual development marginally rehabilitated Lacouturism's good standing, while conversely casting a vague shadow of heterodoxy over the Worker's theological reputation. This phantom heresy, born out of Québécois cultural revivalism and the Catholic mystical tradition, produced some very precious fruit throughout its southward migration, not the least being its evolution into a spiritual combustion engine for Dorothy Day's maximalist practical theology.

Notes

Introduction: Conversion and Catholic Pacifism

1. Mark Zwick and Louise Zwick, *The Catholic Worker Movement: Intellectual and Spiritual Origins* (New York: Paulist Press, 2005), 234. See also, Dorothy Day, "Day after Day," *Catholic Worker*, September, 1941, 1, 3. Cf. William D. Miller, *A Harsh and Dreadful Love: Dorothy Day and the Catholic Worker Movement* (New York: Liveright, 1973); *Dorothy Day: A Biography* (San Francisco: Harper and Row, 1982); *All Is Grace: The Spirituality of Dorothy Day* (Garden City, NY: Doubleday, 1987).

2. John J. Hugo interviewed by William Miller, Pittsburgh, 1976, W-9, box 2, folder 2, Dorothy Day–Catholic Worker Collection, Memorial Library, Marquette University, Milwaukee, WI.

3. Ibid.

4. Joseph T. McNicholas, "A Mighty League," *Catholic Worker*, April, 1938, 1.

5. Jerome Oetgen, *Mission to America: A History of Saint Vincent Archabbey, the First Benedictine Monastery in the United States* (Washington, DC: Catholic University of America Press, 2000).

6. John J. Hugo, *Your Ways Are Not My Ways*, vol. 1 (Pittsburgh, PA: Encounter with Silence), 55–56.

> Why did I become a priest? I wonder how many priests could give a really definite answer to that question; perhaps only the unhappy priests, spoken of above, who thought they were being pushed into it. . . . To explain this, I fall back on the word "attraction," used by older spiritual writers, that is to say, the attraction of god's grace or, better, of God Himself. That makes sense; after all, marriages begin in an attraction that grows until it becomes irresistible. Dorothy Day, in her autobiography, speaks of being haunted by God even in her unlikely girlhood. I recall no such experience, although God was always high and bright in my universe, but like a distant star. . . . If I may use a figure, it would be a magnet, subtle, at first almost unfelt, but growing in force until it became all but overpowering. So perhaps it is simpler and truer just to compare it to falling in love. And genuine love, of whatever kind, exacts a high price.

7. Hugo interviewed by Miller in Pittsburgh, 1976.

8. Judith Butler, *Frames of War: When Is Life Grievable?* (New York: Verso, 2009), 167.

9. Walter Benjamin, "On the Concept of History," in *Selected Writings*, ed. Howard Eiland and Michael W. Jennings, vol. 4, *1938–1940* (Cambridge, MA: Belknap Press, 2003), 392. See also, David Carroll Cochran, *Catholic Realism and the Abolition of War* (Maryknoll, NY: Orbis Books, 2014).

10. Robert A. Orsi, *Between Heaven and Earth: The Religious Worlds People Make and the Scholars Who Study Them* (Princeton, NJ: Princeton University Press, 2005).

11. Hugo, *Your Ways Are Not My Ways*, vol. 1, 14.

12. Zwick and Zwick, *The Catholic Worker Movement*, 75, 97, 177.

13. Nicholas Berdyaev, *The Bourgeois Mind and Other Essays* (Freeport, NY: Books for Libraries Press, 1966), 13.

14. Quoted in Zwick and Zwick, *The Catholic Worker Movement*, 90–91.

15. Emmanuel Levinas, "Ethics as First Philosophy," in *The Levinas Reader*, ed. Seán Hand (Cambridge, MA: Basil Blackwell, 1989), 83–84.

16. Rosalie G. Riegle, *Dorothy Day: Portraits by Those Who Knew Her* (Maryknoll, NY: Orbis Books, 2003), 64. See also, John T. McGreevy, *Catholicism and American Freedom: A History* (New York: W. W. Norton, 2003), 142–45.

17. Robert Coles, *Dorothy Day: A Radical Devotion* (Reading, MA: Addison-Wesley Publishing, 1987), 111.

18. Dorothy Day, "The Scandal of the Works of Mercy," *Commonweal*, November 4, 1949, 99.

19. Ibid. See also, Coles, *Dorothy Day*, 111.

20. Robert A. Orsi, "U.S. Catholics between Memory and Modernity: How Catholics Are American," in *Catholics in the American Century: Recasting Narratives of U.S. History*, ed. R. Scott Appleby and Kathleen Sprows Cummings (Ithaca, NY: Cornell University Press, 2012), 16.

21. Bruno Latour, *We Have Never Been Modern* (Cambridge, MA: Harvard University Press, 1993), 10–12. Although Latour pairs this with a concomitant, albeit apparently contradictory, process of translation or mediation.

22. Norman Sykes, review of *Enthusiasm: A Chapter in the History of Religion with Special Reference to the XVII and XVIII Centuries*, by Ronald A. Knox, *Journal of Theological Studies* 2, no. 2 (1951): 215.

23. Knox, *Enthusiasm*, v–vi.

24. Ibid., 584.

25. Ibid., 584.

26. Jeffrey Jerome Cohen, *Monster Theory: Reading Culture* (Minneapolis: University of Minnesota Press, 1996).

27. Paul Hanly Furfey, *The Respectable Murderers: Social Evil and Christian Conscience* (New York: Herder and Herder, 1966).

28. Leon Hooper has highlighted this historical peculiarity in some of his research. J. Leon Hooper, "Murray and Day: A Common Enemy, a Common Cause?," *U.S. Catholic Historian* 24, no. 1 (Winter 2006): 45–61.

29. Brenna Moore, *Sacred Dread: Raïssa Maritain, the Allure of Suffering, and the French Catholic Revival, 1905–1944* (Notre Dame, IN: University of Notre Dame Press, 2013).

30. R. Scott Appleby, *"Church and Age Unite!": The Modernist Impulse in American Catholicism* (Notre Dame, IN: University of Notre Dame Press, 1992), 9. Jeffrey Jerome Cohen, "Monster Culture (Seven Theses)," in *Monster Theory*, 3–25.

31. Latour, *We Have Never Been Modern*, 10.

32. Robert A. Orsi, "Everyday Religion and the Contemporary World: The Un-Modern, or What Was Supposed to Have Disappeared but Did Not," in *Ordinary Lives and Grand Schemes: An Anthropology of Everyday Religion*, ed. Samuli Schielke and Liza Debevec (New York: Berghahn Books, 2012), 157.

33. Paula Kane, *Sister Thorn and Catholic Mysticism in Modern America* (Chapel Hill: University of North Carolina Press, 2013), 192–93. See also Stephen Schloesser, *Jazz Age Catholicism: Mystic Modernism in Postwar Paris, 1919–1933* (Toronto: University of Toronto Press, 2005), and Svetlana Boym, *The Future of Nostalgia* (New York: Basic Books, 2001).

34. David J. O'Brien, *Public Catholicism* (New York: Macmillan, 1989); James T. Fisher, *The Catholic Counterculture in America, 1933–1962* (Chapel Hill: University of North Carolina Press, 1989).

35. Dorothy Day, "We Are Un-American: We Are Catholics," *Catholic Worker*, April, 1948, 2. See also, Fisher, *The Catholic Counterculture*, 72.

36. David J. O'Brien, "The Pilgrimage of Dorothy Day," *Commonweal*, December 19, 1980, 711.

37. My thoughts regarding the use of this term are owed to Daniel Colucciello Barber, *On Diaspora: Christianity, Religion and Secularity* (Eugene, OR: Cascade Books, 2011).

38. George Yancy, "Looking at Whiteness: Tarrying with the Embedded and Opaque White Racist Self," in *Look, a White!: Philosophical Essays on Whiteness* (Philadelphia: Temple University Press, 2012), 156. George Yancy has nuanced that the declarative statement is necessarily itself performative, or constitutive of the substance contained in the declaration. Yancy's work focused on white privilege and anti-blackness as an example, a white person declaring that they are antiracist is not necessarily, in and of itself, an antiracist act, and does not thereby make that person one of the "good whites"—an antiracist. Similarly, just saying one is anti-modern does not make it so, and it may be worth considering

if even the process of such a declaration is itself a deeply contemporary practice.

39. William M. Halsey, *The Survival of American Innocence: American Catholicism in an Era of Disillusionment, 1920–1940* (Notre Dame, IN: University of Notre Dame Press, 1980).

40. Dan McKanan, *The Catholic Worker after Dorothy: Practicing the Works of Mercy in a New Generation* (Collegeville, MN: Liturgical Press, 2008), 19.

41. It is worth noting that while Miller's groundbreaking writings on Day are a treasure trove of information, often gleaned directly from sources no longer living, and therefore invaluable to *Catholic Worker* historians, factual errors abound in his work, and his distaste for citations make much legwork for anyone interested in doing their due diligence. Jim Forest's recent revised biography is an excellent, very meticulously researched text, that should at least serve as a reference when using Miller, but is a wonderful, highly illustrated, and enlightening read on its own and shows Day not just in her later years, which—and this is just a hypothesis—in our ageist culture, often serves to blunt her radicalism by aesthetically diminishing her strength. Jim Forest, *All Is Grace: A Biography of Dorothy Day* (Maryknoll, NY: Orbis Books, 2011).

42. Paula M. Kane, "'She Offered Herself Up': The Victim Soul and Victim Spirituality in Catholicism," *Church History* 71, no. 1 (March 2002): 101–2.

43. Kenneth L. Woodward, *Making Saints: How the Catholic Church Determines Who Becomes a Saint, Who Doesn't, and Why* (New York: Touchstone, 1996), 36.

44. Benjamin Peters, *John Hugo and an American Catholic Theology of Nature and Grace* (PhD diss., University of Dayton), 2011. Charles Strauss's work has yet to be published but is taking shape in some fascinating directions, so I await it with great anticipation.

1. *Canadien* Identity, Nationalism, and Muscular Catholicism

1. Gregory Baum, *The Church in Quebec* (Ottawa: Novalis, 1991), and David Martin, *A General Theory of Secularization* (New York: Harper & Row, 1978).

2. Jacques Lacoursière and Robin Philpot, *A People's History of Quebec* (Montréal: Baraka Books, 2009), 39–40.

3. Ibid., 71.

4. Ibid., 70–71.

5. Ibid., 73–74.

6. Ibid., 108.

7. Terence J. Fay, *A History of Canadian Catholics: Gallicanism, Romanism, and Canadianism* (Montréal: McGill-Queen's University Press, 2002), 81. See also, Jay P. Dolan, *The American Catholic Experience: A History from Colonial Times to the Present* (Garden City, NY: Doubleday, 1985), 436.

8. Lacoursière and Philpot, *A People's History of Quebec*, 121.

9. "Laurentie" was the poetic name given to an imaginary independent Québec by contemporary secessionists. Max Nemni and Monique Nemni, *Young Trudeau: Song of Quebec, Father of Canada, 1919–1944* (Toronto: McClelland & Steward, 2006), 73.

10. Ibid., 62.

11. John English, *Citizen of the World: The Life of Pierre Elliott Trudeau*, vol. 1, *1919–1968* (Toronto: Vintage Canada, 2007), 29.

12. E.-Martin Meunier and Jean-Philippe Warren, *Sortir de la "Grande noirceur": L'horizon "personnaliste" de la Révolution tranquille* (Sillery, Québec: Les Éditions du Septentrion, 2002), 33.

13. Gauvreau, *The Catholic Origins of Quebec's Quiet Revolution, 1931–1970* (Montréal: McGill-Queen's University Press, 2005), 32.

14. Ibid., 25.

15. Nemni and Nemni, *Young Trudeau*, 64–65.

16. Baum, *The Church in Quebec*, 28.

17. Gauvreau, *The Catholic Origins of Quebec's Quiet Revolution*, 15.

18. Ibid., 16.

19. Nemni and Nemni, *Young Trudeau*, 96. See also, John Hellman, *Emmanuel Mounier and the New Catholic Left, 1930–1950* (Toronto: University of Toronto Press, 1981).

20. Gauvreau, *The Catholic Origins of Quebec's Quiet Revolution*, 27.

21. Ibid., 43.

22. Mason Wade, *The French Canadians* (Toronto: Macmillan, 1955), 863–65.

23. Kevin J. Christiano, "The Trajectory of Catholicism in Twentieth-Century Quebec," in *The Church Confronts Modernity: Catholicism Since 1950 in the United States, Ireland, and Quebec*, edited by Leslie Woodcock Tentler (Washington, DC: Catholic University of America Press, 2007), 45.

24. Wade, *The French Canadians*, 1. See also, Lionel Groulx, *Notre Maître, le Passé* (Montréal: Granger frères, 1936).

25. Garth Stevenson, "The Politics of Remembrance in Irish and Quebec Nationalism," *Canadian Journal of Political Science / Revue canadienne de science politique* 37, no. 4 (December 2004): 907.

26. Lionel Groulx quoted in Wade, *The French Canadians*, 871.

27. Osman Bilen, *The Historicity of Understanding and the Problem of Relativism in Gadamer's Philosophical Hermeneutics* (Washington, DC: Council for Research in Values and Philosophy, 2000), 55. See also, Hans-Georg Gadamer, "On the Circle of Understanding," in *Hermeneutics versus Science?: Three German Views*, edited by John M. Connolly and Thomas Keutner (Notre Dame, IN: University of Notre Dame Press, 1988), 72–74.

28. Lionel Groulx quoted in Wade, *The French Canadians*, 874. See also, J. R. Miller, *Reflections on Native-Newcomer Relations: Selected Essays* (Toronto: University of Toronto Press, 2004), 875, and Olivar Asselin, *L'oeuvre de l'abbé Groulx* (Montréal: Bibliothèque de l'Action française, 1923), 62–63.

29. Robert Bothwell, ed., *Canada and Quebec: One Country, Two Histories* (Vancouver: University of British Columbia Press, 1998), 79.

30. Michael D. Behiels, *Prelude to Quebec's Quiet Revolution: Liberalism versus Neo-nationalism, 1945–1960* (Montréal: McGill-Queen's University Press, 1985), 26.

31. Nemni and Nemni, *Young Trudeau*, 73.

32. Janet Ajzenstat, "Liberalism and Nationality," *Canadian Journal of Political Science / Revue canadienne de science politique* 14, no. 3 (September 1981): 607.

33. Marcel Fournier, "Quebec Sociology and Quebec Society: The Construction of a Collective Identity," *Canadian Journal of Sociology / Cahiers canadiens de sociologie* 26, no. 3 (Summer 2001): 338.

34. Bothwell, *Canada and Quebec*, 28.

35. Everett C. Hughes, "The French-English Margin in Canada," *American Journal of Sociology* 39, no. 1 (July 1933): 9–10, and Behiels, *Prelude to Quebec's Quiet Revolution*, 3.

36. John C. Super, "'Rerum Novarum' in Mexico and Quebec," *Revista de Historia de América* 126 (January-June 2000): 72–73.

37. Stevenson, "The Politics of Remembrance in Irish and Quebec Nationalism," 917–18.

38. Lower, "New France in New England," 280.

39. Lucia Ferretti, *Brève histoire de l'Église catholique au Québec* (Montréal: Boréal, 2000), 102.

40. Mark A. Noll, *A History of Christianity in the United States and Canada* (Grand Rapids, MI: W. B. Eerdmans, 1992), 255.

41. Francis Parkman, *The Old Régime in Canada*, vol. 2 (Boston: Little, Brown, and Company, 1902), 203–4.

42. Gregory Baum, "Comparing Post–World War II Catholicism in Quebec, Ireland, and the United States," in *The Church Confronts Modernity: Catholicism Since 1950 in the United States, Ireland, and Quebec*, ed. Leslie Woodcock Tentler (Washington, DC: Catholic University of America Press, 2007), 269.

43. Leslie Woodcock Tentler, introduction to *The Church Confronts Modernity: Catholicism Since 1950 in the United States, Ireland, and Quebec*, ed. Leslie Woodcock Tentler (Washington, DC: Catholic University of America Press, 2007), 5.

44. Wilfrid Laurier quoted in Lacoursière and Philpot, *A People's History of Quebec*, 124.

45. Desmond Bowen, *Paul Cardinal Cullen and the Shaping of Modern Irish Catholicism* (Dublin: Gill and Macmillan, 1983), 269–70.

46. Asselin, *L'oeuvre de l'abbé Groulx*, 54–55. See also, Wade, *The French Canadians*, 38.

47. Thomas Flanagan, *Louis 'David' Riel: 'Prophet of the New World'* (Toronto: University of Toronto Press, 1996), 3.

48. Fay, *A History of Canadian Catholics*, 48.

49. Yvan Lamonde, *Histoire Sociale des Idées au Québec (1896–1929)*, vol. 2 (Montréal: Les Éditions Fides, 2004), 57.

50. Peter L. Berger, *The Sacred Canopy: Elements of a Sociological Theory of Religion* (Garden City, NY: Doubleday, 1967), 45.

51. Fay, *A History of Canadian Catholics*, 77.

52. Ibid., 77–78.

53. Ibid., 78.

54. Wade, *The French Canadians*, 4.

55. Lower, "New France in New England," 279.

56. Louis Riel, *The Collected Writings of Louis Riel*, ed. George F. G. Stanley (Edmonton: University of Alberta Press, 1985), 52–56. See also, Flanagan, *Louis 'David' Riel.*

57. Ferretti, *Brève histoire de l'Église catholique au Québec*, 102.

58. Tentler, *The Church Confronts Modernity*, 7. See also, Hughes, "The French-English Margin in Canada," 5.

59. Hughes, "The French-English Margin in Canada," 2.

60. Susan Mann, *The Dream of Nation: A Social and Intellectual History of Quebec* (Montréal: McGill-Queen's University Press, 2002), 223–24.

61. Ramsay Cook quoted in Bothwell, *Canada and Quebec*, 42. See also, John Dickinson and Brian Young, *A Short History of Quebec*, 4th ed. (Montréal: McGill-Queen's University Press, 2008), 231.

62. Villeneuve quoted in Lacoursière and Philpot, *A People's History of Quebec*, 152.

63. Dickinson and Young, *A Short History of Quebec*, 239.

64. Fay, *A History of Canadian Catholics*, 109.

65. Arthur Silver quoted in Bothwell, *Canada and Quebec*, xxiv.

66. Behiels quoted in Bothwell, *Canada and Quebec*, 85.

67. Jean Hamelin and Nicole Gagnon, *Histoire du catholicisme québécois: Le XXe siècle*, vol. 1, *1898–1940* (Montréal: Boréal Express, 1984), 32.

68. Lower, "New France in New England," 284.

69. Lacoursière and Philpot, *A People's History of Quebec*, 121.

70. Lower, "New France in New England," 285.

71. Lower, "New France in New England," 294–95.

72. Pierre Savard, *Jules-Paul Tardivel, la France et les États-Unis: 1851–1905* (Québec: Les presses de l'Université Laval, 1967), 207.

73. Ibid., 217.

74. Savard, *Jules-Paul Tardivel*, 220.

75. Dickinson and Young, *A Short History of Quebec*, 274–75.

76. Lamonde, *Histoire Sociale des Idées au Québec*, 34.

77. Wade, *The French Canadians*, 865.

78. Peter Gay, *Modernism: The Lure of Heresy, From Baudelaire to Beckett and Beyond* (New York: W. W. Norton, 2008), 70.

79. Silver quoted in Bothwell, *Canada and Quebec*, 69.

80. Lamonde, *Histoire Sociale des Idées au Québec*, 33.

81. Robert J. Brym and Rhonda L. Lenton, "The Distribution of Anti-Semitism in Canada in 1984," *Canadian Journal of Sociology / Cahiers canadiens de sociologie* 16, no. 4 (Autumn 1991): 413–14.

82. Super, "'Rerum Novarum' in Mexico and Quebec," 78–79.

83. Wade, *The French Canadians*, 351–52.

84. Silver quoted in Bothwell, *Canada and Quebec*, xv.

85. Ibid., xv.

86. Jules-Paul Tardivel, *"Pour la patrie": An 1895 Religious and Separatist Vision of Quebec in the Mid-Twentieth Century* (Toronto: University of Toronto Press, 1975), 33.

87. Silver quoted in Bothwell, *Canada and Quebec*, xv.

88. Savard, *Jules-Paul Tardivel*, 281–82 (*La Vérité*, November 24, 1894).

89. Le Docteur Bataille, *Le Diable au XIXe Siècle: La franc-maçonnerie Luciférienne* (Paris: Delhomme and Briguet, 1893).

90. Savard, *Jules-Paul Tardivel*, 275. See also, R. A. Gilbert in Edward A. Waite, *Devil-Worship in France, with Diana Vaughn and the Question of Modern Palladism* (York Beach, ME: Red Wheel/Weiser, 2003), xii–xiii.

91. Bataille, *Le Diable au XIXe Siècle*, 27.

92. Ibid., 36–37.

93. Pope Leo XIII, *Inimica vis* (December 8, 1892), 9. http://www.vatican.va/holy_father/leo_xiii/encyclicals/documents/hf_l-xiii_enc_08121892_inimica-vis_en.html.

94. Waite, *Devil-Worship in France*, 143.

95. Savard, *Jules-Paul Tardivel*, 300–1.

96. R. A. Gilbert quoted in Waite, *Devil-Worship in France*, ix.

97. Richard Hofstadter, *The Paranoid Style in American Politics and Other Essays* (Cambridge, MA: Harvard University Press, 1996).

98. Fay, *A History of Canadian Catholics*, 136.

99. Ibid., 136–37.

100. Mark S. Massa, SJ, *Anti-Catholicism in America: The Last Acceptable Prejudice* (New York: Crossroad, 2003), 22–23.

101. Lacoursière and Philpot, *A People's History of Quebec*, 134.

102. Michael Gauvreau, *The Catholic Origins of Quebec's Quiet Revolution, 1931–1970* (Montréal: McGill-Queen's University Press, 2005), 20.

103. Kevin J. Christiano quoted in Tentler, *The Church Confronts Modernity*, 21.

> In the space of little more than fifty years, between the end of the Second World War and the close of the twentieth century, the Canadian province of Quebec went from being one of the most socially traditional, politically conservative, and religiously devout regions of the developed world to one of the least.

104. Ibid., 44.

105. English, *Citizen of the World*.

106. Nemni and Nemni, *Young Trudeau*, 16.

107. Ibid., 31.

108. Trudeau quoted in Nemni and Nemni, *Young Trudeau*, 49.

109. Super, "'Rerum Novarum' in Mexico and Quebec," 77–78. See also, Wade, *The French Canadians*, 37.

110. Behiels, *Prelude to Quebec's Quiet Revolution*, 21–22. See also, Gauvreau, *The Catholic Origins of Quebec's Quiet Revolution*, 53.

111. Behiels, *Prelude to Quebec's Quiet Revolution*, 21–22. See also, Baum, *The Church in Quebec*, 18–19.

112. Wade, *The French Canadians*, 781.

113. English, *Citizen of the World*, 47.

114. Fay, *A History of Canadian Catholics*, 156.

115. Michel Bock, "Dix utopies qui ont forgé le Québec—Lionel Groulx, à la recherche d'une mystique national," *Le Devoir*, August 8, 2005. See also, Lionel Groulx, *Orientations* (Montréal: Éditions du Zodiaque, 1935), 266–67. Translated in Nemni and Nemni, *Young Trudeau*, 61–62. http://www.ledevoir.com/non-classe/87773/dix-utopies-qui-ont-forge-le-quebec-lionel-groulx-a-la-recherche-d-une-mystique-nationale.

116. Mann, *The Dream of Nation*, 219.

117. Hamelin and Gagnon, *Histoire du catholicisme Québécois*, 419. Full text is available online at: http://faculty.marianopolis.edu/c.belanger/quebechistory/docs/1930s/Manifestedelajeunegeneration-LesJeune-Canada-HistoireduQuebec.htm. An English translation of the *Manifesto of the Young Generation* is available in Ramsay Cook and Michael Behiels, eds., *The Essential Laurendeau* (Vancouver: Copp Clark, 1976), 34–36.

118. Super, "'Rerum Novarum' in Mexico and Quebec," 80.

119. Dickinson and Young, *A Short History of Quebec*, 198. See also, Wade, *The French Canadians*, 885.

120. Behiels, *Prelude to Quebec's Quiet Revolution*, 9.

121. Blair Fraser, "Labor and the Church in Quebec," *Foreign Affairs* 28, no. 2 (January 1950): 247.

122. Fraser, "Labor and the Church in Quebec," 249.

123. Lacoursière and Philpot, *A People's History of Quebec*, 157.

124. Fraser, "Labor and the Church in Quebec," 250.

125. Philippe Desranleau quoted in Fraser, "Labor and the Church in Quebec," 248–49.

126. English, *Citizen of the World*, 203.

127. Fraser, "Labor and the Church in Quebec," 254.

128. Stevenson, "The Politics of Remembrance in Irish and Quebec Nationalism," 922.

129. Christiano quoted in Tentler, *The Church Confronts Modernity*, 55. See also, Fraser, "Labor and the Church in Quebec," 249.

2. Onésime Lacouture and Conversion in the White Desert

1. Anselme Longpré, *Un mouvement spirituel au Québec (1931–1962): Un retour à l'Évangile* (Montréal: Fides, 1976), 8–9.

2. Lacouture, *Mon séjour en Alaska*, 12. See also, Karl Strauch, *La Thème de la "folie de la Croix" dans l'œuvre du Père Onésime Lacouture (1881–1951)* (Montréal: Cahiers Scivias, 1998), 22.

3. Lacouture, *Mon séjour en Alaska*, 13.

4. Kane, *Sister Thorn*, 234. See also, Michael Freze, SFO, *They Bore the Wounds of Christ: The Mystery of the Sacred Stigmata* (Huntington, IN: Our Sunday Visitor, 1989), 274–76, and Onesime Alfred Boyer, *She Wears a Crown of Thorns* (New York: Benziger Bros., 1949).

5. Hugo, *Your Ways Are Not My Ways*, vol. 1, 285.

6. Lacouture, *Mon séjour en Alaska*, 13–14.

7. Ibid., 14.

8. Augustine of Hippo, *The Confessions*, trans. Maria Boulding, OSB (New York: Random House, 1998), x.6.8, 2.

9. Lacouture, *Mon séjour en Alaska*, 108.

10. Ibid., 15.

11. Peter McDonough, *Men Astutely Trained: A History of the Jesuits in the American Century* (New York: Free Press, 1992), 146–47.

12. Hugo, *Your Ways Are Not My Ways*, vol. 1, 288.

13. Ibid., 32.

14. Patrick W. Carey, *Avery Cardinal Dulles, SJ: A Model Theologian* (Mahwah, NJ: Paulist Press, 2010), 95.

> Like many of the Jesuit novitiates in the United States, it was situated in a bucolic setting, far removed from city life. The rural atmosphere, the rolling hills and fertile fields, the beauty of the Hudson River Valley, the quiet, and the slow pace of life that mirrored the rhythms of nature provided an ideal atmosphere for an introduction to a religious way of life that had its own regular cycle of prayer, study, manual labor, exercise, recreation, and rest.

15. McDonough, *Men Astutely Trained*, 149.

16. Thomas Cahill, *How the Irish Saved Civilization: The Untold Story of Ireland's Heroic Role from the Fall of Rome to the Rise of Medieval Europe* (New York: Doubleday, 1995).

17. Dorothy Day, *The Long Loneliness* (New York: HarperCollins, 1952), 59.

18. Augustine, *The Confessions*, i.1.1, 3.

19. William James, *The Varieties of Religious Experience* (New York: Modern Library, 1999), 79, 414. See also, Knox, *Enthusiasm*, 8, and Francis W. Newman, *The Soul, Its Sorrows and Its Aspirations* (London: J. Chapman, 1852), 89, 91.

20. James, *The Varieties of Religious Experience*, 163.

21. Ibid., 94.

22. Ibid., 101.

23. Ibid., 167, 159–60.

24. Thomas T. McAvoy, *The Americanist Heresy in Roman Catholicism, 1895–1900* (Notre Dame, IN: University of Notre Dame Press, 1963).

25. Lacouture, *Mon séjour en Alaska*, 88.

26. Ibid., 57–58.

27. John W. O'Malley, SJ, *The First Jesuits* (Cambridge, MA: Harvard University Press, 1993), 30. See also, Melbournensis, "St. Francis Xavier," *Irish Monthly* 9, no. 97 (July 1881): 338.

28. Lacouture, *Mon séjour en Alaska*, 6–7.

29. Paul Giles, *American Catholic Arts and Fictions: Culture, Ideology, Aesthetics* (New York: Cambridge University Press, 1992), 28.

30. David Tracy, *The Analogical Imagination: Christian Theology and the Culture of Pluralism* (New York: Crossroad, 1981), 412–15.

31. Woodward, *Making Saints*, 397.

32. Lacouture, *Mon séjour en Alaska*, 8–10.

33. Marjorie Reeves, *The Influence of Prophecy in the Later Middle Ages: A Study in Joachimism* (South Bend, IN: University of Notre Dame Press, 1993), 16.

34. Bernard McGinn, *Apocalyptic Spirituality: Treatises and Letters of Lactantius, Adso of Monier-en-Der, Joachim of Fiore, the Spiritual Franciscans, Savonarola*

(New York: Paulist Press, 1979), 105. See also, E. Randolph Daniel, "The Double Procession of the Holy Spirit in Joachim of Fiore's Understanding of History," *Speculum* 55, no. 3 (July 1980): 469–83.

35. Lacouture, *Mon séjour en Alaska*, 88.

36. Hugo, *Your Ways Are Not My Ways*, vol. 1, 288–89.

37. Lacouture, *Mon séjour en Alaska*, 4–5.

38. Ibid., 87.

39. Hugo, *Your Ways Are Not My Ways*, vol. 1, 199–200.

40. Ibid., 293.

41. Ibid., 292–93.

42. Mary Annette Pember, "The Last Orphans of Holy Cross," *Indian Country Today Media Network*, February 6, 2014, http://indiancountrytodaymedianetwork.com/2014/02/06/last-orphans-holy-cross-153438?page=0%2C0.

43. Lacouture, *Mon séjour en Alaska*, 84, 118.

44. Ibid., 23.

45. Ibid., 32.

46. Ibid., 96.

47. Ibid., 95.

48. Ibid., 57.

49. Ibid., 128.

50. Kallistos Ware, "The Way of the Ascetics: Negative or Affirmative?," in *Asceticism*, ed. Vincent L. Wimbush and Richard Valantasis (New York: Oxford University Press, 1998), 44.

51. John of the Cross, "The Dark Night," in *The Collected Works of St. John of the Cross*, trans. Kieran Kavanaugh, OCD, and Otilio Rodriguez, OCD (Washington, DC: ICS Publications, 1991), 386.

52. Gillian Clark, "Women and Asceticism in Late Antiquity: The Refusal of Status and Gender," in *Asceticism*, 44.

53. Kieran Kavanaugh, OCD, "Spanish Sixteenth Century: Carmel and Surrounding Movements," in *Christian Spirituality: Post-Reformation and Modern*, ed. Louis Dupré, Don E. Saliers, and John Meyendorff (New York: Crossroad, 1987), 82–83.

54. John of the Cross, "The Dark Night," 416–17.

55. Jean Orcibal, *Saint Jean de la Croix et les mystiques rhéno-flamands* (Bruges, Belgium: Desclée de Brouwer, 1966), 177.

56. James J. Buckley, "On Being a Symbol: An Appraisal of Karl Rahner," *Theological Studies* 40, no. 3 (September 1979): 453–73.

57. Bernard McGinn, *The Growth of Mysticism: Gregory the Great through the 12th Century* (New York: Crossroad, 2007), 326–27. McGinn distinguishes between spiritual visions and "mysticism" proper. While both categories claim "to have had contact with the divine realm in special ways not available through

the ordinary sacramental and liturgical channels,"(327) and there is considerable overlap between the two, the relationship is not one-to-one (i.e., not every visionary is a mystic, and vice versa).

58. Lacouture, *Mon séjour en Alaska*, 104.

59. John of the Cross, "The Spiritual Canticle," in *The Collected Works of St. John of the Cross*, 472. See also, Luis M. Girón-Negrón, "Dionysian Thought in Sixteenth-Century Spanish Mystical Theology," in *Re-Thinking Dionysius the Areopagite*, ed. Sarah Coakley and Charles M. Stang (Malden, MA: Wiley-Blackwell, 2009), 169–73, and Michael A. Sells, *Mystical Languages of Unsaying* (Chicago: University of Chicago Press, 1994), 215.

60. John of the Cross, "The Dark Night," 436.

61. Hugo, *Your Ways Are Not My Ways*, vol. 1, 293.

62. Augustine of Hippo, *On Christian Teaching*, trans. R. P. H. Green (New York: Oxford University Press, 1997) i.xxvii, 21.

63. Augustine, *The Confessions*, vii.3.4, 123–24.

64. Ibid., 202.

65. Bernard of Clairvaux, "On Loving God," in *Bernard of Clairvaux: Selected Works*, trans. G. R. Evans (New York: Paulist Press, 1987), 204.

66. Benedicta Ward, SLG, "The New Orders," in *The Study of Spirituality*, ed. Cheslyn Jones, Geoffrey Wainwright, and Edward Yarnold, SJ (New York: Oxford University Press, 1986), 288.

67. McGinn, *The Growth of Mysticism*, 219.

> Ordered love, then, means not that we have to choose *between* God and creatures, or to reject totally the body and the material world, but rather that we need to put all our affections and desires in the proper relation. Whether or not we think that Bernard and his twelfth-century contemporaries, with the deep ambivalences of their views about materiality and the body, managed to create a consistent and viable order of love, we cannot deny how hard they struggled to attain this ideal.

68. Ibid., 163.

69. Lacouture, *Mon séjour en Alaska*, 98–99.

70. Ibid., 131.

71. Ibid., 121.

72. Ibid., 125.

73. Ibid., 126.

74. Barbara Newman, *God and the Goddesses: Vision, Poetry, and Belief in the Middle Ages* (Philadelphia: University of Pennsylvania Press, 2003), 295.

75. Lacouture, *Mon séjour en Alaska*, 130.

76. Lacouture, *Mon séjour en Alaska*, 140.

3. Onésime Lacouture and the "Return to the Gospel"

1. Lacouture, *Mon séjour en Alaska*, 153.

2. Hugo, *Your Ways Are Not My Ways*, 294.

3. Longpré, *Un mouvement spirituel au Québec*, 18.

4. Hugo, *Your Ways Are Not My Ways*, 295.

5. Ibid., 296.

6. Longpré, *Un mouvement spirituel au Québec*, 18.

7. Hugo, *Your Ways Are Not My Ways*, 297.

8. Ibid., 197–98.

9. Longpré, *Un mouvement spirituel au Québec*, 18.

10. Longpré, *Un mouvement spirituel au Québec*, 23.

11. Ibid., 25–26.

12. Onésime Lacouture, SJ, *Mes retraites, première série: Doctrine Surnaturelle pour se défaire de toute mentalité païenne* (Québec: Éditions Scivias, 1998), 5.

13. Longpré, *Un mouvement spirituel au Québec*, 8.

14. Onésime Lacouture, "Are Creatures Dung . . . . or Dessert?" (AJC [BO-0167-1,1], 24 November 1941), 10.

15. Lacouture, *Mes retraites*, 145.

16. Longpré, *Un mouvement spirituel au Québec*, 26–27.

17. 1 Cor. 1:17–29.

18. H. Richard Niebuhr, *Christ and Culture* (New York: HarperCollins, 2001), 117.

19. Knox, *Enthusiasm*, 580–81.

20. Strauch, *Le thème de la "folie de la Croix,"* 99.

21. Ibid., 100. See also, Lacouture, *Mes retraites*, 160.

22. Lacouture, *Mes retraites*, 55. Blaise Pascal, *Pensées*, trans. A. J. Krailsheimer (New York: Penguin Books, 1995), 43.

23. Lacouture, *Mes retraites*, 22.

24. Augustine of Hippo, *On Christian Teaching*, 25–26.

25. Ron Highfield, "The Freedom to Say 'No'? Karl Rahner's Doctrine of Sin," *Theological Studies* 56 (1995): 495.

26. John of the Cross, "The Dark Night," in *The Collected Works of St. John of the Cross*, 366.

27. Lacouture, *Mes retraites*, 71–72.

28. Ibid., 405.

29. Matt. 6:5–8.

30. Lacouture, *Mes retraites*, 408.

31. Augustine of Hippo, *The Confessions*, 7.

32. Lacouture, *Mes retraites*, 133.

33. Ibid., 136–37.

34. Ibid., 137.

35. Ibid., 70–71.

36. Ibid., 131–33.

37. Ibid., 119, 150.

38. Peter Brown, *The Body and Society: Men, Women, and Sexual Renunciation in Early Christianity* (New York: Columbia University Press, 1988), 411.

39. Lacouture, *Mes retraites*, 97.

40. Ibid., 75.

41. Ibid., 39.

42. Richard Valantasis, "A Theory of the Social Function of Asceticism," in *Asceticism*, eds. Vincent L. Wimbush and Richard Valantasis (New York: Oxford University Press, 1998), 548. See also, Richard Schechner, "Magnitude of Performance," in *The Anthropology of Experience*, eds. Victor W. Turner and Edward M. Bruner (Urbana: University of Illinois Press, 1986), 345.

43. Lacouture, *Mes retraites*, 419.

44. Ibid., 264. Heb. 12:1–8.

45. Lacouture, *Mes retraites*, 264, 266.

46. Ibid., 421.

47. David Brakke, *Demons and the Making of the Monk: Spiritual Combat in Early Christianity* (Cambridge, MA: Harvard University Press, 2006), 10–11. Emphasis added.

48. Ibid., 241.

49. Lacouture, *Mes retraites*, 56.

50. Ibid., 72.

51. Ibid., 85.

52. Ibid., 125.

53. Ignatius of Loyola, "Helpful Notes for the Perception and Understanding of Scruples and of the Insinuations of Our Enemy," in *Personal Writings*, trans. Joseph A. Munitz and Philip Endean (New York: Penguin Books, 1996), 355–56.

54. Ibid., 188.

55. Lacouture, *Mes retraites*, 70. See also, Simon Tugwell, OP, *Ways of Imperfection: An Exploration of Christian Spirituality* (Springfield, IL: Templegate, 1985), vii, and Andrew Louth, *The Origins of the Christian Mystical Tradition: From Plato to Denys* (New York: Oxford University Press, 2007), xiii–xiv.

56. John of the Cross, "The Ascent of Mount Carmel," in *The Collected Works of St. John of the Cross*, 123–24.

57. Lacouture, *Mes retraites*, 38. See also, Thomas à Kempis, *The Imitation of Christ*, trans. Leo Sherley-Price (London: Penguin Books, 1952), 168.

58. Lorenzo Scupoli, *The Spiritual Combat* (Mesa, AZ: Scriptoria Books, 2009), 16–17.

59. Lacouture, *Mes retraites*, 37.

60. Ibid., 268.

61. Ibid., 177, 218. See also, Onésime Lacouture, SJ, *Mes retraites II: La vie de Jésus* (Québec: Scivias, 1998), 16, 115, and Onésime Lacouture, SJ, *Mes retraites III: L'activité du Saint-Esprit* (Québec: Scivias, 1999), 64.

62. Onésime Lacouture (11 May 1941) quoted in Longpré, *Un mouvement spirituel au Québec*, 53.

63. Hugo, *Your Ways Are Not My Ways*, 159. See also, Jean-Marie-Rodrigue Villeneuve to Emile Papillon (AJC [BO-0167-1,1], 25 July 1937).

64. Hamelin and Gagnon, *Histoire du catholicisme québécois*, 386.

65. Adélard Dugré to Onésime Lacouture (AJC [BO-0167-1,1], 9 November 1931).

66. Wlodimir Ledóchowski to Adélard Dugré (AJC [BO-0167-1,1], 24 May 1933).

67. Anonymous to Adélard Dugré (AJC [BO-0167-1,1], 15 April 1933).

68. Ibid.: "Je retrouve cette note qu'un philosophe m'a envoyée: Cette retraite m'a fait un grand bien, surtout par son idée de fond, abandon à la volonté de Dieu."

69. Longpré, *Un mouvement spirituel au Québec*, 38.

70. Adélard Dugré to Onésime Lacouture (AJC [BO-0167-1,1], 30 August 1933).

71. Emile Papillon to Onésime Lacouture (AJC [BO-0167-1,1], 11 September 1937).

72. Ibid.

73. Anonymous to Emile Papillon (AJC [BO-0165-1,1], 19 October 1937).

74. Onésime Lacouture (BANQ [P9/C7], n.d.). Lacouture wrote an account of his pilgrimage to the Holy Land and eventually published it as an appendix to his memoirs from his Alaskan mission. Onésime Lacouture, "Mon Voyage en Terre Sainte," *Mon séjour en Alaska*, 154.

75. Onésime Lacouture to Émile Yelle (AJC [BO-0167-1,2], 4 June 1938).

76. Emile Papillon to Onésime Lacouture (AJC [BO-0167-1,1], 28 September 1938).

77. Ibid.

78. Adélard Dugré to Onésime Lacouture (AJC [BO-0167-1,1], 11 November 1938).

79. Ibid.

80. Emile Papillon to Onésime Lacouture (AJC [BO-0167-1,1], 6 December 1938).

81. Emile Papillon to Onésime Lacouture (AJC [BO-0167-1,1], 4 March 1939).

82. Ibid.

83. Emile Papillon to Onésime Lacouture (AJC [BO-0167-1,3], 25 August 1939).

84. Longpré, *Un mouvement spirituel au Québec*, 44.

85. Hugo, *Your Ways Are Not My Ways*, 159.

86. Walter Brueggemann, *The Prophetic Imagination* (Minneapolis, MN: Fortress Press, 2001), 81. Abraham J. Heschel, *The Prophets* (New York: Harper and Row, 1962), 9.

87. Hugo, *Your Ways Are Not My Ways*, 159. Raymond A. Schroth, SJ, *The American Jesuits: A History* (New York: New York University Press, 2007), 141–42.

88. Zacheus J. Maher to Emile Papillon (AJC [BO-0167-1,1], 5 April 1941).

89. Emile Papillon to Joseph R. Stack (AJC [BO-0167-1,2], 24 January 1940).

90. Francis J. Seeliger to Emile Papillon (AJC [BO-0167-1,1], 14 August 1940).

91. Emile Papillon to Francis J. Seeliger (AJC [BO-0167-1,2], 20 September 1940).

92. Longpré, *Un mouvement spirituel au Québec*, 55.

93. D. L. Crenier, OSB, English translation of "Grâce et Nature," in *Bulletin de Saint Benôit* (BANQ [P9/D4], 29 September 1941), 2.

94. Onésime Lacouture, SJ, "Les Creatures . . . . Fumier ou Dessert?" (BANQ [P9/A37], 17 October 1941).

95. Ibid., 3.

96. Ibid., 9–10.

97. Zacheus J. Maher to Emile Papillon and Francis J. Seeliger (AJC [BO-0167-1,1], 4 November 1941).

98. Zacheus J. Maher to Onésime Lacouture (AJC, BO-0167-1,1], 4 November 1941).

99. Emile Papillon to Zacheus J. Maher (AJC [BO-0167-1,1], n.d.).

100. Ildebrando Antoniutti to Emile Papillon (AJC [BO-0167-1,1], 14 February 1942).

101. Emile Papillon to Ildebrando Antoniutti (AJC [BO-0167-1,1], 20 February 1942).

102. Emile Papillon to Jean-Marie-Rodrigue Villeneuve (AJC [BO-0167-1,1], 22 February 1942). Emile Papillon to Guido Leclaire (AJC [BO-0167-1,1], 23 February 1942).

103. Emile Papillon to Zacheus J. Maher (AJC [BO-0167-1,1], 14 May 1942).

104. Zacheus J. Maher to Emile Papillon (AJC [BO-0167-1,1], 19 May 1942).

105. Ibid.

106. Emile Papillon to Onésime Lacouture (AJC [BO-0167-1,1], 1 June 1942).

You have to answer the following questions, *sub gravi*

1. Did you prepare this translation?
2. If it was done by another, did you know about it? Did you approve it? Revise, correct? Adapt it?
3. Did you know this translation would be distributed in the U.S.?
4. Did you submit it to the approval of Fr. Seeliger, or a local superior?
5. Were you authorized by one of them to distribute this document?

Was it on November 24, 1941 that you signed or read this document or permitted the translation? More importantly, was it after you received the letter from Fr. Maher informing you that you had been suspended from all priestly functions, in virtue of holy obedience?

107. Onésime Lacouture to Emile Papillon (AJC [BO-0167-1,1], 5 June 1942).

108. Ibid.

109. Zacheus J. Maher to Emile Papillon (AJC [BO-0167-1,1], 21 June 1942).

110. Onésime Lacouture, SJ, "Philosophe ou Théologien?" (AJC [BO-0167-1,1], 4 July 1942).

111. Ildebrando Antoniutti to Emile Papillon (AJC [BO-0167-1,1], 12 October 1942).

112. Emile Papillon to Ildebrando Antoniutti (AJC [BO-0167-1,1], 14 October 1942).

113. Onésime Lacouture to Emile Papillon (AJC [BO-0167-1,1], 19 October 1942).

114. This prophecy was given at Lacouture's final retreat, prior to his exile in 1939.

115. Onésime Lacouture to Emile Papillon (AJC [BO-0167-1,1], 12 October 1943).

116. Onésime Lacouture to Norbert de Boynes (AJC [BO-0167-1,3], 6 June 1944).

117. Ibid.

118. Ibid.

119. Ibid.

120. Robert A. Orsi, *The Madonna of 115th Street: Faith and Community in Italian Harlem, 1880–1950* (New Haven, CT: Yale University Press, 1985), xiii–xiv.

121. Hugo, *Your Ways Are Not My Ways*, 30.

4. Mackerel Snappers in the US Industrial Era

1. See Mircea Eliade, *The Sacred and the Profane: The Nature of Religion*, trans. Willard R. Trask (New York: Harcourt Brace, 1959).

2. Robert A. Markus, *The End of Ancient Christianity* (Cambridge: Cambridge University Press, 1991), 17.

3. Judith Halberstam, *The Queer Art of Failure* (Durham, NC: Duke University Press, 2011), 3. See also, Barbara Ehrenreich, *Bright-Sided: How Positive Thinking Is Undermining America* (New York: Metropolitan Books, 2009).

4. See Lauren Gail Berlant, *Cruel Optimism* (Durham, NC: Duke University Press, 2011).

5. Sydney E. Ahlstrom, "National Trauma and Changing Religious Values," in "A New America?," special issue, *Daedalus* 107, no. 1 (Winter 1978), 15–16.

6. Michael McGerr, *A Fierce Discontent: The Rise and Fall of the Progressive Movement in America, 1870–1920* (New York: Free Press, 2003), 151.

7. Charles R. Morris, *The Tycoons: How Andrew Carnegie, John D. Rockefeller, Jay Gould, and J. P. Morgan Invented the American Supereconomy* (New York: Henry Holt, 2005), 265.

8. Jackson Lears, *Rebirth of a Nation: The Making of Modern America, 1877–1920* (New York: HarperCollins, 2009), 296.

9. Upton Sinclair, *The Jungle* (New York: Doubleday, Page & Co., 1906).

10. Paul Boyer, *When Time Shall Be No More: Prophecy and Belief in Modern American Culture* (Cambridge, MA: Harvard University Press, 1992), 67–68.

11. Christopher H. Evans, *The Kingdom Is Always but Coming: A Life of Walter Rauschenbusch* (Grand Rapids, MI: William B. Eerdmans, 2004), 119.

12. Walter Rauschenbusch, *Christianity and the Social Crisis* (New York: MacMillan, 1913), 352.

13. Edwin S. Gaustad and Leigh E. Schmidt, *The Religious History of America* (San Francisco: HarperCollins, 2002), 242.

14. Nick Salvatore, *Eugene V. Debs: Citizen and Socialist* (Urbana: University of Illinois Press, 1982), 64–65.

15. Lears, *Rebirth of a Nation*, 306.

16. Edward Behr, *Prohibition: Thirteen Years That Changed America* (New York: Arcade, 2011), 66.

17. Ronald C. White Jr. and C. Howard Hopkins, *The Social Gospel: Religion and Reform in Changing America* (Philadelphia: Temple University Press, 1976); Henry F. May, *The End of American Innocence: A Study of the First Years of Our Own Time, 1912–1917* (New York, Columbia University Press, 1992), 12–13.

18. Richard M. Gamble, *The War for Righteousness: Progressive Christianity, the Great War, and the Rise of the Messianic Nation* (Wilmington, DE: ISI Books, 2003), 5.

19. Henri de Lubac, SJ, *La postérité spirituelle de Joachim de Flore, tome II: de Saint-Simon à nos jours* (Paris: Éditions Lethielleux, 1979), 438–39.

20. Hans Urs von Balthasar, *The Theology of Henri de Lubac* (San Francisco: Ignatius Press, 1991), 123.

21. Halsey, *The Survival of American Innocence*, 2. See also, Ehrenreich, *Bright-Sided*, 13.

22. Gaustad and Schmidt, *The Religious History of America*, 318.

23. Barry Hankins, *Jesus and Gin: Evangelism, the Roaring Twenties and Today's Culture Wars* (New York: Palgrave Macmillan, 2010), 63. See also, William Werpehowski, "Reinhold Niebuhr," in *The Blackwell Companion to Political Theology*, ed. Peter Scott and William T. Cavanaugh (Malden, MA: Blackwell, 2004), 182.

24. George M. Marsden, *Fundamentalism and American Culture* (New York: Oxford University Press, 2006), 210–11.

25. Halsey, *The Survival of American Innocence*, 38.

26. Henry F. May, "The Rebellion of the Intellectuals, 1912–1917," *American Quarterly* 8, no. 2 (Summer 1956): 125.

27. T. J. Jackson Lears, *No Place of Grace: Antimodernism and the Transformation of American Culture, 1880–1920* (New York: Pantheon, 1983), 31.

28. See also, Mark S. Massa, SJ, and Catherine Osborne, eds., *American Catholic History: A Documentary Reader* (New York: New York University Press, 2008), 139–48.

29. James Hennessey, SJ, *American Catholics: A History of the Roman Catholic Community in the United States* (New York: Oxford University Press, 1981), 243.

30. Joseph P. Chinnici, OFM, "Spiritual Capitalism and the Culture of American Catholicism," in "American Catholic Social Thought," special issue, *U.S. Catholic Historian* 5, no. 2 (1986): 134.

31. David J. O'Brien, *American Catholics and Social Reform: The New Deal Years* (New York: Oxford University Press, 1968), 148.

32. Patrick W. Carey, *Catholics in America: A History* (New York: Rowan and Littlefield, 2004), 86–87.

33. James Gibbons, "Cardinal Gibbons' Defense of the Knights of Labor, 20 February 1887," in *Documents of American Catholic History*, ed. John Tracy Ellis (Milwaukee, WI: Bruce Publishing, 1962), 464, 471. See also, Henry J. Browne, *The Catholic Church and the Knights of Labor* (New York: Arno Press, 1976), 182–274.

34. McGreevy, *Catholicism and American Freedom*, 132–33. See also, Henry George, *Progress and Poverty: An Inquiry into the Cause of Industrial Depressions, and of Increase of Want with Increase of Wealth* (New York: D. Appleton, 1886), and Henry George, *The Conditions of Labor: An Open Letter to Pope Leo XIII* (New York: C. Webster, 1893), 29.

35. O'Brien, *Public Catholicism*, 130. See also, Dolan, *The American Catholic Experience*, 335.

36. Elzéar-Alexandre Taschereau, "Condemned by the Church: Cardinal Taschereau's Letter on the Knights of Labor," *New York Times*, August 14, 1886, 5.

37. Jay P. Dolan, *Catholic Revivalism* (Notre Dame, IN: University of Notre Dame Press, 1978); O'Brien, *Public Catholicism*; McGreevy, *Catholicism and Ameri-*

can Freedom; Massa, *Anti-Catholicism in America*; Orsi, *The Madonna of 115th Street*; Fisher, *The Catholic Counterculture in America.*

38. Chinnici, "Spiritual Capitalism," 134.

39. R. Emmett Curran, SJ, "Confronting 'The Social Question': American Catholic Thought and the Socio-Economic Order in the Nineteenth Century," in "American Catholic Social Thought," special issue, *U.S. Catholic Historian* 5, no. 2 (1986): 168–69.

40. Thomas J. Shelley, "Archbishop John Hughes and the Church in New York," *Catholic New York*, July 6, 2000.

41. Curran, "Confronting 'The Social Question,'" 165.

42. Charles R. Morris, *American Catholic: The Saints and Sinners Who Built America's Most Powerful Church* (New York: Random House, 1997), 84.

43. Kevin Kenny, *Making Sense of the Molly Maguires* (New York: Oxford University Press, 1998).

44. Bowen, *Paul Cardinal Cullen and the Shaping of Modern Irish Catholicism*, 13.

45. Morris, *American Catholic*, 87.

46. Ibid., 92. See also, C. Joseph Nuesse, "Henry George and 'Rerum Novarum': Evidence is Scant That the American Economist Was a Target of Leo XIII's Classic Encyclical," *American Journal of Economics and Sociology* 44, no. 2 (April 1985): 241–54.

47. Will Herberg, *Protestant, Catholic, Jew: An Essay in American Religious Sociology* (Garden City, NY: Doubleday, 1955); Eric Rauchway, *The Great Depression and the New Deal: A Very Short Introduction* (New York: Oxford University Press, 2008), 25.

48. McGreevy, *Catholicism and American Freedom*, 198.

49. John Tracy Ellis, "American Catholics and the Intellectual Life," *Thought* 30, no. 118 (Autumn 1955): 351–88. See also, Massa and Osborne, *American Catholic History*, 100–1.

50. Carey, *Catholics in America*, 83.

51. McGreevy, *Catholicism and American Freedom*, 203.

52. Halsey, *The Survival of American Innocence*, 6.

53. Ibid., 142.

54. Carey, *Catholics in America*, 84.

55. Mark S. Massa, SJ, *Catholics and American Culture: Fulton Sheen, Dorothy Day, and the Notre Dame Football Team* (New York: Crossroad, 1999).

56. Mark Oppenheimer, *Knocking on Heaven's Door: American Religion in the Age of Counterculture* (New Haven, CT: Yale University Press, 2003), 68–69.

57. Andrew M. Greeley, *The Catholic Imagination* (Berkeley: University of California Press, 2000), 1.

58. Halsey, *The Survival of American Innocence*, 18.

59. Fisher, *The Catholic Counterculture in America*, 54. See also, Dolan, *Catholic Revivalism*.

60. Joseph P. Chinnici, OFM, *Living Stones: The History and Structure of Catholic Spiritual Life in the United States* (New York: Macmillan, 1989), 157.

61. James M. O'Toole, *The Faithful: A History of Catholics in America* (Cambridge, MA: Harvard University Press, 2008), 146. See also, Jeremy Bonner, Christopher D. Denny, and Mary Beth Fraser Connolly, eds., *Empowering the People of God: Catholic Action before and after Vatican II* (New York: Fordham University Press, 2014).

62. Chinnici, *Living Stones*, 167.

63. Ibid., 163.

64. Dolan, *Catholic Revivalism*, 53.

65. O'Toole, *The Faithful*, 11–49.

66. The Catholic revival was an evangelical summons to conversion. To say this, however, introduces a term, *evangelical*, that has a variety of meanings. It can be so rigidly defined theologically as to become a test of orthodoxy, or it can be described more generically as a perspective from which religion is viewed primarily as "an experience of personal conversion" that issues forth "in a pursuit of personal piety." Understood in this sense the term *evangelical* represents a mood or style of religion which is not peculiar to any one denomination and thus best describes the central thrust of the revival tradition in American history. Catholic revivalism fostered such a religious experience, and for this reason it deserves to be included in the history of American evangelicalism (Dolan, *Catholic Revivalism*, 91).

67. O'Brien, *Public Catholicism*, 125.

68. James T. Fisher, *On the Irish Waterfront: The Crusader, the Movie, and the Soul of the Port of New York* (Ithaca, NY: Cornell University Press, 2009), 20.

69. Hennessey, *American Catholics*, 254.

70. Kenneth J. Heineman, "A Catholic New Deal: Religion and Labor in 1930s Pittsburgh," *Pennsylvania Magazine of History and Biography* 118, no. 4 (October 1994): 376; Dorothy Day, *All the Way to Heaven: The Selected Letters of Dorothy Day*, ed. Robert Ellsberg (Milwaukee, WI: Marquette University Press, 2010), 18.

71. Heineman, "A Catholic New Deal," 378.

72. Ibid., 378.

73. Kenneth J. Heineman, *A Catholic New Deal: Religion and Reform in Depression Pittsburgh* (University Park: Pennsylvania State University Press, 1999), 16.

74. "National Affairs: Cox's Army," *Time*, January 18, 1932, 12.

75. Heineman, *A Catholic New Deal*, 25.

76. Heineman, "A Catholic New Deal," 373–74.

77. Heineman, *A Catholic New Deal*, 30.

78. Charles O. Rice, "Reflections of a Labor Priest," in "American Catholic Social Thought," special issue, *U.S. Catholic Historian* 5, no. 2 (1986): 231–32.

79. Charles H. McCormick, "From Seeing Reds to Being Feds: The Pittsburgh Bureau of Investigation Field Office in Transition, 1920–1925," *Pennsylvania History* 69, no. 3 (Summer 2002): 367.

80. Pittsburgh was the dynamo from which radical energy flowed to the countryside, so the potential danger lay not just in the giant mills and factories that loomed and bellowed smoke near the city. For a hundred miles around lay coal camps and mill towns whose soot and grime and gob piles and waste runoff despoiled the streams and valleys. The immigrant workers in such places where other immigrant institutions such as churches were weak or nonexistent, were susceptible to the appeals of economic and political radicals. Because radicals sometimes seemed the only ones to care, they acted as mediating agents in the process of Americanization and, not coincidentally, in the spread of socialism and anarchism (Charles H. McCormick, *Seeing Reds: Federal Surveillance of Radicals in the Pittsburgh Mill District, 1917–1921* [Pittsburgh: University of Pittsburgh Press, 1997], 27).

81. Heineman, "A Catholic New Deal," 368.

82. O'Brien, *American Catholics and Social Reform*, 109–10.

83. Heineman, "A Catholic New Deal," 368.

84. Kenneth J. Heineman, "Iron City Trinity: The Triumph and the Trials of Catholic Social Activism in Pittsburgh, 1932–1972," *U.S. Catholic Historian* 22, no. 2 (Spring 2004): 126.

The Steel Workers Organizing Committee (SWOC) was a predecessor of the United Steel Workers of America Union, formed in 1936 as an organ of the CIO, absorbing the floundering Amalgamated Association of Iron and Steel Workers (AA). See Carroll D. Wright, "The Amalgamated Association of Iron and Steel Workers," *Quarterly Journal of Economics* 7, no. 4 (July 1893): 400–32, and Steve Rosswurm, *The FBI and the Catholic Church, 1935–1962* (Amherst: University of Massachusetts Press, 2009), 228.

85. Neil Betten, *Catholic Activism and the Industrial Worker* (Gainesville: University Presses of Florida, 1976), 77.

86. Charles Owen Rice to the Textile Workers Organizing Committee in Utica, NY (1938), quoted in Heineman, "A Catholic New Deal," 381–82.

87. Charles Owen Rice, quoted in Max M. Kampelman, *The Communist Party Vs. The C.I.O.: A Study in Power Politics* (New York: Frederick A. Praeger, 1957), 135–36.

> Place your people carefully in the meeting hall. Try to have a good-sized bunch down front. . . . Place others on each side and place a nice contingent

in the back. This is called the Diamond, the oldest meeting strategy in the world. It makes it look as if the entire meeting is filled with your people. ("The Labor Priests," *Fortune* 39 [January–June 1949]: 175–77)

88. O'Brien, *American Catholics and Social Reform*, 125–26.

89. Betten, *Catholic Activism and the Industrial Worker*, 124–25. See also, John C. Cort, *Dreadful Conversions: The Making of a Catholic Socialist* (New York: Fordham University Press, 2003).

90. Douglas P. Seaton, *Catholics and Radicals: The Association of Catholic Trade Unionists and the American Labor Movement, from Depression to Cold War* (Lewisburg, PA: Bucknell University Press, 1981), 111–12.

91. Paul Hanly Furfey, *Fire on the Earth* (New York: Macmillan, 1936).

92. Colman McCarthy, "Furfey, P. H.: Love and the Urban Ghetto," *Washington Post*, July 30, 1978, F3. See also, Claudia Levy, "Paul Hanly Furfey Dies at 95; Catholic U. Sociology Chairman," *Washington Post*, June 11, 1993, C6, and Loretta Morris, "Celebration of a Life: Paul Hanly Furfey," *Sociology of Religion* 54, no. 2 (1993): 219–20.

5. John Hugo and the Retreat's Southward Migration

1. Hugo, *Your Ways Are Not My Ways*, 48.

2. O'Brien, *Public Catholicism*.

3. Hugo, *Your Ways Are Not My Ways*, 49.

4. Oetgen, *Mission to America*.

5. Hugo, *Your Ways Are Not My Ways*, 51.

6. Ibid., 55–56.

7. David J. O'Brien and Thomas A. Shannon, *Catholic Social Thought: The Documentary Heritage* (Maryknoll, NY: Orbis Books, 1992), 40.

8. Hugo, *Your Ways Are Not My Ways*, 99–100.

9. Ibid., 60.

10. Ibid., 14.

11. Benjamin Peters, "Nature and Grace in the Theology of John Hugo," in *God, Grace, and Creation*, ed. Philip J. Rossi (Maryknoll, NY: Orbis Books, 2010), 60.

12. John J. Hugo interviewed by William Miller in Pittsburgh, 1976 (DD-CW [W-9, Box 2, Folder 2]).

13. John J. Hugo, *A Sign of Contradiction: As the Master so the Disciple* (Québec: Éditions Scivias, 1999), 23–24.

14. Hugo, *Your Ways Are Not My Ways*, 298–99.

15. John J. Hugo, *Applied Christianity* (New York: n.p., 1944), 11.

16. Ibid., 95.

17. Peters, "Nature and Grace in the Theology of John Hugo," 63.

18. Peter Tyler, *St. John of the Cross* (New York: Continuum, 2010), 148; John of the Cross, "The Living Flame of Love," in *The Collected Works of St. John of the Cross*, 638–39.

19. Peters, "Nature and Grace in the Theology of John Hugo"; Benjamin Peters, *John Hugo and an American Catholic Theology of Nature and Grace* (PhD diss., University of Dayton, 2011). See also, Henri de Lubac, SJ, *The Mystery of the Supernatural*, trans. Rosemary Sheed (New York: Crossroad, 1998), xxxv.

20. Hugo, *Your Ways Are Not My Ways*, 34.

21. Ibid., 38.

22. Ibid., 38.

23. Fyodor Dostoevsky, *The Brothers Karamazov*, trans. Constance Garnett (New York: Macmillan, 1922), 55.

24. Hugo, *Your Ways Are Not My Ways*, 45.

25. Ibid., 105.

26. Ibid., 106.

27. John Hugo to Dorothy Day (DD-CW [Hugo folder], 12 October 1941).

28. John Cooney, *The American Pope: The Life and Times of Francis Cardinal Spellman* (New York: New York Times Books, 1984); Robert I. Gannon, SJ, *The Cardinal Spellman Story* (Garden City, NY: Doubleday, 1962). On Scanlon's tenure as rector at Dunwoodie see, Thomas J. Shelley, *Dunwoodie: The History of St. Joseph's Seminary, Yonkers, New York* (Westminster, MD: Christian Classics, 1993), 188–90.

29. John J. Hugo, *Nature and the Supernatural: A Defense of the Evangelic Ideal* (n.p., 194—), and Hugo, *Your Ways Are Not My Ways.*

30. Francis J. Connell, CSsR, review of *Applied Christianity* by John J. Hugo, in *American Ecclesiastical Review* 113 (July 1945): 69.

31. Ibid., 69.

32. Ibid., 70–71.

33. The Jansenist controversy will be investigated in greater depth, but it is worth noting that while Pelagianism and Jansenism might appear to be diametrically opposed, Henri de Lubac contends that the latter is the organic progeny of Pelagius. Henri de Lubac, SJ, *Augustinianism and Modern Theology*, trans. Lancelot Sheppard (London: Geoffrey Chapman, 1969), 31, 40. See also, Louis K. Dupré, "The Case for Jansenism," *Journal of Religion*, 76, no. 4 (October 1996): 607–10.

34. Ephraim Radner, *Spirit and Nature: The Saint-Médard Miracles in 18th-Century Jansenism* (New York: Crossroad, 2002), 26.

35. William Doyle, *Jansenism* (New York: St. Martin's, 2000), 20.

36. Ibid., 91.

A. Some of God's commandments are impossible for the Just to obey, because they lack the grace to make it possible.

B. In the state of fallen nature, there can be no resistance to interior grace.

C. For merit and demerit after the fall, it is not necessary to have freedom from necessity, it is enough to have freedom from constraint.

D. The Semi-Pelagians admitted the necessity of an interior and prevenient grace, even for the beginning of faith, but they were heretical in holding that it might be either resisted or obeyed.

E. It is a Semi-Pelagian error to say that Christ died for all men.

37. Jonathan Wright, *God's Soldiers: Adventures, Politics, Intrigue, and Power—A History of the Jesuits* (New York: Doubleday, 2004), 163, 169.

38. The Jesuits created Jansenism, in the sense that they gave this name to a collection of doctrines and attitudes propounded by their self-proclaimed enemies. And whereas the famous definition of cardinal Giovanni Bona (1609–74) that a Jansenist was merely a Catholic who did not like Jesuits, was an oversimplification, it was based on the undeniable fact that many Jesuits tended to regard those who were not explicitly their allies as Jansenist fellow-travellers (Doyle, *Jansenism*, 36).

39. Knox, *Enthusiasm*, 2.

40. Ibid., 588.

41. Dorothy Day, "Poverty and Precarity," *Catholic Worker* (May 1952): 2, 6. See also, Dorothy Day, *By Little and By Little: The Selected Writings of Dorothy Day* (New York: Alfred A. Knopf, 1983), 106–9.

42. Joseph Clifford Fenton, "Nature and the Supernatural Life," *American Ecclesiastical Review* 114 (January 1946): 54–68.

43. Ibid., 55.

44. Ibid., 63.

45. Ibid., 56–57.

46. Ibid., 66.

47. Ibid., 66.

48. Ibid., 67.

49. R. Scott Appleby and John H. Haas, "The Last Supernaturalists: Fenton, Connell, and the Threat of Catholic Indifferentism," *U.S. Catholic Historian* 13, no. 2 (Spring 1995): 27, 36.

50. Hooper, "Murray and Day," 45–61.

51. Hugo, *Nature and the Supernatural*, 129.

52. Ibid., 154–55.

53. Hofstadter, *The Paranoid Style*.

54. Ibid., 29–30.

55. Ibid., 3.

56. Ibid., 6.

57. Richard Hofstadter, *Anti-intellectualism in American Life* (New York: Alfred A. Knopf, 1963), 18–19.

58. Ellis, "American Catholics and the Intellectual Life." See also, Thomas J. Shelley, "The Young John Tracy Ellis and American Catholic Intellectual Life," in "The Intellectual Life: Essays in Memory of John Tracy Ellis, Part One," special issue, *U.S. Catholic Historian* 13, no. 1 (Winter 1995): 1–18.

59. Pascal P. Parente, "Nature and Grace in Ascetical Theology," *American Ecclesiastical Review* (June 1943): 434.

60. Gerald Vann, OP, "Nature and Grace," *Orate Fratres* 21, no. 3 (January 26, 1947): 97–105.

61. Ibid., 101.

62. Ibid., 101, 97.

63. Ibid., 101.

64. Hugo, *Nature and the Supernatural*, 228.

65. Ibid., 228.

66. Joseph P. Donovan, CM, "A Bit of Puritanical Catholicity," *Homiletic and Pastoral Review* 48, no. 11 (August 1948): 807–14. See also, Leo J. Trese, "Ten Forty-Five," *Emmanuel* 54, no. 10 (October 1948): 297–98, and Louis A. Farina, "Is Detachment Puritanical?," *Homiletic and Pastoral Review* 49, no. 5 (February 1949): 356–67.

67. Hugo, *Nature and the Supernatural*, i.

68. Farina, "Is Detachment Puritanical?," 359.

69. Anonymous, *Brother Nathaniel Has a Brainstorm*, 23.

70. Donovan, "A Bit of Puritanical Catholicity," 807–14.

71. Ibid., 811.

72. Trese, "Ten Forty-Five."

73. Ibid., 298.

74. Farina, "Is Detachment Puritanical?," 356–68.

75. Ibid., 357.

76. Kavanaugh, "Spanish Sixteenth Century," 78; Girón-Negrón, "Dionysian Thought," 165–74; Alastair Hamilton, "The *Alumbrados: Dejamiento* and its Practitioners," in *A New Companion to Hispanic Mysticism*, ed. Hilaire Kallendorf (Boston: Brill, 2010), 103–24.

77. Farina, "Is Detachment Puritanical?," 358.

78. Apropos of the critic's plea for moderation, it is only necessary to recall that the rule of moderation, while it is valid for the moral virtues, does not apply to the theological virtues. We are not to believe in God or love Him in a moderate degree, but without limit. The only thing that imposes a restraint on us here is our capacity to love; since this capacity is finite, our wildest excessive love will fall pitifully short of the infinite love which God deserves. . . .

Furthermore, what is true of charity is inevitably true of that virtue which is simply the reverse and underside of charity, namely, detachment. As Christian charity should be total, so also Christian detachment should be universal (Ibid., 360).

79. Hugo, *Your Ways Are Not My Ways*, 183.

80. Hugo interviewed by William Miller in Pittsburgh, 1976 (DD-CW [W-9, Box 2, Folder 2]).

> Father Lacouture was very jealous of me because he wanted me to keep my mind fixed right on what we now call evangelization. He admired Dorothy Day but he didn't want me to become absorbed in the Catholic Worker. He felt that this was more important, that all those works were an issue and a byproduct or a result but that somebody had to keep the minds on evangelization, which is a hard thing for priests to do and for bishops to do today. They are off on the issues; they want the fruit. But I couldn't exactly do that because I was personally involved with my age.

6. Dorothy Day, Anti-triumphalism, and a Personalist Approach to Voluntary Poverty

1. Day, *The Long Loneliness*, 245–46.

2. Ibid., 243–44.

3. Dorothy Day, "Requiem for Father Roy," *Catholic Worker*, November 1954, 1, 6.

4. Father Roy talked to us of nature and the supernatural, how God became man that man might become God, how we were under the obligation of putting off the old man and putting on Christ, how we had been made the sons of God, by the seed of supernatural life planted in us at our baptism, and of the necessity we were under to see that the seed grew and flourished. We had to aim at perfection; we had to be guided by the folly of the Cross. (Day, *The Long Loneliness*, 246–47)

5. Day, "Requiem for Father Roy," 1, 6. See also, Brigid O'Shea Merriman, OSF, *Searching for Christ: The Spirituality of Dorothy Day* (Notre Dame: University of Notre Dame Press, 1994), 155, and Day, *The Long Loneliness*, 272–73.

6. Heineman, *A Catholic New Deal*, 108.

7. Miller, *A Harsh and Dreadful Love*, 188; John J. Hugo interviewed by William D. Miller in Pittsburgh, 1976 (DD-CW [W-9, Box 2, Folder 2]). In Miller's interview, Hugo dates his first meeting with Dorothy Day to "about 1940."

8. Dorothy Day, *All Is Grace* (DD-CW [D-3:6]: undated fragments), 3.

9. John J. Hugo interviewed by William D. Miller, 1976 (DD-CW [W-9, Box 2, Folder 2]).

10. Dorothy Day, "The Death of Father Onésime Lacouture, S.J.," *Catholic Worker* 107, December 12, 1951, 1.

11. Dorothy Day, *Loaves and Fishes* (Maryknoll, NY: Orbis Books, 1997), 87.

12. Jim Forest, *All Is Grace: A Biography of Dorothy Day* (Maryknoll, NY: Orbis Books, 2011), 18.

13. Day, *The Long Loneliness*, 37.

14. Barbara Ehrenreich, *Nickel and Dimed: On (Not) Getting By in America* (New York: Metropolitan Books, 2001).

15. Staughton Lynd and Andrej Grubacic, *Wobblies and Zapatistas* (Oakland, CA: PM Press, 2008), 15–16.

16. Mike Gold, *Jews Without Money* (New York: International Publishers, 1930).

17. Gerald W. McFarland, *Inside Greenwich Village: A New York City Neighborhood, 1898–1918* (Amherst: University of Massachusetts Press, 2001), 159, 179.

18. Forest, *All Is Grace*, 44.

19. Malcolm Cowley, *Exile's Return* (New York: Penguin Books, 1934), 69.

20. Day, *The Long Loneliness*, 84.

21. Day, *The Long Loneliness*, 84. See also, Thomas J. Shelley, *Greenwich Village Catholics: St. Joseph's Church and the Evolution of an Urban Faith Community, 1829–2002* (Washington, DC: Catholic University of America Press, 2003), 147.

22. Day, *The Long Loneliness*, 84–85.

23. William James, *The Varieties of Religious Experience* (New York: Modern Library, 1999), 166–85. See also, Dorothy Day, *From Union Square to Rome* (Silver Spring, MD: Preservation of the Faith Press, 1938), 4.

24. Paul Elie, *The Life You Save May Be Your Own: An American Pilgrimage* (New York: Farrar, Straus and Giroux, 2003), 28.

25. Forest, *All Is Grace*, 48.

26. Ibid., 50.

27. Dorothy Day, *The Eleventh Virgin* (New York: Albert and Charles Boni, 1924), III.iv.

28. Dwight Macdonald, "Revisiting Dorothy Day," *New York Review of Books*, January 28, 1971, 18.

29. Dorothy Day, *The Duty of Delight: The Diaries of Dorothy Day*, ed. Robert Ellsberg (Milwaukee, WI: Marquette University Press, 2008), 629. Forest, *All Is Grace*, 58.

30. Day, *The Long Loneliness*, 99. Day, *From Union Square to Rome*, 104–5.

31. Day, *The Long Loneliness*, 104.

32. Ibid., 105.

33. Day, *All the Way to Heaven*, 3. See also, Forest, *All Is Grace*, 63.

34. Day, *All the Way to Heaven*, 7.

35. Forest, *All Is Grace*, 65.

36. Day, *The Long Loneliness*, 113.

37. Robert Ellsberg, in Day, *All the Way to Heaven*, 9.

38. Miller, *A Harsh and Dreadful Love*, 67, 69, 72. At times, both Day and Hugo grew weary of Miller, and Day temporarily halted her partnership with the Marquette University Archives upon hearing that it had accepted money from the Rockefeller family, which was consistent with her habitual refusal of honorary doctorates from universities that hosted on-campus ROTC. Hugo thought that Miller's affected spirituality was annoyingly bourgeois. See Day to Miller in *All the Way to Heaven* (2010), 428–29.

> I had a letter from Professor Miller telling me that he is under contract to write a commentary on the manuscript of Dorothy's "All is Grace" and he has taken up the work, inviting some suggestions from me and asking me to read the MS. I have agreed. But I have also urged him to make the retreat, a request to which he turns a deaf ear, as he has to you. He tells me that he takes care of his spiritual needs by listening to Mozart. This marks an incomprehension of the spiritual life so gross that it guarantees the failure of his effort. And will deeply misrepresent Dorothy. He and his friend . . . seem to think that the mere fact of being educated in history makes them also final judges in Catholic spirituality. The book, I fear, would be a disaster. (John J. Hugo to Sr. Peter Claver Fahey, June 17, 1984 [DD-CW (PCF Papers, Series 1, Box 1)])

39. Day, *The Long Loneliness*, 85.

40. Dorothy Day to Forster Batterham (March 15, 1929), in Day, *All the Way to Heaven*, 25. See also, Fisher, *The Catholic Counterculture*, 17.

41. Day, *The Long Loneliness*, 120.

42. Augustine of Hippo, *On Christian Teaching*, i.xxxv, 26–27.

43. Bruce Watson, *Sacco and Vanzetti: The Men, the Murders, and the Judgment of Mankind* (New York: Penguin Books, 2007), 25.

44. Day, *The Long Loneliness*, 147.

45. Watson, *Sacco and Vanzetti*, 294.

46. Dorothy Day, quoted in Coles, *Dorothy Day*, 59.

47. Forest, *All Is Grace*, 78.

48. Day, *The Long Loneliness*, 135–36. See also, Forest, *All Is Grace*, 74.

49. Dorothy Day to Forster Batterham, in Day, *All the Way to Heaven*, 9.

50. Day, *The Long Loneliness*, 136.

51. Dorothy Day, quoted in Coles, *Dorothy Day*, 61–62.

52. Forest, *All Is Grace*, 75.

53. Day, *The Long Loneliness*, 139.

54. Ibid., 144, 148. Although she specifies her Catholic "conditional baptism" occurred in 1927 in *From Union Square to Rome*, in *The Long Loneliness* Day seems to indicate that another summer passed between Sacco and Vanzetti's execution and her reception into the Church, which would imply a December 1928 baptism. Day, *From Union Square to Rome*, 146.

55. Forest, *All Is Grace*, 84. Jim Fisher deserves credit for noting the confusion among the historical literature. Jim Fisher, "Up the Hill, with Phil (and Charlie)," *The Irish Waterfront* (blog), February 17, 2011, http://irishwaterfront.wordpress.com/2011/02/17/up-the-hill-with-phil/. Thankfully, Jim Forest has laid the matter to rest by going to the source and retrieving Day's baptismal record from Our Lady Help of Christians in Tottenville, Staten Island—dated December 29, 1927 (although they did mistakenly record her birth year to be 1898).

56. Dorothy Day to Forster Batterham (December 10, 1932), in Day, *All the Way to Heaven*, 47–49.

57. Day, *The Long Loneliness*, 256.

58. Fisher, *The Catholic Counterculture*, 10.

59. Day, *The Long Loneliness*, 142.

60. Fisher, *The Catholic Counterculture*, 15.

61. Ibid., 165.

62. Forest, *All Is Grace*, 100–1. See also, Fisher, *The Catholic Counterculture*, 25–26. Actually Maurin had been directed to Dorothy Day by then *Commonweal* editor, George Shuster, who thought they might be well-disposed toward one another.

63. Peter Maurin, "Self-Organization," in *The Green Revolution* (Fresno, CA: Academy Guild Press, 1961), 7. Maurin recited this "Easy Essay" to Day at their first meeting, immediately after she had returned from Washington, DC, where she had covered a hunger march protest for *America*.

64. Day, *The Duty of Delight*, 524. See also, Dorothy Day and Francis J. Sicius, *Peter Maurin: Apostle to the World* (Maryknoll, NY: Orbis Books, 2004).

65. James M. O'Toole, *The Faithful: A History of Catholics in America* (Cambridge, MA: Belknap Press, 2008), 145–46. Zwick and Zwick, *The Catholic Worker Movement*, 25.

66. Marc Ellis, *Peter Maurin: Prophet in the Twentieth Century* (New York: Paulist Press, 1981); Arthur Sheehan, *Peter Maurin: Gay Believer* (Garden City, NY: Hanover House, 1959); Day and Sicius, *Peter Maurin*; Marc H. Ellis, "Peter Maurin; To Bring the Social Order to Christ," in *A Revolution of the Heart: Essays on the Catholic Worker*, ed. Patrick G. Coy (Philadelphia: Temple University Press, 1988), 15–46; Geoffrey B. Gneuhs, "Peter Maurin's Personalist Democracy," in *A Revolution of the Heart: Essays on the Catholic Worker*, ed. Patrick G. Coy (Philadelphia: Temple University Press, 1988), 47–68.

67. Day, *Loaves and Fishes*, 5.

68. Stanley Vishnewski interviewed by Marc Ellis, New York (DD-CW [W-9, Box 2, Folder 25], May 1978).

69. Merriman, *Searching for Christ*, 52–53, 57. See also, Hellman, *Emmanuel Mounier and the New Catholic Left*; O'Brien, *Public Catholicism*, 189; Emmanuel Mounier, *Personalism*, trans. Philip Mairet (Notre Dame, IN: University of Notre Dame Press, 1952).

70. Dorothy Day, "On Pilgrimage—May 1948," *Catholic Worker*, May 1948, 3.

71. Stanley Vishnewski, "The Day I Met Peter Maurin," *Catholic Worker*, May 1976, 5.

72. Elie, *The Life You Save May Be Your Own*, 71.

73. Forest, *All Is Grace*, 105.

74. Finley Peter Dunne, *Observations by Mr. Dooley* (New York: R. H. Russell, 1902), 240.

75. Coles, *Dorothy Day*, 120–21.

76. Dorothy Day, *The Duty of Delight: The Diaries of Dorothy Day*, ed. Robert Ellsberg (Milwaukee, WI: Marquette University Press, 2008), 524.

77. Forest, *All Is Grace*, 113.

78. *Catholic Worker*, May 1933, 4.

79. Forest, *All Is Grace*, 125.

80. Fisher, *The Catholic Counterculture*, 55. See also, Merriman, *Searching for Christ*, 145.

81. Fisher, *The Catholic Counterculture*, 38.

82. Day, "All Is Grace" (DD-CW [D-3:6]: n.d.), 25.

83. Fisher, *The Catholic Counterculture*, 52.

84. Merriman, *Searching for Christ*, 155.

85. Day, *All Is Grace*, 241–42.

86. Day, *All Is Grace*, 149.

87. Dorothy Day, 1942 retreat notes (DD-CW [D-4, Box 9]).

88. Day, *The Long Loneliness*, 263.

89. Dorothy Day, "On Pilgrimage—December 1965," *Catholic Worker*, December 1965, 1, 2, 7. See also, Dorothy Day, *Therese* (Springfield, IL: Templegate, 1979).

90. John J. Hugo, "The Will of God," audio recording (SGPA: n.d.), 11.2.

91. John J. Hugo, *Pruning* (n.p., n.d.). Hugo, *Why Must I Suffer?*

92. Hugo, *Why Must I Suffer?*, 18.

93. Ibid., 21.

94. Ibid., 25–26.

95. Dorothy Day, "On Pilgrimage—September 1952," *Catholic Worker*, September 1952, 2, 6.

96. Day, *The Long Loneliness*, 274–75.

97. John J. Hugo, "The Immorality of Conscription," *Catholic Worker*, November 1944, 3–10. Patrick G. Coy, "Conscription and the Catholic Conscience in World War II," in *American Catholic Pacifism: The Influence of Dorothy Day and the Catholic Worker Movement*, edited by Anne Klejment and Nancy L. Roberts (Westport, CT: Praeger, 1996), 57.

98. Day, *The Long Loneliness*, 245.

99. Dorothy Day to Thomas Merton (October 10, 1960) in Day, *All the Way to Heaven*, 268.

100. Stanley Vishnewski, *Wings of the Dawn* (New York: Catholic Worker Press, 1984), 209–10.

101. Ibid., 211–12.

102. Ibid., 212.

103. Ibid., 221–22.

104. John J. Hugo interviewed by William Miller in Pittsburgh, 1976 (DD-CW [W-9, Box 2, Folder 2]).

105. Each day I realize what a tremendous thing the truths of the retreat are and what they have meant and mean to my priestly life. God has been good above measure to send them into my life at the very time that my hands were anointed with oil to consecrate. We have made so terribly many mistakes though and many of them seem almost irreparable.

I believe that the Retreat is dynamite . . . T.N.T. and then some. I backed out of the retreat because the closer it came the more I realized what damage can be done by throwing around dynamite without knowing how to use it. . . . I do not yet know how to throw dynamite so that it will do only good and no harm (Paul Judge to Dorothy Day, no date [DD-CW (Series D-1, Box 11, Folder 4)]).

106. John J. Hugo to anonymous, June 12, no year (DD-CW [W-49, Box 1]).

107. Dorothy Day, "Oh the Bitter Scorn that Religion Calls Up" (DD-CW [D3, Box 6]), 1.

108. Vishnewski, *Wings of the Dawn*, 221.

109. Day, *All Is Grace*, 46–47.

110. Ware, "The Way of Ascetics," 6–7.

111. Forest, *All Is Grace*, 177–80.

112. Harvey Egan to Dorothy Day, no date (DD-CW [Series D-1, Box 6, Folder 1]).

113. Dorothy Day, "C. W. Retreat," *Catholic Worker*, September 1939, 4.

Epilogue: To Afflict the Comfortable and Comfort the Afflicted: Catholic Worker Pacifism as a Form-of-Life

1. Francis J. Sicius, "Prophecy Faces Tradition: The Pacifist Debate during World War II," in *American Catholic Pacifism: The Influence of Dorothy Day and the Catholic Worker Movement*, ed. Anne Klejment and Nancy L. Roberts (Westport, CT: Praeger, 1996), 71–72.

2. "Gaudium et Spes," in *Vatican II: Constitutions, Decrees, Declarations*, ed. Austin Flannery (Northport, NY: Costello, 1996), 163–282.

3. Patricia McNeal, "Catholic Peace Organizations and World War II" in *American Catholic Pacifism*, 41.

4. Dorothy Day (August 10, 1940) in *By Little and By Little*, 151.

5. Tom Cornell, "Dorothy Day Recalled: Worker Leader 'Didn't Want Any Sugar Coating,'" *National Catholic Reporter*, November 27, 1981), 16.

6. Nicholas Rademacher, "Apostle of Social Justice: Paul Hanly Furfey and the Construction of a Catholic Culture" (PhD diss., Catholic University of America, 2006).

7. Day, *The Duty of Delight*, 61–62.

8. John Cogley, *A Canterbury Tale: Experiences and Reflections, 1916–1976* (New York: Seabury Press, 1976), 31.

9. Francis J. Sicius, "Prophecy Faces Tradition," in *American Catholic Pacifism*, 73.

10. John J. Hugo interviewed by William Miller, 1976 (DD-CW [W-9, Box 2, Folder 2]).

11. Dorothy Day, "Our Stand," *Catholic Worker*, June 1940, 1, 4.

12. J. Edgar Hoover letter to Assistant Attorney General Wendell Berge (13 January 1943) FBI-FOIA 62-61208-3.

13. Giorgio Agamben, *The Highest Poverty: Monastic Rules and Form-of-Life*, trans. Adam Kotsko (Stanford, CA: Stanford University Press, 2013), xi. See also, Adam Kotsko, "How to Read Agamben," *Los Angeles Review of Books*, June 4, 2013, https://lareviewofbooks.org/essay/how-to-read-agamben, and Nathan Schneider, "Commies for Christ," *New Inquiry*, December 13, 2013, http://thenewinquiry.com/essays/commies-for-christ/.

14. Day, *The Duty of Delight*, 59. See also, Ugolino of Quintvalle, "How St. Francis, Walking One Day with Brother Leo, Explained to Him What Things Are Perfect Joy," in *The Little Flowers of St. Francis of Assisi*, trans. Raphael Brown (Garden City, NY: Image Books, 1958), 58–59.

15. Dorothy Day, "Why Do the Members of Christ Tear One Another?," *Catholic Worker*, February 1942, 1, 4, 7.

16. Day, *The Long Loneliness*, 254–55.

17. Fisher, *The Catholic Counterculture in America*, 59. Kane, "'She Offered Herself Up,'" 101–2.

18. Reinhold Niebuhr, *Moral Man and Immoral Society: A Study in Ethics and Politics* (Louisville, KY: Westminster John Knox Press, 1932), 242–44.

19. Thomas Merton, foreword to Dorothy Day, *Loaves and Fishes* (Maryknoll, NY: Orbis Books, 1963), ix; Dorothy Day, "Poverty and Precarity," *Catholic Worker*, May 1952, 2, 6.

20. Day, "We Are Un-American," 2.

21. Judith Butler, "The Claim of Non-Violence," in *Frames of War*, 165–84.

22. Dorothy Day to John Cogley (1940), in Day, *All the Way to Heaven*, 54.

23. Day, *The Long Loneliness*, 84–85.

24. Zwick and Zwick, *The Catholic Worker Movement*, 234. See also, Day, "Day after Day," 1, 3.

25. Dorothy Day, "April 18 [1948]," in *On Pilgrimage* (Grand Rapids, MI: William B. Eerdmans, 1997), 136.

> A great controversy has arisen about this retreat which is not settled yet, mainly because of the implications of the teaching that we are sons of God and must so behave. The controversy is over nature and the supernatural and man's death and resurrection to a new life, putting off the old man and putting on the new man.
>
> The teaching has been that love which is of the lover for the Beloved can only be between equals, and so to achieve this we must die to the natural and live supernatural lives, doing everything for the love of God.
>
> Not being a theologian or a philosopher, I have written little on the subject and wish to talk and write less.

26. Dorothy Day, "Our Country Passes from Undeclared War to Declared War: We Continue Our Christian Pacifist Stand," *Catholic Worker*, January 1942, 4.

27. Merriman, *Searching for Christ*, 131.

28. Dorothy Day, quoted in Coles, *Dorothy Day*, 97.

Bibliography

Archival Sources

Bibliothèque et Archives Nationales du Québec (BANQ).

Dorothy Day–Catholic Worker Collection (DD-CW). Memorial Library, Marquette University.

Fonds Onésime Lacouture, S.J./Anselme Longpré [formerly housed in the Centre de recherche Lionel-Groulx]. Archives des jésuites au Canada / The Archive of the Jesuits in Canada (AJC).

Freedom of Information Act files (FBI-FOIA). Federal Bureau of Investigation.

Saint Germaine Parish Archive (SGPA). Bethel Park, Pennsylvania.

Books, Articles, and Dissertations

Agamben, Giorgio. *The Highest Poverty: Monastic Rules and Form-of-Life*. Translated by Adam Kotsko. Stanford, CA: Stanford University Press, 2013.

Ahlstrom, Sydney E. "National Trauma and Changing Religious Values." In "A New America?" Special issue. *Daedalus* 107, no. 1 (Winter 1978): 13–29.

Ajzenstat, Janet. "Liberalism and Nationality." *Canadian Journal of Political Science / Revue canadienne de science politique* 14, no. 3 (September 1981): 587–609.

Anonymous. *Brother Nathaniel Has a Brainstorm: A Story*. Oakmont, PA: Father Louis Farina, 1944.

Appleby, R. Scott. *"Church and Age Unite!": The Modernist Impulse in American Catholicism*. Notre Dame, IN: University of Notre Dame Press, 1992.

Appleby, R. Scott, and John H. Haas. "The Last Supernaturalists: Fenton, Connell, and the Threat of Catholic Indifferentism." *U.S. Catholic Historian* 13, no. 2 (Spring 1995): 23–48.

Asselin, Olivar. *L'oeuvre de l'abbé Groulx*. Montréal: Bibliothèque de l'Action française, 1923.

Augustine of Hippo. *On Christian Teaching*. Translated by R. P. H. Green. New York: Oxford University Press, 1997.

———. *The Confessions of Saint Augustine*. Translated by Maria Boulding, OSB. New York: Random House, 1998.

Barber, Daniel Colucciello. *On Diaspora: Christianity, Religion and Secularity*. Eugene, OR: Cascade Books, 2011.

Barbour, John D. "Character and Characterization in Religious Autobiography." *Journal of American Academy of Religion* (Summer 1987): 307–30.

Bataille, Le Docteur. *Le Diable au XIXe Siècle: La franc-maçonnerie Luciférienne*. Paris: Delhomme and Briguet, 1893.

Baum, Gregory. *The Church in Quebec*. Ottawa: Novalis, 1991.

———. "Comparing Post–World War II Catholicism in Quebec, Ireland, and the United States." In *The Church Confronts Modernity: Catholicism since 1950 in the United States, Ireland, and Quebec*, edited by Leslie Woodcock Tentler, 268–96. Washington, DC: Catholic University of America Press, 2007.

Behiels, Michael D. *Prelude to Quebec's Quiet Revolution: Liberalism versus Neo-nationalism, 1945–1960*. Montréal: McGill-Queen's University Press, 1985.

Behr, Edward. *Prohibition: Thirteen Years That Changed America*. New York: Arcade, 2011.

Benjamin, Walter. *Selected Writings, Volume 4, 1938–1940*. Edited by Howard Eiland and Michael William Jennings. Cambridge, MA: Belknap Press, 2003.

Berdyaev, Nicholas. *The Bourgeois Mind and Other Essays*. Freeport, NY: Books for Libraries Press, 1966).

Berger, Peter L. *The Sacred Canopy: Elements of a Sociological Theory of Religion*. Garden City, NY: Doubleday, 1967.

Berlant, Lauren Gail. *Cruel Optimism*. Durham, NC: Duke University Press, 2011.

Bernard of Clairvaux. *Bernard of Clairvaux: Selected Works*. Translated by G. R. Evans. New York: Paulist Press, 1987.

Betten, Neil. *Catholic Activism and the Industrial Worker*. Gainesville, FL: University Presses of Florida, 1976.

Bilen, Osman. *The Historicity of Understanding and the Problem of Relativism in Gadamer's Philosophical Hermeneutics*. Washington, DC: Council for Research in Values and Philosophy, 2000.

Bonner, Jeremy, Christopher D. Denny, and Mary Beth Fraser Connolly, eds. *Empowering the People of God: Catholic Action before and after Vatican II*. New York: Fordham University Press, 2014.

Bothwell, Robert, ed. *Canada and Quebec: One Country, Two Histories*. Vancouver: University of British Columbia Press, 1998.

Bowen, Desmond. *Paul Cardinal Cullen and the Shaping of Modern Irish Catholicism*. Dublin: Gill and Macmillan, 1983.

Boyer, Onesime Alfred. *She Wears a Crown of Thorns*. New York: Benziger Bros., 1949.

Boyer, Paul. *When Time Shall Be No More: Prophecy and Belief in Modern American Culture*. Cambridge, MA: Harvard University Press, 1992.

Boym, Svetlana. *The Future of Nostalgia*. New York: Basic Books, 2001.

Brakke, David. *Demons and the Making of the Monk: Spiritual Combat in Early Christianity*. Cambridge, MA: Harvard University Press, 2006.

Brown, Peter. *The Body and Society: Men, Women, and Sexual Renunciation in Early Christianity*. New York: Columbia University Press, 1988.

Browne, Henry J. *The Catholic Church and the Knights of Labor*. New York: Arno Press, 1976.

Brueggemann, Walter. *The Prophetic Imagination*. Minneapolis, MN: Fortress Press, 2001.

Brym, Robert J., and Rhonda L. Lenton. "The Distribution of Anti-Semitism in Canada in 1984." *Canadian Journal of Sociology / Cahiers canadiens de sociologie*, 16, no. 4 (Autumn 1991): 411–18.

Buckley, James J. "On Being a Symbol: An Appraisal of Karl Rahner." *Theological Studies* 40, no. 3 (September 1979): 453–73.

Burrell, David, and Stanley Hauerwas. "Self-deception and Autobiography: Theological and Ethical Reflections on Speer's 'Inside the Third Reich.'" *Journal of Religious Ethics* 3, no. 1 (Spring 197 4): 99–117.

Butler, Judith. *Frames of War: When Is Life Grievable?* New York: Verso, 2009.

Cahill, Thomas. *How the Irish Saved Civilization: The Untold Story of Ireland's Heroic Role from the Fall of Rome to the Rise of Medieval Europe*. New York: Doubleday, 1995.

Carey, Patrick W. *Avery Cardinal Dulles, SJ: A Model Theologian*. Mahwah, NJ: Paulist Press, 2010.

———. *Catholics in America: A History*. New York: Rowan and Littlefield, 2004.

Chinnici, OFM, Joseph P. *Living Stones: The History and Structure of Catholic Spiritual Life in the United States*. New York: Macmillan, 1989.

———. "Spiritual Capitalism and the Culture of American Catholicism." In "American Catholic Social Thought." Special issue. *U.S. Catholic Historian* 5, no. 2 (1986): 131–61.

Christiano, Kevin J. "The Trajectory of Catholicism in Twentieth-Century Quebec." In *The Church Confronts Modernity: Catholicism Since 1950 in the United States, Ireland, and Quebec*, edited by Leslie Woodcock Tentler, 21–61. Washington, DC: Catholic University of America Press, 2007.

Clark, Gillian. "Women and Asceticism in Late Antiquity: The Refusal of Status and Gender." In *Asceticism*, edited by Vincent L. Wimbush and Richard Valantasis, 33–48. New York: Oxford University Press, 1998.

Cochran, David Carroll. *Catholic Realism and the Abolition of War*. Maryknoll, NY: Orbis Books, 2014.

Cogley, John. *A Canterbury Tale: Experiences and Reflections, 1916–1976*. New York: Seabury Press, 1976.

Cohen, Jeffrey Jerome. *Monster Theory: Reading Culture*. Minneapolis: University of Minnesota Press, 1996.

Coles, Robert. *Dorothy Day: A Radical Devotion*. Reading, MA: Addison-Wesley, 1987.

Connell, CSSR, Francis J. Review of *Applied Christianity*, by John Hugo. *American Ecclesiastical Review* 113 (July 1945): 69–72.

Cook, Ramsay, and Michael Behiels, eds. *The Essential Laurendeau*. Vancouver, BC: Copp Clark, 1976.

Cooney, John. *The American Pope: The Life and Times of Francis Cardinal Spellman*. New York: New York Times Books, 1984.

Cort, John C. *Dreadful Conversions: The Making of a Catholic Socialist*. New York: Fordham University Press, 2003.

Cowley, Malcolm. *Exile's Return*. New York: Penguin Books, 1934.

Coy, Patrick G. "Conscription and the Catholic Conscience in World War II." In *American Catholic Pacifism: The Influence of Dorothy Day and the Catholic Worker Movement*, edited by Anne Klejment and Nancy L. Roberts. Westport, CT: Praeger, 1996.

Crenier, OSB, D. L. *Bulletin de Saint-Benoît*. Special supplement (September 1941), 1–8.

Curran, SJ, R. Emmett. "Confronting 'The Social Question:' American Catholic Thought and the Socio-Economic Order in the Nineteenth Century." In "American Catholic Social Thought." Special issue. *U.S. Catholic Historian* 5, no. 2 (1986): 165–93.

Daniel, E. Randolph. "The Double Procession of the Holy Spirit in Joachim of Fiore's Understanding of History." *Speculum* 55, no. 3 (July 1980): 469–83.

Day, Dorothy. *All the Way to Heaven: The Selected Letters of Dorothy Day*. Edited by Robert Ellsberg. Milwaukee, WI: Marquette University Press, 2010.

———. *By Little and By Little: The Selected Writings of Dorothy Day*. New York: Alfred A. Knopf, 1983.

———. *The Duty of Delight: The Diaries of Dorothy Day*. Edited by Robert Ellsberg. Milwaukee, WI: Marquette University Press, 2008.

———. *The Eleventh Virgin*. New York: Albert and Charles Boni, 1924.

———. *From Union Square to Rome*. Silver Spring, MD: Preservation of the Faith Press, 1938.

———. *Loaves and Fishes*. Maryknoll, NY: Orbis Books, 1997.

———. *The Long Loneliness*. New York: HarperCollins, 1952.

———. *On Pilgrimage*. Grand Rapids, MI: William B. Eerdmans, 1997.

———. "The Scandal of the Works of Mercy." *Commonweal* 51 (November 4, 1949): 99–102.

———. *Therese*. Springfield, IL: Templegate, 1979.

Day, Dorothy, and Francis J. Sicius. *Peter Maurin: Apostle to the World*. Maryknoll, NY: Orbis Books, 2004.

de Lubac, SJ, Henri. *Augustinianism and Modern Theology.* Translated by Lancelot Sheppard. London: Geoffrey Chapman, 1969.

———. *The Mystery of the Supernatural.* Translated by Rosemary Sheed. New York: Crossroad, 1998.

———. *La Posterité spirituelle de Joachim de Flore, tome II: de Saint-Simon à nos jours.* Paris: Éditions Lethielleux, 1979.

Dickinson, John, and Brian Young. *A Short History of Quebec.* 4th ed. Montréal: McGill-Queen's University Press, 2008.

Dolan, Jay P. *The American Catholic Experience: A History from Colonial Times to the Present.* Garden City, NY: Doubleday, 1985.

———. *Catholic Revivalism.* Notre Dame, IN: University of Notre Dame Press, 1978.

Donovan, CM, Joseph P. "A Bit of Puritanical Catholicity." *Homiletic and Pastoral Review* 48, no. 11 (August 1948): 807–14.

Dostoevsky, Fyodor. *The Brothers Karamazov.* Translated by Constance Garnett. New York: Macmillan, 1922.

Doyle, William. *Jansenism.* New York: St. Martin's Press, 2000.

Dunne, Finley Peter. *Observations by Mr. Dooley.* New York: R. H. Russell, 1902.

Dupré, Louis K. "The Case for Jansensism." *Journal of Religion* 76, no. 4 (October 1996): 607–10.

Ehrenreich, Barbara. *Bright-Sided: How Positive Thinking Is Undermining America.* New York: Metropolitan Books, 2009.

———. *Nickel and Dimed: On (Not) Getting by in America.* New York: Metropolitan Books, 2001.

Eliade, Mircea. *The Sacred and the Profane: The Nature of Religion.* Translated by Willard R. Trask. New York: Harcourt Brace, 1959.

Elie, Paul. *The Life You Save May Be Your Own: An American Pilgrimage.* New York: Farrar, Straus, and Giroux, 2003.

Ellis, John Tracy. "American Catholics and the Intellectual Life." *Thought* 30, no. 118 (Autumn 1955): 351–88.

Ellis, Marc. "Peter Maurin: To Bring the Social Order to Christ." In *A Revolution of the Heart: Essays on the Catholic Worker,* edited by Patrick G. Coy, 15–46. Philadelphia: Temple University Press, 1988.

———. *Peter Maurin: Prophet in the Twentieth Century.* New York: Paulist Press, 1981.

English, John. *Citizen of the World: The Life of Pierre Elliott Trudeau, Volume One: 1919–1968.* Toronto: Vintage Canada, 2007.

Evans, Christopher H. *The Kingdom Is Always but Coming: A Life of Walter Rauschenbusch.* Grand Rapids, MI: William B. Eerdmans, 2004.

Farina, Louis A. "Is Detachment Puritanical?" *Homiletic and Pastoral Review* 49, no. 5 (February 1949): 356–67.

Fay, Terence J. *A History of Canadian Catholics: Gallicanism, Romanism, and Canadianism.* Montréal: McGill-Queen's University Press, 2002.

Fenton, Joseph Clifford. "Nature and the Supernatural Life." *American Ecclesiastical Review* 114 (January 1946): 54–68.

Ferretti, Lucia. *Brève histoire de l'Église catholique au Québec.* Montréal: Boréal, 2000.

Fisher, James T. *The Catholic Counterculture in America, 1933–1962.* Chapel Hill: University of North Carolina Press, 1989.

———. *On the Irish Waterfront: The Crusader, the Movie, and the Soul of the Port of New York.* Ithaca, NY: Cornell University Press, 2009.

Flanagan, Thomas. *Louis 'David' Riel: 'Prophet of the New World.'* Toronto: University of Toronto Press, 1996.

Flannery, Austin, ed. *Vatican II: Constitutions, Decrees, Declarations.* Northport, NY: Costello, 1996.

Forest, Jim. *All Is Grace: A Biography of Dorothy Day.* Maryknoll, NY: Orbis Books, 2011.

Fournier, Marcel. "Quebec Sociology and Quebec Society: The Construction of a Collective Identity." *Canadian Journal of Sociology / Cahiers canadiens de sociologie* 26, no. 3 (Summer 2001): 333–48.

Fournier, PSS, Roland. "Grâce et Nature." *Le Séminaire* (August 15, 1941): 140–51.

Fraser, Blair. "Labor and the Church in Quebec." *Foreign Affairs* 28, no. 2 (January 1950): 247–54.

Freze, SFO, Michael. *They Bore the Wounds of Christ: The Mystery of the Sacred Stigmata.* Huntington, IN: Our Sunday Visitor, 1989.

Furfey, Paul Hanly. *Fire on the Earth.* New York: Macmillan, 1936.

———. *The Respectable Murderers: Social Evil and Christian Conscience.* New York: Herder and Herder, 1966.

Gadamer, Hans-Georg. "On the Circle of Understanding." In *Hermeneutics versus Science?: Three German Views*, edited by John M. Connolly and Thomas Keutner, 68–78. Notre Dame, IN: University of Notre Dame Press, 1988.

Gamble, Richard M. *The War for Righteousness: Progressive Christianity, the Great War, and the Rise of the Messianic Nation.* Wilmington, DE: ISI Books, 2003.

Gannon, SJ, Robert I. *The Cardinal Spellman Story.* Garden City, NY: Doubleday, 1962.

Gaustad, Edwin S., and Leigh E. Schmidt. *The Religious History of America.* San Francisco: HarperCollins, 2002.

Gauvreau, Michael. *The Catholic Origins of Quebec's Quiet Revolution, 1931–1970.* Montréal: McGill-Queen's University Press, 2005.

Gay, Peter. *Modernism: The Lure of Heresy, from Baudelaire to Beckett and Beyond.* New York: W. W. Norton, 2008.

George, Henry. *The Conditions of Labor: An Open Letter to Pope Leo XIII*. New York: C. Webster, 1893.

———. *Progress and Poverty: An Inquiry into the Cause of Industrial Depressions, and of Increase of Want with Increase of Wealth*. New York: D. Appleton, 1886.

Gibbons, James. "Cardinal Gibbons' Defense of the Knights of Labor, 20 February 1887." In *Documents of American Catholic History*, edited by John Tracy Ellis. Milwaukee, WI: Bruce Publishing, 1962.

Giles, Paul. *American Catholic Arts and Fictions: Culture, Ideology, Aesthetics*. New York: Cambridge University Press, 1992.

Gneuhs, Geoffrey B. "Peter Maurin's Personalist Democracy." In *A Revolution of the Heart: Essays on the Catholic Worker*, edited by Patrick G. Coy, 47–68. Philadelphia: Temple University Press, 1988.

Gold, Mike. *Jews Without Money*. New York: International Publishers, 1930.

Greeley, Andrew M. *The Catholic Imagination*. Berkeley: University of California Press, 2000.

Groulx, Lionel. *The Iron Wedge: L'appel de la race*. Translated by Michel Gaulin. Ottawa: Carleton University Press, 1986.

———. *Notre Maître, le Passé*. Montréal: Granger frères, 1936.

———. *Orientations*. Montréal: Éditions du Zodiaque, 1935.

Halberstam, Judith. *The Queer Art of Failure*. Durham, NC: Duke University Press, 2011.

Halsey, William M. *The Survival of American Innocence: American Catholicism in an Era of Disillusionment, 1920–1940*. Notre Dame, IN: University of Notre Dame Press, 1980.

Hamelin, Jean, and Nicole Gagnon. *Histoire du catholicisme québécois, Le XXe siècle, Tome 1, 1898–1940*. Montréal: Boréal, 1984.

Hamilton, Alastair. "The *Alumbrados: Dejamiento* and its Practitioners." In *A New Companion to Hispanic Mysticism*, edited by Hilaire Kallendorf, 103–24. Boston: Brill, 2010.

Hankins, Barry. *Jesus and Gin: Evangelism, the Roaring Twenties and Today's Culture War*. New York: Palgrave Macmillan, 2010.

Heineman, Kenneth J. "A Catholic New Deal: Religion and Labor in 1930s Pittsburgh." *Pennsylvania Magazine of History and Biography* 118, no. 4 (October 1994): 363–94.

———. *A Catholic New Deal: Religion and Reform in Depression Pittsburgh*. University Park: Pennsylvania State University Press, 1999.

———. "Iron City Trinity: The Triumph and the Trials of Catholic Social Activism in Pittsburgh, 1932–1972." *U.S. Catholic Historian* 22, no. 2 (Spring 2004): 121–45.

Hellman, John. *Emmanuel Mounier and the New Catholic Left, 1930–1950*. Toronto: University of Toronto Press, 1981.

Hennessey, James. *American Catholics: A History of the Roman Catholic Community in the United States*. New York: Oxford University Press, 1981.

Herberg, Will. *Protestant, Catholic, Jew: An Essay in American Religious Sociology*. Garden City, NY: Doubleday, 1955.

Heschel, Abraham J. *The Prophets*. New York: Harper and Row, 1962.

Highfield, Ron. "The Freedom to Say 'No'? Karl Rahner's Doctrine of Sin." *Theological Studies* 56 (1995): 485–505.

Hofstadter, Richard. *Anti-intellectualism in American Life*. New York: Alfred A. Knopf, 1963.

———. *The Paranoid Style in American Politics and Other Essays*. Cambridge, MA: Harvard University Press, 1996.

Hooper, SJ, J. Leon. "Murray and Day: A Common Enemy, a Common Cause?" *U.S. Catholic Historian* 24, no. 1 (Winter 2006): 45–61.

Hughes, Everett C. "The French-English Margin in Canada." *American Journal of Sociology* 39, no. 1 (July 1933): 1–11.

Hugo, John J. *Applied Christianity*. New York: n.p., 1944.

———. Letter to the editor. *Emmanuel* 54, no. 12 (December 1948): 378–79.

———. *Nature and the Supernatural: A Defense of the Evangelic Ideal*. N.p.: n.p., 194—.

———. *A Sign of Contradiction: As a Master So the Disciple*. Québec: Éditions Scivias, 1999.

———. *Why Must I Suffer? Or, How to Become a Butterfly*. Kenosha, WI: Marytown Press, 1952.

———. *Your Ways Are Not My Ways*. Vol. 1. Pittsburgh, PA: Encounter with Silence, 1986.

Ignatius of Loyola. *Personal Writings*. Translated by Joseph A. Munitz and Philip Endean. New York: Penguin Books, 1996.

James, William. *The Varieties of Religious Experience*. New York: Modern Library, 1999.

John of the Cross. *The Collected Works of St. John of the Cross*. Translated by Kieran Kavanaugh, OCD. Washington, DC: Institute of Carmelite Studies, 1979.

Kampelman, Max M. *The Communist Party vs. The C.I.O.: A Study in Power Politics*. New York: Frederick A. Praeger, 1957.

Kane, Paula M. "'She Offered Herself Up': The Victim Soul and Victim Spirituality in Catholicism." *Church History* 71, no. 1 (March 2002): 80–119.

———. *Sister Thorn and Catholic Mysticism in Modern America*. Chapel Hill: University of North Carolina Press, 2013.

Kavanaugh, OCD, Kieran. "Spanish Sixteenth Century: Carmel and Surrounding Movements." In *Christian Spirituality: Post-reformation and Modern*, edited by Louis Dupré, Don E. Saliers, and John Meyendorff, 69–92. New York: Crossroad, 1987.

à Kempis, Thomas. *The Imitation of Christ*. Translated by Leo Sherley-Price. London: Penguin Books, 1952.

Kenny, Kevin. *Making Sense of the Molly Maguires*. New York: Oxford University Press, 1998.

Klejment, Anne. "The Radical Origins of Catholic Pacifism: Dorothy Day and the Lyrical Left During World War I." In *American Catholic Pacifism: The Influence of Dorothy Day and the Catholic Worker Movement*, edited by Anne Klejment and Nancy L. Roberts, 15–32. Westport, CT: Praeger, 1996.

Knox, Ronald A. *Enthusiasm: A Chapter in the History of Religion, with Special Reference to the XVII and XVIII Centuries*. New York: Oxford University Press, 1950.

Kotsko, Adam. "How to Read Agamben." *Los Angeles Review of Books*, June 4, 2013. https://lareviewofbooks.org/essay/how-to-read-agamben.

Lacoursière, Jacques, and Robin Philpot. *A People's History of Quebec*. Montréal: Baraka Books, 2009.

Lacouture, SJ, Onésime. *Mes retraites, première série: Doctrine Surnaturelle pour se défaire de toute mentalité païenne*. Québec: Éditions Scivias, 1998.

———. *Mes retraites II: La vie de Jésus*. Québec: Éditions Scivias, 1998.

———. *Mes retraites III: L'activité du Saint-Esprit*. Québec: Éditions Scivias, 1999.

———. *Mon séjour en Alaska, 1910–1913*. Québec: Editions Scivias, 1998.

Lamonde, Yvan. *Histoire Sociale des Idées au Québec (1896–1929)*. Vol. 2. Montréal: Les Éditions Fides, 2004.

Latour, Bruno. *We Have Never Been Modern*. Cambridge, MA: Harvard University Press, 1993.

Lears, T. J. Jackson. *No Place of Grace: Antimodernism and the Transformation of American Culture, 1880–1920*. New York: Pantheon Books, 1983.

———. *Rebirth of a Nation: The Making of Modern America, 1877–1920*. New York: HarperCollins, 2009.

Levinas, Emmanuel. *The Levinas Reader*. Edited by Seán Hand. Cambridge, MA: Basil Blackwell, 1989.

Longpré, Anselme. *Un mouvement spiritual au Québec (1931–1962): Un retour à l'Évangile*. Montréal: Fides, 1976.

Louth, Andrew. *The Origins of the Christian Mystical Tradition: From Plato to Denys*. New York: Oxford University Press, 2007.

Lower, A. R. M. "New France in New England." *New England Quarterly* 2, no. 2 (April 1929): 278–95.

Lynd, Staughton, and Andrej Grubacic. *Wobblies and Zapatistas*. Oakland, CA: PM Press, 2008.

Macdonald, Dwight. "Revisiting Dorothy Day." *New York Review of Books*, January 28, 1971, 12–19.

———. "The Foolish Things of the World—I." *New Yorker*, October 4, 1952, 37–42.

Mann, Susan. *The Dream of Nation: A Social and Intellectual History of Quebec*. Montréal: McGill-Queen's University Press, 2002.

Marcuse, Herbert. *Negations: Essays in Critical Theory*. Boston: Beacon Press, 1968.

Markus, Robert A. *The End of Ancient Christianity*. Cambridge: Cambridge University Press, 1991.

Marsden, George M. *Fundamentalism and American Culture*. New York: Oxford University Press, 2006.

Martin, David. *A General Theory of Secularization*. New York: Harper and Row, 1978.

Massa, SJ, Mark S. *Anti-Catholicism in America: The Last Acceptable Prejudice*. New York: Crossroad, 2003.

———. *Catholics and American Culture: Fulton Sheen, Dorothy Day, and the Notre Dame Football Team*. New York: Crossroad, 1999.

Massa, SJ, Mark S., and Catherine Osborne, eds. *American Catholic History: A Documentary Reader*. New York: New York University Press, 2008.

Maurin, Peter. *The Green Revolution*. Fresno, CA. Academy Guild Press, 1961.

May, Henry F. *The End of American Innocence: A Study of the First Years of Our Own Time, 1912–1917*. New York: Columbia University Press, 1992.

———. "The Rebellion of the Intellectuals, 1912–1917." *American Quarterly* 8, no. 2 (Summer 1956): 114–26.

McAvoy, Thomas T. *The Americanist Heresy in Roman Catholicism, 1895–1900*. Notre Dame, IN: University of Notre Dame Press, 1963.

McCormick, Charles H. "From Seeing Reds to Being Feds: The Pittsburgh Bureau of Investigation Field Office in Transition, 1920–1925." *Pennsylvania History* 69, no. 3 (Summer 2002): 367–92.

———. *Seeing Reds: Federal Surveillance of Radicals in the Pittsburgh Mill District, 1917–1921*. Pittsburgh: University of Pittsburgh Press, 1997.

McDonough, Peter. *Men Astutely Trained: A History of the Jesuits in the American Century*. New York: Free Press, 1992.

McFarland, Gerald W. *Inside Greenwich Village: A New York City Neighborhood, 1898–1918*. Amherst: University of Massachusetts Press, 2001.

McGerr, Michael. *A Fierce Discontent: The Rise and Fall of the Progressive Movement in America, 1870–1920*. New York: Free Press, 2003.

McGinn, Bernard. *Apocalyptic Spirituality: Treatises and Letters of Lactantius, Adso of Monier-en-Der, Joachim of Fiore, the Spiritual Franciscans, Savonarola*. New York: Paulist Press, 1979.

———. *The Growth of Mysticism: Gregory the Great through the 12th Century*. New York: Crossroad, 2007.

McGreevy, John T. *Catholicism and American Freedom: A History*. New York: W. W. Norton, 2003.

McKanan, Dan. *The Catholic Worker after Dorothy: Practicing the Works of Mercy in a New Generation*. Collegeville, MN: Liturgical Press, 2008.

Melbournensis. "St. Francis Xavier." *Irish Monthly* 9, no. 97 (July 1881): 337–49.

Merriman, OSF, Brigid O'Shea. *Searching for Christ: The Spirituality of Dorothy Day*. Notre Dame, IN: University of Notre Dame Press, 1994.

Merton, Thomas. Foreword to *Loaves and Fishes*, by Dorothy Day. Maryknoll, NY: Orbis Books, 1963, xi–x.

Meunier, E.-Martin, and Jean-Philippe Warren. *Sortir de la "Grande Noirceur": L'horizon "personaliste" de la Révolution tranquille*. Sillery, QC: Les Éditions du Septentrion, 2002.

Miller, J. R. *Reflections on Native-Newcomer Relations: Selected Essays*. Toronto: University of Toronto Press, 2004.

Miller, William D. *All Is Grace: The Spirituality of Dorothy Day*. Garden City, NY: Doubleday, 1987.

———. *A Harsh and Dreadful Love: Dorothy Day and the Catholic Worker Movement*. New York: Liveright, 1973.

———. *Dorothy Day: A Biography*. San Francisco: Harper and Row, 1982.

Moore, Brenna. *Sacred Dread: Raïssa Maritain, the Allure of Suffering, and the French Catholic Revival, 1905–1944*. Notre Dame, IN: University of Notre Dame Press, 2013.

Morris, Charles R. *American Catholic: The Saints and Sinners Who Built America's Most Powerful Church*. New York: Random House, 1997.

———. *The Tycoons: How Andrew Carnegie, John D. Rockefeller, Jay Gould, and J. P. Morgan Invented the American Supereconomy*. New York: Henry Holt, 2005.

Morris, Loretta. "Celebration of a Life: Paul Hanly Furfey." *Sociology of Religion* 54, no. 2 (1993): 219–20.

Mounier, Emmanuel. *Personalism*. Translated by Philip Mairet. Notre Dame, IN: University of Notre Dame Press, 1952.

"National Affairs: Cox's Army." *Time*, January 18, 1932.

Nemni, Max, and Monique Nemni. *Young Trudeau: Song of Quebec, Father of Canada, 1919–1944*. Toronto: McClelland and Steward, 2006.

Newman, Barbara. *God and the Goddesses: Vision, Poetry, and Belief in the Middle Ages*. Philadelphia: University of Pennsylvania Press, 2003.

Newman, Francis W. *The Soul, Its Sorrows and Its Aspirations*. London: J. Chapman, 1852.

Niebuhr, H. Richard. *Christ and Culture*. New York: HarperCollins, 2001.

Niebuhr, Reinhold. *Moral Man and Immoral Society: A Study in Ethics and Politics*. Louisville, KY: Westminster John Knox Press, 1932.

Noll, Mark A. *A History of Christianity in the United States and Canada*. Grand Rapids, MI: W. B. Eerdmans, 1992.

Nuesse, C. Joseph. "Henry George and 'Rerum Novarum': Evidence Is Scant That the American Economist Was a Target of Leo XIII's Classical Encyclical." *American Journal of Economics and Sociology* 44, no. 2 (April 1985): 241–54.

O'Brien, David J. *American Catholics and Social Reform: The New Deal Years*. New York: Oxford University Press, 1968.

———. "The Pilgrimage of Dorothy Day." *Commonweal* 107 (December 19, 1980): 711–15.

———. *Public Catholicism*. New York: Macmillan, 1989.

O'Brien, David J., and Thomas A. Shannon. *Catholic Social Thought: The Documentary Heritage*. Maryknoll, NY: Orbis Books, 1992.

O'Malley, SJ, John W. *The First Jesuits*. Cambridge, MA: Harvard University Press, 1993.

O'Toole, James M. *The Faithful: A History of Catholics in America*. Cambridge, MA: Belknap Press, 2008.

Oetgen, Jerome. *Mission to America: A History of Saint Vincent Archabbey, the First Benedictine Monastery in the United States*. Washington, DC: Catholic University of America Press, 2000.

Oppenheimer, Mark. *Knocking on Heaven's Door: American Religion in the Age of Counterculture*. New Haven, CT: Yale University Press, 2003.

Orcibal, Jean. *Saint Jean de la Croix et les mystiques rhéno-flamands*. Bruges, Belgium: Desclée de Brouwer, 1966.

Orsi, Robert A. *Between Heaven and Earth: The Religious Worlds People Make and the Scholars Who Study Them*. Princeton, NJ: Princeton University Press, 2005.

———. "Everyday Religion and the Contemporary World: The Un-Modern, or What Was Supposed to Have Disappeared but Did Not." In *Ordinary Lives and Grand Schemes: An Anthropology of Everyday Religion*, edited by Joska Samuli Schielke and Liza Debevec, 146–61. New York: Berghahn Books, 2012.

———. *The Madonna of 115th Street: Faith and Community in Italian Harlem, 1880–1950*. New Haven, CT: Yale University Press, 1985.

———. "U.S. Catholics between Memory and Modernity: How Catholics Are American." In *Catholics in the American Century: Recasting Narratives of U.S. History*, edited by R. Scott Appleby and Kathleen Sprows Cummings, 11–42. Ithaca, NY: Cornell University Press, 2012.

Parente, Pascal P. "Nature and Grace in Ascetical Theology." *American Ecclesiastical Review* (June 1943): 430–37.

Parkman, Francis. *The Old Régime in Canada*. Vol. 2. Boston: Little, Brown, and Company, 1902.

Pascal, Blaise. *Pensées*. Translated by A. J. Krailsheimer. New York: Penguin Books, 1995.

Pember, Mary Annette. "The Last Orphans of Holy Cross." *Indian Country Today Media Network*. February 6, 2014. http://indiancountrytodaymedianetwork.com/2014/02/06/last-orphans-holy-cross-153438?page=0%2C0.

Peters, Benjamin. *John Hugo and an American Catholic Theology of Nature and Grace*. PhD diss., University of Dayton, 2011.

———. "Nature and Grace in the Theology of John Hugo." In *God, Grace, and Creation*, edited by Philip J. Rossi, 59–78. Maryknoll, NY: Orbis Books, 2010.

Rademacher, Nicholas. *Apostle of Social Justice: Paul Hanly Furfey and the Construction of a Catholic Culture*. PhD diss., Catholic University of America, 2006.

Radner, Ephraim. *Spirit and Nature: The Saint-Médard Miracles in 18th-Century Jansenism*. New York: Crossroad, 2002.

Rauchway, Eric. *The Great Depression and The New Deal: A Very Short Introduction*. New York: Oxford University Press, 2008.

Rauschenbusch, Walter. *Christianity and the Social Crisis*. New York: MacMilan, 1913.

Reeves, Marjorie. *The Influence of Prophecy in the Later Middle Ages: A Study in Joachimism*. South Bend, IN: University of Notre Dame Press, 1993.

Rice, Charles O. "Reflections of a Labor Priest." In "American Catholic Social Thought." Special issue. *U.S. Catholic Historian* 5, no. 2 (1986): 231–34.

Riegle, Rosalie G. *Dorothy Day: Portraits by Those Who Knew Her*. Maryknoll, NY: Orbis Books, 2003.

Riel, Louis. *The Collected Writings of Louis Riel*. Edited by George F. G. Stanley. Edmonton: University of Alberta Press, 1985.

Rosswurm, Steve. *The FBI and the Catholic Church, 1935–1962*. Amherst: University of Massachusetts Press, 2009.

Ryan, John A. *Bishops' Program of Social Reconstruction: A General Review of the Problems and Survey of Remedies*. Washington, DC: National Catholic Welfare Conference, 1919.

Salvatore, Nick. *Eugene V. Debs: Citizen and Socialist*. Urbana: University of Illinois Press, 1982.

Savard, Pierre. *Jules-Paul Tardivel, la France et les Etats-Unis: 1851–1905*. Québec: Les presses de l'Université Laval, 1967.

Schechner, Richard. "Magnitude of Performance." In *The Anthropology of Experience*, edited by Victor W. Turner and Edward M. Bruner, 344–72. Urbana: University of Illinois Press, 1986.

Schloesser, Stephen. *Jazz Age Catholicism: Mystic Modernism in Postwar Paris, 1919–1933*. Toronto: University of Toronto Press, 2005.

Schneider, Nathan. "Commies for Christ." *New Inquiry*, December 13, 2013. http://thenewinquiry.com/essays/commies-for-christ/.

Schroth, Raymond A. *The American Jesuits: A History*. New York: New York University Press, 2007.

Scupoli, Lorenzo. *The Spiritual Combat*. Mesa, AZ: Scriptoria Books, 2009.

Seaton, Douglas P. *Catholics and Radicals: The Association of Catholic Trade Unionists and the American Labor Movement, from Depression to Cold War*. Lewisburg, PA: Bucknell University Press, 1981.

Sells, Michael S. *Mystical Languages of Unsaying*. Chicago: University of Chicago Press, 1994.

Sheehan, Arthur. *Peter Maurin: Gay Believer*. Garden City, NY: Hanover House, 1959.

Shelley, Thomas J. "Archbishop John Hughes and the Church in New York." *Catholic New York*, July 6, 2000. http://www.cny.org/stories/Anniversary,2499?content_source=&category_id=&search_filter=hughes&event_mode=&event_ts_from=&list_type=&order_by=&order_sort=&content_class=&sub_type=stories&town_id=.

———. *Dunwoodie: The History of St. Joseph's Seminary, Yonkers, New York*. Westminster, MD: Christian Classics, 1993.

———. *Greenwich Village Catholics: St. Joseph's Church and the Evolution of an Urban Faith Community, 1829–2002*. Washington, DC: Catholic University of America Press, 2003.

———. "The Young John Tracy Ellis and American Catholic Intellectual Life." In "The Intellectual Life: Essays in Memory of John Tracy Ellis, Part One." Special issue. *U.S. Catholic Historian* 13, no. 1 (Winter 1995): 1–18.

Sicius, Francis J. "Prophecy Faces Tradition: The Pacifist Debate during World War II." In *American Catholic Pacifism: The Influence of Dorothy Day and the Catholic Worker Movement*, edited by Anne Klejment and Nancy L. Roberts, 65–76. Westport, CT: Praeger, 1996.

Sinclair, Upton. *The Jungle*. New York: Doubleday, Page & Co., 1906.

Stevenson, Garth. "The Politics of Remembrance in Irish and Quebec Nationalism." *Canadian Journal of Political Science / Revue canadienne de science politique* 37, 4 (December 2004): 903–25.

Strauch, Karl. *Le Thème de la "folie de la Croix" dans l'œuvre du Père Onésime Lacouture (1881–1951)*. Montréal: Cahiers Scivias, 1998.

Super, John C. "'Rerum Novarum' in Mexico and Quebec." *Revista de Historia de América* 126 (January-June 2000): 63–84.

Sykes, Norman. Review of *Enthusiasm: A Chapter in the History of Religion, with Special Reference to the XVII and XVIII Centuries*, by Ronald A Knox. *Journal of Theological Studies*. N.s.:2 (1951): 215–20.

Tardivel, Jules-Paul. *"Pour la patrie": An 1895 Religious and Separatist Vision of Quebec in the Mid-Twentieth Century*. Toronto: University of Toronto Press, 1975.

Tentler, Leslie Woodcock, ed. *The Church Confronts Modernity: Catholicism Since 1950 in the United States, Ireland, and Quebec*. Washington, DC: Catholic University of America Press, 2007.

Tracy, David. *The Analogical Imagination: Christian Theology and the Culture of Pluralism*. New York: Crossroad, 1981.

Trese, Leo J. "Ten Forty-five." *Emmanuel* 54, no. 10 (October 1948): 297–99.

Tugwell, OP, Simon. *Ways of Imperfection: An Exploration of Christian Spirituality*. Springfield, IL: Templegate Publishers, 1985.

Tyler, Peter. *St. John of the Cross*. New York: Continuum, 2010.

Ugolino of Quintvalle. *The Little Flowers of St. Francis of Assisi*. Translated by Raphael Brown. Garden City, NY: Image Books, 1958.

Valantasis, Richard. "A Theory of the Social Function of Asceticism." In *Asceticism*, edited by Vincent L. Wimbush and Richard Valantasis, 544–52. New York: Oxford University Press, 1998.

Vann, OP, Gerald. "Nature and Grace." *Orate Fratres* 21, no. 3 (January 26, 1947): 97–105.

Vishnewski, Stanley. *Wings of the Dawn*. New York: Catholic Worker Press, 1984.

Von Balthasar, Hans Urs. *The Theology of Henri de Lubac*. San Francisco: Ignatius Press, 1991.

Wade, Mason. *The French Canadians*. Toronto: Macmillan, 1955.

Waite, Edward A. *Devil-Worship in France, with Diana Vaughn and the Question of Modern Palladism*. York Beach, ME: Red Wheel/Weiser, 2003.

Ward, SLG, Benedicta. "The New Orders." In *The Study of Spirituality*, edited by Cheslyn Jones, Geoffrey Wainwright, and Edward Yarnold, SJ, 283–91. New York: Oxford University Press, 1986.

Ware, Kallistos. "The Way of the Ascetics: Negative or Affirmative?" In *Asceticism*, edited by Vincent L. Wimbush and Richard Valantasis, 3–15. New York: Oxford University Press, 1998.

Watson, Bruce. *Sacco and Vanzetti: The Men, the Murders, and the Judgment of Mankind*. New York: Penguin Books, 2007.

Werpehowski, William. "Reinhold Niebuhr." In *The Blackwell Companion to Political Theology*, edited by Peter Scott and William T. Cavanaugh, 180–93. Malden, MA: Blackwell, 2004.

White, Ronald C., and C. Howard Hopkins. *The Social Gospel: Religion and Reform in Changing America*. Philadelphia: Temple University Press, 1976.

Woodward, Kenneth L. *Making Saints: How the Catholic Church Determines Who Becomes a Saint, Who Doesn't, and Why*. New York: Touchstone, 1996.

Wright, Carroll D. "The Amalgamated Association of Iron and Steel Workers." *Quarterly Journal of Economics* 7, no. 4 (July 1893): 400–32.

Wright, Jonathan. *God's Soldiers: Adventures, Politics, Intrigue, and Power—A History of the Jesuits.* New York: Doubleday, 2004.

Yancy, George. "Looking at Whiteness: Tarrying with the Embedded and Opaque White Racist Self." In *Look, a White!: Philosophical Essays on Whiteness.* Philadelphia: Temple University Press, 2012, 152–75.

Zwick, Mark, and Louise Zwick. *The Catholic Worker Movement: Intellectual and Spiritual Origins.* New York: Paulist Press, 2005.

Index

CATHOLIC PRACTICE IN NORTH AMERICA

James T. Fisher and Margaret M. McGuinness (eds.), *The Catholic Studies Reader*

Jeremy Bonner, Christopher D. Denny, and Mary Beth Fraser Connolly (eds.), *Empowering the People of God: Catholic Action before and after Vatican II*

Christine Firer Hinze and J. Patrick Hornbeck II (eds.), *More than a Monologue: Sexual Diversity and the Catholic Church. Volume I: Voices of Our Times*

J. Patrick Hornbeck II and Michael A. Norko (eds.), *More than a Monologue: Sexual Diversity and the Catholic Church. Volume II: Inquiry, Thought, and Expression*

Jack Lee Downey, *The Bread of the Strong:* Lacouturisme *and the Folly of the Cross, 1910–1985*